# The senses in interior design

Manchester University Press

To buy or to find out more about the books
currently available in this series, please go to:
https://manchesteruniversitypress.co.uk/series/
studies-in-design-and-material-culture/

**STUDIES IN DESIGN & MATERIAL CULTURE**

general editors
*SALLY-ANNE HUXTABLE,*
*NATIONAL TRUST*
*ELIZABETH CURRIE, ROYAL*
*COLLEGE OF ART/V&A*
*LIVIA LAZZARO REZENDE,*
*UNIVERSITY OF NEW SOUTH*
*WALES*
*WESSIE LING, LONDON*
*METROPOLITAN UNIVERSITY*

founding editor
*PAUL GREENHALGH*

# The senses in interior design

## Sensorial expressions and experiences

Edited by
John Potvin, Marie-Ève Marchand
and Benoit Beaulieu

Manchester University Press

Published by Manchester University Press
Oxford Road, Manchester M13 9PL
www.manchesteruniversitypress.co.uk

British Library Cataloguing-in-Publication Data
A catalogue record for this book is available from the British Library

ISBN    978 1 5261 6782 8    hardback
ISBN    978 1 5261 9077 2    paperback

First published 2023
Paperback published 2025

EU authorised representative for GPSR:
Easy Access System Europe – Mustamäe tee 50, 10621 Tallinn, Estonia
gpsr.requests@easproject.com

Typeset
by Cheshire Typesetting Ltd, Cuddington, Cheshire

# Contents

# Figures

Every reasonable attempt has been made to obtain permission to reproduce copyright images. If any proper acknowledgement has not been made, copyright holders are invited to contact the author via Manchester University Press.

# Contributors

**Benoit Beaulieu** is currently a PhD candidate in the Department of Art History at Concordia University. After receiving his BA in Art History from UQAM, he completed his MA in Art History at the Université Paris I Panthéon-Sorbonne. He is the recipient of a Canada Graduate Scholarship and a Concordia University Graduate Fellowship. His doctoral research focuses on the way French dandy Robert de Montesquiou used his interiors and archives as means of reclaiming control over his story. He is particularly interested in interior decoration and design and its intersection with notions of gender and sexuality in Europe at the end of the nineteenth century.

**Erin J. Campbell** holds a PhD in Art History from the University of Toronto and is Professor of Early Modern European Art in the Department of Art History & Visual Studies, University of Victoria. She has won awards for research and teaching, including the William Nelson Prize for the best article published in *Renaissance Quarterly* and the Faculty of Fine Arts Award for Teaching Excellence. Her publications appear in journals and essay collections, including the *Journal of Art Historiography*, *Sixteenth Century Journal*, *Word & Image*, *Renaissance Quarterly*, *The Cultural Aesthetics of Eighteenth-Century Porcelain*, *To Have and To Hold: Marriage in Premodern Europe 1200–1700* and *Design and Agency: Critical Perspectives on Identities, Histories, Practices*. She is also editor and contributing author of *Growing Old in Early Modern Europe: Cultural Representations* (Ashgate, 2006), co-editor and contributing author of *The Early Modern Italian Domestic Interior: People, Objects, Domesticities* (Ashgate, 2013) and co-editor of *A Cultural History of Furniture*, vol. II, *The Middle Ages and Renaissance, 500–1500*. *Old Women and Art in the Early Modern Italian Domestic Interior* was published by Ashgate in 2015.

**James Deaville** teaches Music in the School for Studies in Art and Culture at Carleton University in Ottawa. He edited *Music in Television* (Routledge, 2010) and with Christina Baade co-edited *Music and the Broadcast Experience* (Oxford University Press, 2016) and is currently co-editing *The Oxford Handbook on Music and Advertising* (2021). His publications have appeared in the *Journal of the American Musicological Society*, *Journal of the Society for American Music*, *American Music*, *Sound and the Moving Image* and *Music and Politics*, and he has contributed to books published by Oxford, Cambridge, Routledge, Chicago and Yale, among others. Last year he received a four-year grant from the Social Sciences and Humanities Research Council of Canada to conduct research on the roles of music and sound in cinematic and televisual representations of disability. He also published the article 'The moaning of (un-)life: Animacy, muteness and eugenics in cinematic and televisual representation' in the Disability and Voice special issue of the *Journal of Interdisciplinary Voice Studies*. Most recently he blogged for the Canadian Federation for the Humanities and Social Sciences about students with disabilities and the pandemic.

**Fiona Fisher** is a design historian and curator. She is a member of the Modern Interiors Research Centre at Kingston School of Art, Kingston University, London, where she is the curator of Dorich House Museum. Her research interests include British post-war domestic interiors in relation to suburban modernity, and the design of the modern public house in England with reference to national identity and evolving relationships of public, private and commercial space. Her work has been published in academic journals including the *London Journal* and *Visual Resources* and her publications include *Designing the British Post-War Home: Kenneth Wood, 1948–1968* (2015) and the co-edited collections *The Routledge Companion to Design Studies* (2016), *British Design: Tradition and Modernity after 1948* (2015) and *Performance, Fashion and the Modern Interior: From the Victorians to Today* (2011).

**Alice T. Friedman** is the Grace Slack McNeil Professor of the History of American Art and Co-Director of the Architecture Program at Wellesley College Emerita. She is the author of numerous articles and books on architecture, gender and social history, including *Women and the Making of the Modern House* (1998) and *American Glamour and the Evolution of Modern Architecture* (2010). These publications broke new ground in feminist architectural history, foregrounding the role played by women clients and their concerns in shaping key examples of twentieth-century architecture and interiors. Friedman's current projects include a book about queer photographers in New York City in the 1920s, entitled *All That Glamour and Loneliness*, and *Poker Faces/Private Spaces: Modern Architecture, Domesticity and Surveillance*, which uses a series of case

studies to introduce the typology of the 'poker-faced house', a new analytical category in which opacity, irony, decoration and other seemingly
'anti-modern' architectural strategies are deployed to protect queer and
other non-conforming households from public scrutiny.

**Ben Highmore** is Professor of Cultural Studies in the School of Media, Arts
and Humanities at the University of Sussex. His most recent books are *The
Art of Brutalism: Rescuing Hope from Catastrophe in 1950s Britain* (Yale
University Press, 2017) and *Cultural Feelings: Mood, Mediation, and
Cultural Politics* (Routledge, 2017). His book *Lifestyle Revolution: How Taste
Changed Class in Late Twentieth-Century Britain* (2023) was recently pub-
lished by Manchester University Press. He is currently writing a book on
the recent history of playgrounds.

**David Howes** is Professor of Anthropology (Concordia University) and
Law (McGill University) and the Co-Director of the Concordia Centre
for Sensory Studies. He is currently heading a research project entitled
'Explorations in Sensory Design'. Recent publications include *Senses and
Sensation: Critical and Primary Sources* (Routledge, 2018) and *The Sensory
Studies Manifesto* (University of Toronto Press, 2022).

**D. J. Huppatz** is Associate Professor in the Department of Architectural
and Industrial Design, Swinburne University of Technology, Melbourne,
Australia. He is the author of *Design: The Key Concepts* (Bloomsbury, 2020)
and *Modern Asian Design* (Bloomsbury, 2018).

**Louisa Iarocci** is Associate Professor in the Department of Architecture
at the University of Washington in Seattle where she teaches architectural
history, theory and design. She is a licensed architect who has worked
in architectural firms in Toronto, New York and Boston. She completed
her Master's in Art History at Washington University in St Louis and
her PhD in the History of Art and Architecture at Boston University. Her
publications included the anthology *Visual Merchandising: The Image
of Selling* (2013) and the monograph *The Urban Department Store in
America* (2014). More recently she has contributed essays to the anthol-
ogies *Epidemic Urbanism: Contagious Diseases in Global Cities*, edited by
Caitlin DeClercq and Mohammad Gharipour (2021), and *Building/Object:
Shared and Contested Territories of Design and Architecture*, edited by Mark
Crinson and Charlotte Ashby (2022).

**Grace Lees-Maffei** MA RCA FRHistS FRSA FHEA is Professor of Design
History and Programme Director for DHeritage, the Professional Doctorate
in Heritage, at the University of Hertfordshire, UK. Her research into
design mediation, domesticity, national identity and globalization in

design has been published in numerous articles and books. She is author of *Design at Home: Domestic Advice Books in Britain and the USA since 1945* and co-author with Nicolas P. Maffei of *Reading Graphic Design*. She edited *Writing Design: Words and Objects* and *Iconic Designs: 50 Stories about 50 Things* and co-edited *Made in Italy* and *Designing Worlds* with Kjetil Fallan and *The Design History Reader* with Rebecca Houze. Professor Lees-Maffei is a Fellow of the Royal Society of Arts, the Royal Historical Society and AdvanceHE. She is founder of the University of Hertfordshire's Network of Women+ Professors, and she was Chair of Hertfordshire's Researcher Development Group (2014–19) and Research Group Leader for the Theorising Visual Art and Design (TVAD) Research Group (2004–18), Managing Editor (2011–17) and Editor (2002–8) of the *Journal of Design History* and Visiting Professor for both the Doctorate in Design at IADE-U, Lisbon and the MA Design Cultures at Vrije University, Amsterdam (2013–15). She is a Peer Review College Member for the Arts and Humanities Research Council (2012–22).

**Marie-Ève Marchand** is Affiliate Assistant Professor in the Department of Art History at Concordia University (Montreal, Canada). She examines the epistemological issues arising from the collecting and display of decorative arts in museums and domestic spaces during the long nineteenth century. After dedicating her doctoral dissertation to the study of period rooms (Université de Montréal, 2015), she is currently working on a book project that probes the singular role played by French eighteenth-century material culture in American domestic interiors during the Gilded Age. Her recent publications include articles in *Journal of Design History*, *Material Culture Review*, *Musées*, *Espace: Art actuel*, *Esse: Art + Opinions* and *RACAR*, as well as book chapters in edited volumes published by Bononia University Press, Bloomsbury and Routledge. She is the co-editor of *Design and Agency: Critical Perspectives on Identities, Histories, and Practices* (Bloomsbury, 2020).

An American resident of Germany, **Serena Newmark** is a doctoral candidate in Art History at the Freie Universität Berlin working on the Prussian and Greater German design diaspora. She holds a Bachelor of Arts degree in Art History from Carleton College and a Master of Arts degree in Decorative Arts, Design, and Culture from the Bard Graduate Center. Her recent publications include 'From the Palaces of Berlin to the Texas Frontier: The Furniture Designs of Prussian Architect Karl Friedrich Schinkel', in *Traditions in Transition: Change and Material Culture in 19th Century Texas, the Lower South, and the Southwest* (The Museum of Fine Arts, Houston, 2018). Newmark's recent presentations include 'Design Scholarship Displaced: Use of the German Domestic Interior in Nazi Propaganda', Design History Society Annual Conference

2018; 'Prussian Stylistic Influences on Ironwork in Gilded Age America', Designing the Gilded Age: Daughters of the American Revolution Museum Symposium 2021; 'Johann Martin Levien: the Prussian Cabinetmaker who brought New Zealand Hardwoods to Europe', Research Symposium 2021, Furniture History Society; and 'A Plagiarist from New Jersey and the Removal of Prussia from the American Architectural Canon', The Power of Sources in Architectural Research and Practice Forum 2022, Netzwerk Architekturwissenschaft Berlin.

**Claire I R O'Mahony** is Associate Professor in the History of Art and Design and founding course director of the MSt in the History of Design in the Department for Continuing Education at the University of Oxford. She was Chair of the Design History Society and thereby served on the editorial board of the *Journal of Design History* published by Oxford University Press (2019–22). Her research focuses upon decoration and regional identity between 1870 and 1968; recent publications include 'Renaissance and Resistance: Modern French Tapestry and Collective Craft', *Journal of Modern Craft* (2016); '"Urbi et orbi": Decentralization and Design in Nancy's International Exposition of Eastern France 1909' in M. Filipova, ed. *Cultures of International Exhibitions 1840–1940: Great Exhibitions in the Margins* (2015); as well as an edited volume, *A Cultural History of Furniture: The Modern Age* (Bloomsbury Press, 2022).

**John Potvin** is Chair and Professor in the Department of Art History at Concordia University, Montreal. He is the author of *Material and Visual Cultures Beyond Male Bonding* (2008), *Giorgio Armani: Empire of the Senses* (2013) and *Bachelors of a Different Sort: Queer Aesthetics, Material Culture and the Modern Interior in Britain* (2014), winner of the Historians of British Art Book Prize. In addition to being editor of *The Places and Spaces of Fashion* (2009) and *Oriental Interiors* (2015) he is also co-editor of both *Material Cultures, 1740–1920: The Meanings and Pleasures of Collecting* (2009), *Fashion, Interior Design and the Contours of Modern Identity* (2010) and *Design and Agency* (2020). He serves on the editorial and advisory boards of several international peer-reviewed journals, was book review editor for *Interiors: Interiors, Design and Architecture* (2011–13) and served as Associate Editor of the *Journal of Design History* (2017–22). In 2021 he was awarded a four-year Social Sciences and Humanities Research Council of Canada Grant to investigate 'Primitivism and Design: Art Deco, Hybridity and the Decolonization of the Modern Interior in France 1909–1939'.

**Änne Söll** is Full Professor for Modern Art History at Ruhr University Bochum, Germany. Her areas of research include art of the Weimar Republic, gender studies (masculinities), portraiture, fashion photography, video installations, artists' magazines, museum architecture and period rooms. Recent publications are *Revisiting the Past in Museums and at Historic Sites* (Routledge), edited with Anca Lasc and Andrew McClellan, and *Materials, Practices and Politics of Shine in Modern Art and Popular Culture* (Bloomsbury), edited with Antje Krause-Wahl und Petra Löffler.

**Michael Windover** is Associate Professor and Head of Art and Architectural History in the School for Studies in Art and Culture at Carleton University. He is cross-appointed to the Institute for Comparative Studies in Literature, Art and Culture and the School of Industrial Design at Carleton and is adjunct curator of design at Ingenium. A historian of modern architecture and design, he is author of *Art Deco: A Mode of Mobility* (Presses de l'Université du Québec, 2012) and co-editor with Bridget Elliott of *The Routledge Research Companion to Art Deco* (2019). He is also co-author with Anne MacLennan of *Seeing, Selling, and Situating Radio in Canada, 1922–1956* (Dalhousie Architectural Press, 2017). His research has appeared in *The Journal of the Society for the Study of Architecture in Canada, Architectural History, RACAR, Buildings & Landscapes* and *The Journal of Architecture* as well as in book chapters dealing with issues of architecture or design history.

# Introduction:
# sensorial interactions: interior design through the five senses

*Marie-Ève Marchand*

One of the primary ways to experience and understand the physical world is through the five senses. Sight, touch, smell, taste and hearing can be defined as 'the faculties by which external or internal stimuli are perceived, involving the transmission of nerve impulses from specialized neurons (receptors) to the brain'.[1] In the case of interior design, the stimulation of the senses is bound up with a myriad of elements including colour, light, fabric, appliances, furniture and fragrances among countless others. These are brought together to negotiate, play against or enhance the existing structure and form of buildings in a way that acts upon architectural volumes and shapes interior spaces and their atmospheres. It is in this spirit that decorators and designers, both professional and amateur, have long experimented with, embraced and harnessed new materials, objects and technologies to enhance or heighten sensory awareness and well-being. However, the impact of interior design is not one-sided: it affects and imposes itself as much on the bodily senses as the human sensorium affects the way one designs, uses and perceives designed interiors. In other words, senses are central not only to the experience of interior design but also to its practice. *The senses in interior design* proposes to shed light on and help chart the somewhat fragmentary histories of how the senses have been mobilized within various experiences, whether lived or idealized, as well as expressions of interior design and decoration.

Already in the eighteenth century in *The Genius of Architecture; or, The Analogy of That Art with Our Sensations*, Nicolas Le Camus de Mézières examined how each room of a wealthy town house, from the vestibule to the servants' quarters, should be distributed and decorated to please the senses. De Mézières carefully describes the location of a room within the house, its proportions in relation to the whole, its shape, layout, content, decoration and, in some instances, ideal colour scheme and best practices to please sight, sound and smell.[2] In so doing, the French architect and theoretician showed an early concern for understanding how human beings are sensorially affected by their surroundings. Within this history of interior design and decoration, De Mézières' approach is not unique. For instance, one can think of nineteenth-century physician Max Nordau's harsh diatribes on decadent and symbolist interiors, which threatened to enervate the senses, noting how: '[e]verything in these houses aims at exciting the nerves and dazzling the senses. The disconnected and antithetical effects in all arrangements, the constant contradiction between form and purpose, the outlandishness of most objects, is intended to be bewildering'.[3] More recently, in *Interior Designing for All Five Senses* (1998), interior designer Catherine Bailly Dunne, attempting to address a wide audience, outlines the basics of how to decorate in a way that engages every sense. These three examples, each published in a different century and by authors from differing backgrounds, further confirm that the senses are resolutely endemic to the design and the bodily experience of the interior.

And yet still, to this day, an in-depth discussion of the senses, and even of the body, is too often ignored in the histories and historiography of interior design, decoration and design history. Likely an offshoot of modernist approaches to architectural history, the study of the interior has often focused on star designers or ideal interiors, leaving aside embodied, sensorial agency. Repositioning the senses front and centre, this volume emphasizes sensory expressions and experiences of interior design throughout history. Considering sight, touch, smell, taste and hearing as critical, though until now overlooked, facets of the history of interiors, the fourteen chapters gathered in this volume shed new light on how the senses have been mobilized and how their analysis transforms current understanding of interior design.

## Sensing the field

The literature on the history of interior design, as well as the extant scholarship on the senses, has experienced continued robust growth. Sensory studies is now a legitimate and burgeoning discipline in its own right[4] and disciplines adjacent to the history of interior design, such as art history and architectural history, have gone a long way towards addressing the senses. *Art, History and the Senses: 1830 to the Present*, for instance, edited by Patrizia di Bello and Gabriel Koureas (2010), attempts to critically reappraise the study of art history beyond the supremacy of the visual and sight. In the field of architecture, Juhani Pallasmaa's *The Eyes of the Skin* is an obvious example.[5] In this two-part book, Pallasmaa provides a brief historical survey of how architecture has engaged the senses, followed by considerations about how the senses interact in the experience of architecture. Adopting a phenomenological approach, he critiques the 'ocular bias' of Western culture 'and of architecture in particular', arguing that this lack of consideration for the body and the senses has led to the 'inhumanity of contemporary architecture'.[6] Pallasmaa draws upon philosophical sources and includes several references to various forms of art, thereby formulating a strong theoretical apparatus to explore the role of the senses in connection to the built environment. Yet, despite his expansive survey, he only vaguely refers, if at all, to the question of interior design and decoration.

Scholarship focusing on the senses in interior design includes a mere handful of journal articles. Over the last two decades, only a limited number of papers have been published on the subject in academic venues including the *Journal of Design History, Journal of Interior Design, Design Studies, Design Issues, Design and Culture* or *West 86th: A Journal of Decorative Arts, Design History and Material Culture*, among others. While many authors mention the relevance of the senses to fully understand the interior, as well as the challenges of translating the 'perceptive aspects' of the interior beyond its actual experience,[7] very few dedicate a significant part of their contribution to the senses, let alone the entire article. Sight and touch may be the most frequently addressed within this brief bibliography. For instance, in 'Domesticating Goods from Overseas: Global Material Culture in the Early Modern Netherlands', Anne Gerritsen focuses on vision and touch to demonstrate how the embodied experience of imported objects including carpets, ceramics and furniture contributes to their domestication in the seventeenth-century Dutch interior.[8] Although not addressing interior design specifically, Kate Smith's 'Sensing Design and Workmanship: The Haptic Skills of Shoppers in Eighteenth-Century London' offers another interesting example. In this article, Smith examines how consumers, especially women, used touch as a strategy to further 'their understanding of objects, particularly in terms of design, quality and workmanship',[9] while engaging in what was considered to be the 'work' of browsing from store to store to select quality goods. Hearing, smell and taste are even more rarely dealt with. In 'Sound and Domestic Space in Fifteenth- and Sixteenth-Century Italy', Flora Dennis proposes a rare analysis of the impact of the content, layout and surrounding (exterior) environment of the domestic interior on its soundscape, sometimes to the point of revealing the status and reputation of its inhabitants.[10] For her part, in 'A Sensthetic Approach to Designing for Health', Upali Nanda provides an insight into the importance of considering the interactions between all senses when designing healthcare facilities.[11]

Books published in the field are even more scarce. In their Cooper Hewitt, Smithsonian Design Museum's 2018 exhibition catalogue *Senses: Design beyond Vision*, Ellen Lupton and Andrea Lipps explore how the senses are solicited through design by looking at a plethora of objects and a variety of environments, including offices and cities. Presented as 'a manifesto for inclusive design',[12] their catalogue highlights the benefits for all users of taking the five senses into consideration in design practices. Although a rare example of sensory studies within the field of design studies, it largely sidesteps a consideration of interior design and decoration. Adopting a very different approach, Diana Fuss, in *The Sense of an Interior: Four Writers and the Rooms that Shaped Them* (2004), explores the specific rooms of four acclaimed nineteenth-century literary figures to argue that 'the most critical bridge between the architectural and the psychological interior is the human sensorium: sight, sound, touch, taste, and smell'.[13] These two texts outlined above, at the antipodes of each other, give merely a glimpse of the countless vantage points from which to explore a constellation of interior design practices, theories and uses that have taken the five senses into consideration.

The limits of existing literature in the field are quickly reached and it is undeniable that a sustained historical investigation of the complex relationships between the senses and interior design remains to be undertaken. Many interior design students read, and rightly so, the work of architectural theorists on this topic, including the work of Pallasmaa. Without questioning the relevance of this literature, it is important to stress that it does not fully capture the specificity of interior design as a field which, through its increased professionalization since the late nineteenth century, became independent from the work of the architect.

Over the past 120 years, pioneering interior decorators and designers have worked tirelessly to gain credibility for a field and discipline of its own, distinct and separate from architecture. This, coupled with the post-World War II emergence of design history and design studies as disciplines in their own right, underscores the focus, concern and commitment of this volume to the relationship between the senses and interior design, including its praxis and history. As Penny Sparke has argued, 'the concepts of the interior and of the landscape have, in recent years, become the subjects of studies embracing themes and ideas that sit outside those that have tended to dominate architectural history and theory'.[14] With this in mind, this volume resists the temptation to let interior design be appropriated by or subsumed within a profession which has too often denigrated interior design as merely a feminine and frivolous interest in colour and draperies.[15] Moving further away from architectural studies, this volume is also concerned with the objects that contribute to a spatial whole, rather than focusing exclusively on the spatial dimension of interior design. In contradistinction to modernist inclinations in architecture, decoration is here considered as a critical juncture at which interior design, the subject and the senses come together and are enlivened through their relationship. In addition to decorative effects, chapters in this volume also address sensual techniques and strategies deployed and harnessed by interior design as well as the sensual outcomes produced through decorative and design elements.

## Making sense of the senses

Studies that address the intricate and multilayered relationships between interior design and the senses tend to do so using a wide spectrum of approaches ranging from marketing to philosophy. In this context, the somehow elusive notions of *feelings* and *atmosphere* are often called upon to embrace an undifferentiated collection of stimuli, without necessarily making explicit how the senses are solicited. The commingling of notions such as 'senses' and 'feelings' extends back into history. As David Howes explains, 'Plato, for example, apparently did not distinguish clearly between the senses and feelings.' Referring to the work of Constance Classen, Howes reports that the Greek philosopher did not necessarily make a clear distinction between what is understood today as the five senses from a Western perspective and what could be better described as 'sensations', including 'pleasure, discomfort, desire and fear'.[16]

In a more contemporary context, the (muddled) relationship between feelings, atmosphere and the senses seems to rest upon the close connection between the senses and phenomenology. Building upon the work of German philosopher Edmund Husserl (1859–1938), phenomenology examines the lived and subjective experience as the origin of meaning. As Lupton and Lipps explain in *The Senses: Design beyond Vision*, 'phenomenology situates knowledge in the body: sensual encounters enable consciousness'.[17] In this holistic perception of the surrounding environment, the individual role and contribution of each of the senses are not necessarily dissected and deepened. In addition to being multilayered and ephemeral, feelings and sensations of an interior often commingle in a way that seems to resist scientific analysis. As a result, the senses are too often neglected or viewed with suspicion due to their lack of rationality.

Pushing existing scholarship one step further, the chapters included in this volume seek to unpack which senses are solicited and when, how and to which purposes, thereby challenging the elusive and too often intangible notion of *atmosphere*. For instance, in Chapter 11, Fiona Fisher explains how the atmosphere informs the relationship between the body and its surrounding environment. She provides concrete examples of how designers solicit specific senses with the aim of creating an atmosphere that will achieve a distinct purpose, namely appeal to the customers of the English pub. For his part, Ben Highmore in Chapter 13 further theorizes the notion of atmosphere by attempting to grasp both its sensorial and intellectual complexity in the designed interior. In so doing, he examines how sensory stimuli are orchestrated and explores the agency of the atmosphere and of the subject experiencing it.

The ambition to untangle such complex notions as atmosphere and feelings in connection to the senses does not result in a siloed approach whereby the senses are estranged from one another. Far from being experienced in a vacuum, the senses interact together at all times, even if they may not be all equally solicited or readily perceived. The relationship between the senses opens the door to the notion of synaesthesia, which, albeit mentioned in several chapters, is not discussed at length in this volume. Synaesthesia is understood here as a simultaneous experience or solicitation of two or more of the senses. Neither its neurological, philosophical, sociocultural nor spiritual implications are addressed, although these various angles represent engaging avenues for future research.[18] Nevertheless, by adopting a multisensorial perspective, many contributors to this volume question the historical dominance of the visual and concomitant imbalance between the senses in a Western context. As Howes and Classen remind us, sight has been 'associated with both spiritual and intellectual enlightenment' in Western society, where the correlation between vision and knowledge extends back to the Renaissance.[19] Largely out of necessity, the historiography of interior design depends on sight, given we are often only left with photographs (if we are lucky enough) and/or written sources. However, using written and visual sources does not mean the study of interior design should be limited to sight. One of the purposes of this volume is to go beyond the traditional use of such material to bring forward a variety of sensory experiences and highlight how these might shape methodologies for future analysis of interior design.

Accordingly, this volume uses a thematic rather than a sense-by-sense division or period-centred approach. On the one hand, a fair distribution of scholarship between sight, touch, smell, taste and hearing has yet to be achieved and, as already mentioned, numerous chapters in this volume engage in a polysensory analysis of interiors. On the other hand, to offer an exhaustive portrait of the senses in interior design through time would not be possible given the current scarcity of research in this field. However, by grouping the chapters in three sections exploring sensory politics, aesthetic entanglements and sensual economies respectively, this volume productively engages with overarching themes that showcase some of the similarities, tensions and differences of sensorial experiences within specific temporal and spatial circumstances. Furthermore, combined with a chronological order within each section to avoid potentially distracting time leaps from one chapter to the next, the thematic approach allows for a more nuanced understanding of the interconnections between the senses and interior design, while pointing to their larger sociopolitical stakes.

Finally, given the countless possibilities interior design offers and the polymorphous nature of the senses, this, or any, volume could only ever boast a partial glimpse into the intersections between the senses and interior design. As highlighted by the phrase 'ways of sensing' used by Howes and Classen,[20] cultural circumstances inform the ways in which sensory stimuli are perceived, understood and interpreted, making overgeneralizations across time and place misleading. Far from being the definitive text or the last word on the subject, this collection of essays seeks to initiate a long, provocative and fruitful conversation. A limitation of the present volume is the absence of studies exploring senses and interior design in the non-Western context, a gap that also highlights how young the field is and how much work is left to be done. We hope that by flagging both the importance of this topic and its current Western-centric focus, the volume will foster an expansion of research and analysis beyond a eurocentric framework and serve as a springboard to further studies that will enrich our understanding of how the senses operate in a greater diversity of interior design contexts.

## Senses in contexts

The interior forms an integral part of a broader cultural, social and political programme and agenda, even if not always obvious. Entitled 'Sensory politics', Part I of this volume addresses the political and sociocultural dimension of interior design. One of the threads that run through the five chapters that follow is the connection between the senses and the construction of identities. Exploring questions of gender, class, sexuality, race, colonialism and political propaganda, the authors shed light on how the embodied experience of the interior and the social, cultural and political stakes that inform – or even control – this experience, impact the definition of the self, subjectivity and identity formation.

In 'Heated bodies: fireplaces and the senses in the early modern Italian domestic interior', Erin J. Campbell explores the connections between the five senses and the somatic experience of heat in late sixteenth-century Italy. Campbell examines a central element of interior design, the fireplace, and demonstrates how heat becomes a significant protagonist in the sensual-social dynamics of the home. The importance given to heat echoes the idea of a 'thermal sense' in architecture as formulated by Ulrike Passe in 2009 and according to which 'in addition to the traditional five faculties of sight, hearing, touch, taste and smell the term "sense" includes the means by which bodily position, temperature, pain, balance are perceived'.[21] Interestingly, however, Campbell does not simply argue for the existence of a sixth sense, but rather showcases how the experience of warmth through the senses marks the home with the political dimensions of gender and class.

The notion of gender as it relates to the senses in interior design is also explored by Benoit Beaulieu in 'Sensitive design: Robert de Montesquiou's sensorial installations and their condemnation'. Beaulieu examines the nineteenth-century Parisian apartment of Count Robert de Montesquiou

(1855–1921) through the lens of queer agency and describes how each room was designed with a unique atmosphere that triggered the senses in multiple ways. While de Montesquiou's detractors – who feared nothing less than contamination at the contact of his exuberant interior – condemned what they considered to be an overstimulation of senses as a sign of effeminacy and decadence, the Count himself argued quite the contrary and thought of his interior as a therapeutic environment. Beaulieu describes how the Count's 'idiosyncratic sensorial installations' have been fiercely used against him and demonstrates how the complex stimulation of the senses in interior design actually served as a strategy of self-affirmation and legitimization in a sociopolitical context suspicious of the expression of queer identity.

In 'Reassessing Pierre Legrain's "Black Deco": sensual luxury, primitivism and the French bourgeois interior', John Potvin explores the complex connections between the senses, specifically the haptic, the decorative and the so-called primitive. Examining luxurious objects borrowed directly from African sources and intended for the French bourgeois domestic interior, Potvin tackles the colonial and racist agenda of the '*style moderne*' or art deco style. Seats designed by Pierre Legrain (1889–1929) are the cornerstone of this chapter, which goes beyond the touched surface to unveil how, using a sometimes ethically questionable decorative vocabulary, the art deco approach to interior design celebrated sensuality through luxury. As Potvin demonstrates, while it gave ammunition to critics equating art deco with degeneration, the emphasis given to the senses allowed the occupants to singularly perform their modern identity. By insisting on the importance of the embodied experience of the art deco interior, Potvin sheds new light on a version of French domesticity that challenged the ideal homogeneity and whiteness of modernism.

Queer identity is central to Alice Friedman's '"Brother and I in bed": queer photography at home in New York, 1925–35'. In this chapter, Friedman explores how sensory experience contributed to the expression, performance and celebration of queer masculine identity among cultural and social elite circles. Looking specifically at photographic portraits, including male nudes, and the carefully curated interiors where they were produced, displayed and enjoyed, the author develops the idea of a 'queer sensorium'. In this context, the friendship between Max Ewing (1903–34), who could today be described as an interdisciplinary artist, and Carl Van Vechten (1880–1964), who would later be known as a photographer, provides an intimate angle through which Friedman considers the impact of sight, sound and touch on the experience of sensual pleasure in the domestic interior.

With 'Conquering the home front: Nazi propaganda and sensory experiences in the German domestic interior 1933–45', Serena Newmark looks at the use of the senses in the construction of a very different kind of identity, that of the traditional – and idealized – family under the Third Reich. While the decisive role of politics may have seemed less straightforward in some of the previous chapters, it plays a particularly conspicuous role in this one. Newmark examines the multiple ways in which National Socialist propaganda permeated all spheres of life, and specifically the domestic realm, by dictating what was deemed appropriate for being seen, heard, touched, smelled and tasted. Manipulating Germans in their home through what could be described as a politics of the five senses was key to the dictatorship's attempt at instilling a paradoxical Nazi aesthetic that combined what Newmark describes as the 'return to a pre-industrial, pre-Christian, agrarian, self-sufficient past and the creation of a modern and prosperous consumer society'.

The four chapters that comprise Part II, 'Aesthetic entanglements', highlight some of the tensions that are raised through the stimulation of the senses in the interior and looks at the sometimes deceptive, sometimes subversive play between them. One significant aspect that links these chapters together is the practices through which the senses are harnessed to help fashion the body's and subject's interface with designed interiors. In many ways, this section brings together aesthetic concerns within specific and highly loaded social and cultural contexts, thereby bridging some of the concerns endemic to the previous Part I and following Part III.

This section begins with an examination of the tensions between sight and touch. With 'Into the sensorium: scenes from the dressing room', Louisa Iarocci demonstrates how an apparatus intended primarily for sight, namely stereoscopic photographs, actually goes beyond vision to solicit other senses, more specifically touch. Iarocci's focus on dressing room scenes is of particular interest given the importance of the (female) body in this space and the voyeuristic appeal of the activities that took place in it. As she analyses various activities occurring in the dressing room, Iarocci highlights the proximity between the spatial environment and the bodies occupying it. She shows how the interior frames and extends the occupants, but also how they intimately interact and mirror one another, at times entering into a symbiotic relationship. Design plays a significant role in this (inter)connection as it complements the sensuous qualities of the bodies depicted in the image while echoing the viewer's own relationship with its surrounding environment in a way that ultimately enhances the haptic impact, even the tangibility, of the stereoscopic view.

In 'Site-reading: placing the piano in middle-class homes, 1890–1930', Michael Windover and James Deaville bring together interior design and music history. Music affects an individual emotionally as much as physically and transforms their experience of the space, how they perceive it and feel inside it. Taking the example of the domestic parlour or living room, Windover and Deaville explore how the piano impacted the design of a room and structured its surrounding environment visually, spatially, audibly as well as socially. In addition to impacting the soundscape of an interior, the piano has a visual and haptic appeal. It also informs how the room is furnished and designed to accommodate it – thanks to strategies such as the 'piano window' to provide the player with sufficient light – or even enhance it visually and magnify its sonority with built-in alcoves, for instance. As Windover and Deaville demonstrate, the piano activated the domestic space and articulated a variety of sociocultural narratives, performances and experiences involving the senses in the home. The care dedicated to interior design, visual aesthetic and architectural features around the piano, as well as the transformation of the repertoire to be played at home, reveal its cultural imprint and social role.

The 'master's room' or 'men's room' is the focus of Änne Söll's chapter 'The *Herrenzimmer*: masculinity, the senses and interior design in turn-of-twentieth-century Germany'. This room, which can be described as a study or a gathering space for implicitly white, well-off and heterosexual men, could be used to work, read and write as well as drink, smoke and engage in leisure pursuits. Analysing the *Herrenzimmer* as constructed by magazines and advice books, Söll challenges the common Western assumption that men's rooms of the early twentieth century were all about the intellect and that the sensory experience they provided was ancillary to the greater ideal of 'disembodied (male) thinking'. Söll also reveals that the actual, privately owned *Herrenzimmer* turned out to be much more diverse in their design than the idealized versions disseminated in the glossy pages of design publications. In light of this variety, Söll argues that it was not so much thanks to its 'style' as to its appeal to the senses that the *Herrenzimmer* revealed itself as a men's space. With her investigation, Söll demonstrates how, through interior design, the senses actively contributed to the construction of masculinity within the domestic sphere.

With 'Hands at home? Textures, tactility and touch in interior design', Grace Lees-Maffei explores the relevance of touch, understood as a 'whole-body sense' which goes beyond manual activities performed by the hand. Although Lees-Maffei underlines that all the senses work collectively, by isolating touch she foregrounds the variety of experiences brought by this sense, which is fundamental not only to the ways in which one interacts with their surrounding environment but also to how one engages with design. Lees-Maffei argues that there exists a mutually constitutive relationship between touch and interior design. While this sense is key to grasping the meaning of an interior, it is also central to the very process of its design, even during the ideation stage. Lees-Maffei supports her argument with modernist examples where, as she demonstrates, by encouraging the removal of sensory stimuli, minimalism also contributes to intensify sensory experience. This is particularly true of the haptic where less is more. The chapter concludes with a series of brief vignettes through which the author highlights different experiences of interior design wherein touch is (un)solicited in unexpected ways, such as magazines, shops and museums.

Finally, Part III, 'Sensual economies', looks at the solicitation of the senses in the marketing and consumption of design, with a special interest in the creation of commercial interiors. Kate Smith explains that, already in the eighteenth century, sensory interactions with goods for sale – and especially handling, as visual assessment did not suffice at a time when production had yet to be standardized – were not only a source of idle pleasure: they were also a strategy to increase one's knowledge about design and a key aspect of social performance.[22] Although looking at an object, touching it, smelling it, listening to it or even tasting it, in the case of food, are still an integral part of the in-person shopping experience, senses are solicited in myriad ways by commercial environments and their surrogates in the form of catalogues and advice books.

With 'Forging foam at the 1925 Paris Exhibition', Claire O'Mahony offers a sensorial history of the Nancy and Eastern France Pavilion presented at the Paris Exposition Internationale des Arts Décoratifs et Industriels Modernes. Paying close attention to the sociopolitical context of eastern France during the interwar period, O'Mahony analyses how the spatial organization, materiality and iconography of this pavilion solicited the senses so as to translate the economic and cultural identity of a borderland region devastated during the war. The theoretical notions of 'flow', 'symbiosis' and 'foam' are defined and used by O'Mahony to provide a new understanding of the articulation between various forms of artistic expression – especially iron and glass – industry and the pavilion's tripartite interior space comprised of a central hall flanked by a commercial museum and a conference hall. In the context of this volume, O'Mahony's contribution on the role of art deco design for self-definition within a collective and commercial space also complements Potvin's postcolonial examination of the *style moderne* domestic interior provided in Part I.

The distinctive sensory experience of the English pub is the focus of Fiona Fisher's 'The stimulating atmosphere of the English public house, *c*.1945–75'. In this chapter, Fisher combines an overview of the theoretical understanding of the impact of interior design on consumers' experience and behaviour post-World War II with case studies. In so doing, she explores various approaches to pub design and underlines how atmosphere can be a 'boundary-blurring phenomenon that encompasses emotional, sensory, social and spatial experience and which mediates the relationship between the body and the interior'. One of the significant challenges Fisher brings to the fore is the desire to create an ambience that recalls the pub's tradition but within new architectural settings. As designers solicited the senses to achieve this endeavour, they also supported the commercial ambitions of brewers while initiating what Fisher describes as a 'playful multisensory relationship with the past'.

David Howes' contribution to this volume, 'Interiorizing the senses', raises the veil on the impact of sensory design, sensory marketing and the ensuing aestheticization of everyday life in contemporary society. Drawing from sociology and anthropology, Howes looks at the omnipresence of design and the appeal to the senses in both commodities and the venues where they are sold, while providing a critique of evolutionary psychology as it pertains to interior design. To do so, he covers a wide range of ideas and examples, extending from the sensual features of products by companies that led the aestheticization of everyday life – for example, paint, coloured appliances and shag carpeting – to Catherine Bailly Dunne's advice on how to engage with all five senses when designing one's domestic space. Howes concludes his chapter with a plea for an increased awareness of history and ethnography as a complement to aesthetic concerns in design pedagogy.

With 'Sensorial worlds and atmospheric scenes in Terence Conran's *The House Book*', Ben Highmore's objective is twofold: first, to expose how the 'feeling' of an interior is contingent on a synaesthetic experience and second, to offer a methodological foundation to appreciate what he describes as this 'synaesthetic effect and affect of space'. A close examination of vocabulary used to translate the multisensorial dimension of interior design is key to Highmore's study. Drawing on existential phenomenology, he attempts to capture the sensorial complexity of elusive and ambient notions including 'feeling', 'atmosphere' and 'attunement'. More importantly, he demonstrates how productive they are when trying to make sense of interior design. Terence Conran's *The House Book* (1974) as well as the marketing strategies developed by Conran and the shop Habitat from the early 1960s are used as a case in point. As he dissects Conran's commercial and pedagogical endeavour, Highmore shows how the latter managed to create a sensuality that was specific to Habitat and had the power of 'retuning' objects already known to the customers by changing both their meaning and their sensorial experience.

In the concluding chapter of the volume, 'Aesop's sensory experience', D. J. Huppatz examines how the luxury skincare brand Aesop challenged the rise of online shopping by betting on the way it offers its clients an unparalleled sensory, bodily experience in store. Rather than defining its brand through uniform design, Aesop takes advantage of the specificity of each store's location to make a design statement that is both singular and in communion with its neighbourhood. Each branch is committed to offering an engaging multisensory experience in symbiosis with an immersive and unique interior. Informed by phenomenology and theories of 'experience economy', which aims to create a compelling experience thanks to the integrative work of the designer, Huppatz argues that the meticulously curated stores impact the affect and subjectivity of the customers in a way that reveals itself as transformative.

The three thematic clusters chosen to organize the chapters that comprise this volume build bridges that go beyond geographic, temporal and even sensory specificity. By transcending boundaries, this grouping brings to the fore considerations about identities, social structures and politics that shed new light on the significance of the senses in all aspects of interior design and decoration. The variety of methodologies and theoretical approaches used to tackle the sensorial dimension of the interior is not trivial. Some authors rely on archival sources, other on printed material or a combination of both and their approaches range from descriptive to highly critical. While this balance gives a glimpse of the richness of the field, it also showcases the extent of the work that remains to be undertaken. Each in their unique way, the authors of *The senses in interior design* contribute to this endeavour. And yet, despite their singularity, the chapters brought together here all have at least one thing in common: they give back to the body its central role in the practices, experiences, uses and histories of interior design and decoration.

## Notes

1  'Sense', *Oxford English Dictionary*, online (accessed 12 March 2022).
2  See, for instance, the section on the boudoir. N. Le Camus de Mézières, *The Genius of Architecture; or, The Analogy of That Art with Our Sensations*, introduction by R. Middleton, transl. D. Britt (Santa Monica, CA: The Getty Center; University of Chicago Press, 1992 [1780]), p. 118.
3  See M. Nordau, *Degeneration*, transl. from the second edition of the German work (London: William Heinemann, 1895), p. 11.
4  See, for instance, Concordia University's Centre for Sensory Studies founded in 2012.
5  Other titles include E. Betts (ed.), *Senses of the Empire: Multisensory Approaches to Roman Culture* (London and New York: Routledge, 2017); A. McMahon, 'Space, Sound and Light: Toward a Sensory Experience of Ancient Monumental Architecture', *American Journal of Archaeology*, 117:2 (April 2013), pp. 163–79; N. Atkinson, *The Noisy Renaissance: Sound, Architecture, and Florentine Urban Life* (University Park, PA: Penn State University Press, 2017); R. Muchembled, *Smells: A Cultural History of Odours in Early Modern Times*, transl. S. Pickford (Cambridge and Medford, MA: Polity Press, 2020).
6  J. Pallasmaa, *The Eyes of the Skin: Architecture and the Senses* (Chichester: Wiley, 2005), p. 17.
7  K. Pint, 'The Experience of the Interior: Outlines of an Alternative Anthropology', *Interiors: Design/Architecture/Culture*, 7:1 (2016), pp. 55–72.
8  A. Gerritsen, 'Domesticating Goods from Overseas: Global Material Culture in Early Modern Netherlands', *Journal of Design History*, 29:3 (2016), pp. 228–44.
9  K. Smith, 'Sensing Design and Workmanship: The Haptic Skills of Shoppers in Eighteenth-Century London', *Journal of Design History*, 25:1 (2012), p. 3.
10  F. Dennis, 'Sound and Domestic Space in Fifteenth- and Sixteenth-Century Italy', *Studies in the Decorative Arts* (Fall/Winter 2008–9), pp. 7–19.
11  U. Nanda, 'A Sensthetic Approach to Designing for Health', *Journal of Interior Design*, 42:2 (2017), pp. 7–12.
12  E. Lupton and A. Lipps, *The Senses: Design beyond Vision* (New York: Cooper Hewitt, Smithsonian Design Museum; Princeton Architectural Press, 2018), p. 6.

13  Cited in *ibid.*

14  P. Sparke, 'Introduction' in P. Sparke et al. (eds), *Flow: Interior, Landscape and Architecture in the Era of Liquid Modernity* (London: Bloomsbury, 2018), p. 1.

15  See J. Sanders, 'Curtain Wars: Architects, Decorators, and the Twentieth-Century Domestic Interior', *Design Magazine* (Winter/Spring 2002), pp. 14–20; P. Sparke, *As Long as It's Pink: The Sexual Politics of Taste* (London and San Francisco: Pandora/HarperCollins, 1995).

16  D. Howes, 'The Senses: Polysensoriality' in F. E. Mascia-Lees, *A Companion to the Anthropology of the Body and Embodiment* (Oxford: Wiley-Blackwell, 2011), p. 435.

17  Lupton and Lipps, *The Senses: Design beyond Vision*, p. 4, referring to D. Abram, *The Spell of the Sensuous: Perception and Language in a More-Than-Human World* (1997).

18  D. Howes and C. Classen, 'Synaesthesia Unravelled: The Union of the Senses from a Cultural Perspective' in *Ways of Sensing: Understanding the Senses in Society* (London and New York: Routledge, 2013), pp. 152–74.

19  D. Howes and C. Classen, 'Introduction: Ways and Meanings' in *Ways of Sensing*, p. 1.

20  *Ibid.*, p. 5.

21  U. Passe, quoting the *Collins English Dictionary*, in 'Designing Sensual Spaces: Integration of Spatial Flows Beyond the Visual', *Design Principles and Practices: An International Journal*, 3 (2009), p. 7.

22  K. Smith, 'Sensing Design and Workmanship', pp. 6–8.

# PART I

## Sensory politics

# 1

# Heated bodies: fireplaces and the senses in the early modern Italian domestic interior

*Erin J. Campbell*

## Introduction

Annibale Carracci's sketch (early 1580s) in the Metropolitan Museum in New York provides a rare glimpse into a humble domestic interior [Figure 1.1]. As a demonstration of the artist's interest in genre scenes, the drawing is typically passed over quickly in the scholarship on the artist.[1] Yet, it is invaluable evidence for the role of the senses in constituting the life of the interior. In the image, we are given access to an intimate family scene of a mother drying the clothing of a small child enveloped in her skirts in front of a large fireplace with a roaring fire, while an older child and a cat draw close to enjoy the warmth. Especially striking is the way Annibale captures the transformation of the space of the interior into a place that is synonymous with family through the fireplace and its life-giving heat.[2] Pointing to the fireplace as defining the home, Raffaella Sarti notes that in eighteenth-century Bologna 'the minimum space for renting was called a *camino* ("fireplace")' which included a fireplace and perhaps a storeroom and lavatory.[3] In Annibale's drawing, the fireplace evokes Gaston Bachelard's phenomenology of the home in which the lamp on the family table is 'a little world in itself'.[4]

Fireplaces, such as we see in Annibale's drawing, which were built into a side wall and could be used for both cooking and heating, were invented in Italy sometime between the twelfth and thirteenth centuries.[5] By the late sixteenth century wall fireplaces were no longer restricted to elite residences,[6] although fireplaces in the centre of the room persisted.[7] Sarti underscores that beyond their practical purposes for cooking and heating, fireplaces played a social and symbolic role in the household. The introduction of wall fireplaces into more than one room in larger residences, and the differentiation of fires for cooking, heating and display 'meant giving

**Figure 1.1**  Annibale Carracci, *Domestic Scene*, early 1580s, pen and ink, grey and brown wash, black chalk, 32.8 x 23.6 cm.

life to environments that allowed different ways of socializing for family members'.[8] The sociability of fireplaces recalls the Bolognese Renaissance architect Sebastiano Serlio's (*c.*1475–1554) prescription for a fireplace in the centre of the room in a wealthy peasant's house, where he proposes 'there be a room common to all in the middle, and at its centre there shall be a fire, so that more people can get round it and everyone can see the others' faces when engaging in their amusements and storytelling'.[9] In addition to sociability, Sarti draws attention to the imaginative life of fireplaces, which she explains 'made it possible to transform and diversify the world of the imagination'.[10] Evoking the domestic imaginary, Sarti notes that fireplaces could hold metaphorical and symbolic meaning, allowing them to 'alter the symbolic harmony of the home not only in relation to its internal space but also in its cosmic dimension'.[11]

Building on these ideas about the metaphorical, symbolic and imaginative role of the fireplace and its potential to affect social relations in the interior, this chapter will explore the fireplace and its life-giving heat as significant protagonists in the sensual-social dynamics of the elite early modern Italian home. Curiously, the sense of heat is not often identified as one of the primary senses, and yet thermal sensation is essential to life. While fire activates the senses of touch, sight, sound and smell through its various physical properties and effects, heat activates the sensory receptors of the skin, which respond to heat and cold. Moreover, thermal sensation is also created by the movement of hair follicles, the evaporation of water from the skin and the activity of sweat glands.[12] Typically, fireplaces in early modern Italy are studied for their design elements, with little attention to the synergy between design and the senses, which is surprising given not only the transformative effect of the heat, light, sound, smell and touch of a blazing fire but also the importance of thermal sensation within an environment.[13] By focusing on a case study of the fireplace in the *sala grande* (principal reception room) of the Palazzo Magnani in Bologna [Figures 1.2 and 1.3], considered one of the most spectacular fireplaces in late sixteenth-century Italy,[14] I ask: how does the sensual-somatic experience of heat intertwine with both metaphor and materiality to shape the people and things, practices and representations, meanings and values that transform abstract space into places that come to life through the senses?[15]

## The fireplace in the *sala grande* of the Palazzo Magnani

The Magnani family, like other elite citizens of Bologna in the late sixteenth century, enjoyed a comfortable standard of living, in a city with a distinguished university community, a solid mercantile and agricultural base, and a relatively stable senatorial government.[16] The Magnani were a noble, senatorial family that distinguished themselves in public life, law,

**Figure 1.2** *Sala grande, c.*1590–92, Palazzo Magnani, Bologna.

**Figure 1.3** Fireplace, *c.*1590–92, *sala grande*, Palazzo Magnani, Bologna.

diplomacy, the university, religion and the military.[17] However, the family was removed from the senate in 1513 by Pope Leo X (1475–1521; papacy: 1513–21) because of their alliance with the Bentivoglio, the tyrannical family who were ultimately exiled from Bologna in the early sixteenth century.[18] As part of a campaign to restore the Magnani family honour, the new palace was commissioned by Lorenzo Magnani (1533–1604) to be built on Via Donato (now Via Zamboni 20), with construction starting in 1577 under the direction of Domenico Tibaldi (1541–83), a Bolognese painter and architect.[19] In 1590 the family regained their senatorial status when Lorenzo was reappointed to the senate by Pope Sixtus V (1521–90; papacy: 1585–90) in May 1590. The decorative programme of the *sala grande* was begun in 1590 [Figure 1.2] and has been linked to the Magnani reinstatement to the senate.[20] It includes a painted frieze of the legendary founding of Rome by Romulus and Remus,[21] created by Agostino Carracci (1557–1602), Annibale Carracci (1560–1609) and Ludovico Carracci (1555–1619) and completed by 1592 when Lorenzo was installed in the distinguished position of Gonfaloniere di Giustizia on the first of July in 1592,[22] the same year as Lorenzo's marriage to his third wife, Isabella Campeggi.[23] Samuel Vitali, who has published the most recent scholarship on the patronage and iconography of the *sala grande*, interprets the fresco cycle in didactic and moralizing terms, and views the subject of the founding of Rome as an expression of Lorenzo's gratitude to the pope who elevated him to the senate.[24]

Remarkably, the fireplace is preserved *in situ* in the *sala grande* of the palace [Figure 1.3]. The principal reception room in the Renaissance palazzo was typically located at the front of the house, at the top of the stairs on the *piano nobile*, and included a fireplace, as we see at the Palazzo Magnani. These large halls were devoted to important ceremonial events,[25] such as the ceremony that the newly installed Gonfaloniere was expected to host, which was held at the Palazzo Magnani upon Lorenzo's appointment.[26] In addition to ceremonies, banquets and formal entertainment, the *sala* could also be used for more informal activities, such as dining, playing cards, needlework or simply for standing at the fire.[27] The fireplace in the Palazzo Magnani is the focal point of the room, vying for significance both then and now with the celebrated Carracci frieze. As a multimedia installation, the fireplace involved many different artists and craftsmen from Bologna and elsewhere. It was designed by the Bolognese architect Floriano Ambrosini (1567–1621), who took over the role as architect upon the death of Tibaldi in 1583. The stonework was executed by the family of Veronese stonemasons Adamo, Gherardo and Giovanni Battista Giorgi.[28] The Lombard stuccoist and sculptor Ruggero Bascapè (active 1580–99) created the sculptural elements.[29] Composed of coloured marbles, stucco and gilding, the fireplace includes sculptures of Mars and Minerva on the mantel flanking a fresco by the Carracci of the ancient festival of the *Lupercalia*,[30] which is topped by a broken pediment emblazoned with the Magnani coat of arms and the Latin inscription LAURENTIUS MAGN[ANIVS] / SENATOR / M.D.XCII (Lorenzo Magnani Senator, 1592). The *stemme* is suspended and crowned by two reclining, naked youths. Despite its commanding presence in the room, the fireplace has received far less attention than the Carracci fresco cycle.[31] Yet, the fireplace transforms the entire *sala* into a multisensory, somatic experience. In the following analysis I will examine the design elements of the fireplace in light of the somatic effects of heat.

## Guardians of the hearth

The fireplace is located on the wall where the story of the founding of Rome begins in the painted frieze above. This prominent placement demonstrates the significance of the fireplace not only to the decorative programme as a whole but also to the activities that took place within the hall. This wall is the one that would be seen first by those who entered the hall from the main entrance off the loggia. The monumental sculptures of the Roman divinities Mars and Minerva, which stand on guard fully armed and ready to defend, immediately engage those who enter the hall. Executed by the sculptor Bascapè,[32] the commanding figures are placed on pedestals on top of the mantel and therefore tower over the viewer, a position which amplifies their intimidating effect.[33] Their aggressive stances are further heightened by the glaring, open-mouthed masks below, carved on the marble of the fireplace surround. Both sculptures are rendered in white stucco in contrast to the vividly painted fresco, the polychrome marbles of the fireplace and the gilding of the architectural features. The absence of colour evokes the restrained purity of white marble typical of classical statuary, heightening their authority. On the pedestals under each god, inscriptions underscore their role as warrior divinities, highlighting their duty to guard and defend. Under Mars, the inscription exhorts: ARCEAT / HOSTES (repel enemies); and under Minerva: MUNIAT / URBEM (defends, or, arms the city). Flanking the fresco of the *Lupercalia*, the gods appear to be guarding both the fire below and the fertility rite unfolding in the painting.

While the role of Mars in the saga of the founding of Rome and his relationship to Minerva as the other warrior divinity in the pantheon of antique gods may be enough to explain their presence in the *sala*,[34] Vitali suggests that these martial figures may bear a political meaning, referring to the cities of Rome (Mars) and Bologna (Minerva).[35] For Vitali, harmony between the two gods of war could represent the harmony of the two cities, as the most important cities within the Papal States, or the harmony between the papal legate and the senate defending Bologna against its enemies.[36] We could also read these figures in the context of the household. Thus, the political harmony proposed by Vitali could also represent marital harmony, a theme that is emphasized in the widely circulated prescriptive writings on the family in this period.[37]

## Heat for healthy living

Such iconographic readings, however, can be further enriched by attending to the sensorial, embodied experiences taking place in the room itself. Significantly, space is transformed into place through our sensorial experiences. Places speak to lived experience: they are felt and perceived, understood and imagined, interpreted and narrated.[38] Places are sensorial sites of memory and imagination, rich with metaphor.[39] Approaching the home as a *place* that is continually being created through the intertwining of the social, emotional and imaginative with the material,[40] the senses are key to the experience and making of the interior. The sense of place conjured by the senses recalls Henri Lefebvre's category of representational space in *The Production of Space*, which foregrounds space as arising from the experience of the inhabitants, mediated by the imagination.[41] Like place, which ensues from life and experience, representational spaces are organic, alive and fluid.[42] As a form of space that is created through everyday experiences, memories, feelings, associations and values, it is especially relevant to our understanding of the senses in the processes of place-making in the home.[43] Through our senses we inhabit the home environment and create relationships with family and others who enter the home.[44]

Fireplaces such as the one in the *sala grande* of Palazzo Magnani contribute to the processes of place-making through the intertwining of imagination, metaphor and the somatic effect of heated air. Heat played several roles in early modern Italy. Perhaps the most essential quality of heat was that it was required for healthful living. The temperature of the air was believed to play an important role in the maintenance of health. Cold air was feared because it was thought to have a serious impact on the body by closing the pores.[45] By contrast, heated air was valued for its ability to relax the body, opening the pores and rendering the body soft and limp.[46] In addition to the immediate healthful effect of hot air on the body, fire in particular was thought to correct and purify the air. The action of heat on the air made it mobile, helping to thin, clarify and dissipate the air, which assisted in the elimination of bad vapours or deleterious heavy particles that were believed to exist in damp air.[47]

Given the widely held belief in the value of heated air for health, fireplaces played a key role in maintaining the health of the household.[48] Indeed, such health-giving properties of heated air and fire were visually reinforced by the ornamentation and design of fireplaces.[49] Fireplace iconography could include subjects that underscored the value of fire to humankind, such as Vulcan, the Greek and Roman god of fire and the forge, recommended by the Florentine Renaissance architect Filarete (1400–69),[50] or Prometheus, one of the Titans and a Greek god of fire.[51] While such decorations reinforced the importance of the fire to the development of civilization, they could also emphasize key healthful benefits. For example, an early sixteenth-century fireplace in the Palazzo Doria in Genoa included the Latin inscription SORDID PURGAT (it purges dirty things), underscoring the power of heat to purify the air.[52] Other ornamental motifs including foliage and flowers alluded to the healthful scents of plants integral to the period's medicines. Such images reference the faith in the curative properties of plant-based aromatics, inciting the sense of smell and reinforcing the role of the fireplace in maintaining health.[53]

Reflecting on the desire to create decorative features for the fireplace that expressed the healing and purifying power of heat and fire, we can imagine that the martial stance of Mars and Minerva in their proximity to the flame casts them as guardians of the warming, purgative and aromatic functions of the precious sensation of heat, which was essential to the health and therefore the wellbeing of the household. Such an interpretation considers the sensual, embodied experience of the sculptures as part of a shared environment of heated air. This approach does not exclude understanding the figures as symbolic of civic or domestic harmony; however, considering the effect of the senses on their reception opens up the possibility of meanings that are sensually activated by the heated air emanating from the fireplace.

## Heated bodies

In addition to its role in preserving health by heating the air, heat in medical discourse was also believed to be the basis for physiology during this period. The source of heat in the body was thought to be the heart, which was compared to a hearth. Using the metaphor of guards on a citadel, which reminds us of the martial stance of Mars and Minerva on the mantel, Aristotle advises that the heart 'is necessary because there must be a source of heat: there must be, as it were, a hearth, where that which kindles the whole organism shall reside; and this part must be well guarded, being as it were the citadel (*akropolis*) of the body'.[54] Galen similarly made the association between the heart, bodily heat and the hearth: 'The heart is, as it were, the hearthstone and source of the innate heat by which the animal is governed'.[55]

Even more significant to understanding the somatic force of heat generated by the fireplace in the Magnani *sala* is the fact that the bodily heat generated by the heart was thought to be the source of sexual difference in the early modern period. Within this discourse on the thermal basis for sexuality, women were believed to be innately cold, while heat was considered innately male.[56] Masculine heat was the cause of facial hair, a key marker of male adulthood and therefore virility.[57] Heat, in tandem with the testicles, was intimately involved in the production and quality of semen,[58] so that masculinity and potency were based on heat.[59] The medical writings of Aristotle and Galen, which formed the foundation of early modern medicine, emphasized the quality of masculine heat in the reproductive process.[60] According to Aristotle, heat was essential to the formation and discharging of semen.[61] Thus, masculine heat was the basis for procreation. For Aristotle, semen itself possessed heat. In other words, heated air or pneuma was the main component of semen: it contained the 'soul-heat' which generated new life.[62]

The metaphorical association between the hearth, heat and virility provides a filter through which to interpret the activity of the warrior gods Mars and Minerva. From this perspective, they evoke the guardians of heat alluded to by Aristotle above, and its role in generating masculine virility. In this context, their swords and lances represent the weaponry of sexual warfare, operating as phallic symbols for the sexual activity of the male genitals and signalling male readiness for sexual intercourse.[63] The allusion to sexual arousal evoked by the pointy lance and thrusting sword would be intensified by the quality of heat emanating from the fire. In other words, the increased intensity of the heat of the actual fire, a heat which could be made to burn brighter and with more efficacy through bellows, firedogs, tongs and pokers, which are widely documented in household inventories of the period,[64] metaphorically evoked a more powerful virility.

Contributing to the parallel between the heat of the fireplace and virility are metaphors that use the artisanal creative process to convey the shaping force of male heat as it acts on the female body.[65] Aristotle records several such artisanal metaphors that convey the generative force of male heat, such as the father as a 'swordsmith, carpenter, painter or modeler'.[66] Such parallels between the artisanal shaping of wares and virility resonate with the imagery in the Carracci fresco of the *Lupercalia* above the mantel, between the figures of Mars and Minerva [Figure 1.3]. In this depiction of an ancient Roman fertility rite that formed part of a festival devoted to puri-fication, one of the priests known as the *luperci* beats a woman with strips of goatskin, an action associated with fertility and ease of childbirth.[67] The inscription on the base of the altar in the background where a dog is being sacrificed reads 'UT IUCUNDA SIC FOECENDA' or 'as you are joyous so may you be fertile'. The theme of fertility conveyed by the image has been associated with Lorenzo Magnani's aspiration for heirs.[68] In combination with the heat of the fire below, the image of a man beating a woman evokes the metaphors discussed above that express the shaping force of virile heat, such as the blacksmith pounding on the anvil. As Simons notes, what these artisanal metaphors convey is that 'The female body was to be repet-itively beaten and stamped with masculine impress' or that 'warm liquids' were to be 'poured within'.[69] Significantly, the action of beating in the *Lupercalia* is reinforced by the scene of *Remus and the Cattle Thieves* in the painted frieze directly above the *Lupercalia* [Figure 1.2]. These two images are linked, for in Ovid's *Fasti*, the *Lupercalia*, the suckling of Romulus and Remus by the she-wolf and the incident of the cattle thieves all take place in the same location.[70] In *Remus and the Cattle Thieves*, Remus is represented in the guise of Hercules: he wears a lionskin, wields a club and is portrayed in an active, aggressive pose based on conventions drawn from representations of Hercules in Renaissance art.[71] The phallic significance of his club and the activity of beating is paralleled by the goatskin whips in the *Lupercalia*. The association of beating with virility in these interlinked images is reinforced by the parallel between the club and erect penis in the sculpture of Hercules in the ground-floor vestibule that greets visitors to the palace [Figure 1.4]. Significantly, Hercules is flanked by two small boys, who embody the results of the 'beating'.[72]

Reinforcing the association of beating with virility in the *Lupercalia* and in *Remus and the Cattle Thieves* are the somatic effects of the heat itself, emanating from the fireplace and warming the air of the room. As noted above, heated air has the effect of opening the pores and relaxing the body. In this context, the action of the heated air opening the pores of the body parallels the desired effect of the virile pneuma mixing with heated bodily fluid to create semen, which infuses the female body.[73] In effect, the heat of the fireplace literally achieves what is indicated in the *Lupercalia* by heating and opening the female body, for, as Simons notes: 'Intercourse from the male point of view was not so much represented as penile penetration through flesh into a deep interior as the outward projection of a naturally more heated body whose chief coital function was to direct a stream of precious fluid to a feminized receptacle.'[74] Tellingly, the fireplace is surmounted by two nude reclining youths, placed between the scene of the cattle thieves and the *Lupercalia*, who are crowning the Magnani coat of arms. They provide the material manifestation of the metaphorical somatic infusion of heat from the flame below, ensuring the perpetuity of the Magnani lineage.

Significantly, the parallel between the heated air of the fireplace and virility may be evoked in representations of confinement rooms on maiolica childbirth wares.[75] For example, a maiolica *tagliere* (tray) by Francesco Duratino [Figure 1.5][76] draws us into a comfortably furnished chamber, including a *cassone* (chest), mirror, a canopied bed with brightly patterned bedding and a soft pillow, and a carved cradle. Recalling the Carracci drawing with which we began this chapter, there is a wall fireplace where the swaddling clothes of the newborn are being warmed by the fire, its cradle brought close to the glow of the fire while it is being cuddled in the arms of an attendant. The sensation of heat as literally constituting the room itself is made plain by the use of the same orange colour of the flame throughout

**Figure 1.4**   Gabriele Fiorini (?) and Ruggero Bascapè, *Hercules with Two Children*, *c.*1590, bronze, Palazzo Magnani, Bologna.

the details of the interior, including the canopy, the ceiling, the bedframe, various garments worn by the figures assisting with the newborn and even the skin tones of the attendants. Echoing the transformative firing process in the artisanal creative process of maiolica itself, the heat from the blazing

**Figure 1.5** Francesco Duratino, Italian (active Urbino and elsewhere), 1543–75, tray from a childbirth set.

fire transforms the chamber into a metaphor for conception and fertility. Recalling the metaphors of conception in which a woman's womb is like an oven,[77] the room itself has become the container which 'cooks' the male seed, heated by the virile heat of the fireplace.

## Conclusion

The chapter has shown that the fireplace in the *sala grande* of the Palazzo Magnani and its sensory effects must be seen as central to the transformation of the space of the *sala* into a heated place of masculine virility. This conclusion is supported by Lorenzo's relentless pursuit of an heir, which led him to naturalize three illegitimate sons (all of whom were dead by the time the *sala* was completed), before finally having a son by his third bride, whom he married just before the decoration of the room was complete.

Along with fire tools designed to amplify the heat of the fire burning in the fireplace, as mentioned above, inventories sometimes also mention furnishings located near the fireplace, including chairs, benches and tables.[78] Here, in this semi-public room, which could be used to host important receptions and family events, one can imagine the women, who were considered inherently cold in contrast to the heat of men (even putting burning embers in containers under their clothes to warm up),[79] dragging a bench or a chair closer to the fire, blissfully unaware of or perhaps welcoming the action of masculine virility on their heat-seeking, sensate bodies.

## Notes

1  C. Robertson, *The Invention of Annibale Carracci* (Milan: Silvana Editoriale, 2008), p. 73. Robertson devotes just one sentence to the drawing.
2  On the hearth as synonymous with the family see R. Sarti, *Europe at Home: Family and Material Culture 1500–1800*, trans. A. Cameron (New Haven, CT and London: Yale University Press, 2002), p. 95 and J. M. Malnar and F. Vodvarka, *Sensory Design* (Minneapolis: University of Minnesota Press, 2004), p. 184.
3  Sarti, *Europe at Home*, p. 118.
4  G. Bachelard, *The Poetics of Space*, trans. M. Jolas (Boston, MA: Beacon Press, 1994), p. 171.
5  Sarti, *Europe at Home*, p. 92.
6  S. Cavallo and T. Storey, *Healthy Living in Late Renaissance Italy* (Oxford: Oxford University Press, 2013), p. 95.
7  E. S. Cohen and T. V. Cohen, *Daily Life in Renaissance Italy* (Westport, CT and London: Greenwood Press, 2001), p. 219.
8  Sarti, *Europe at Home*, p. 95.
9  Quoted in *ibid.*, p. 95.
10  *Ibid.*, p. 95.
11  *Ibid.*
12  B. L. Ong, 'Warming up to Heat', *The Senses and Society*, 7:1 (April 2015), p. 10.
13  *Ibid.*, p. 7.
14  R. J. Tuttle, 'I camini' in S. Bettini (ed.), *Palazzo Magnani in Bologna* (Milan: Federico Motta Editore, 2009), p. 137.
15  T. Gieryn, 'A Place for Space in Sociology', *Annual Review of Sociology*, 26 (2000), p. 465; M. M. Degen, *Sensing Cities: Regenerating Public Life in Barcelona and Manchester* (New York and Abingdon: Routledge, 2008), p. 19.
16  G. Angelozzi, 'Nobili, mercanti, dottori, cavalieri, artigiani: stratificazione sociale e ideologia a Bologna nei secoli XVI *e* XVIII' in W. Tega (ed.), *Storia illustrata di Bologna*, vol. II (Milan: Aiep Editore, 1989), p. 54.
17  For the Magnani family see S. Vitali, 'Lorenzo Magnani: "nobile e uno de' senatori della città di Bologna": tasselli per un ritratto' in Bettini (ed.), *Palazzo Magnani in Bologna*, pp. 13–31.
18  G. Roversi, *Palazzi e case nobili del '500 a Bologna: la storia, le famiglie, le opera d'arte* (Bologna: Grafis Edizioni, 1986), pp. 127–8.
19  Roversi, *Palazzi*, p. 129. Floriano Ambrosini took over in 1583 when Tibaldi died. It is now a bank headquarters, Rolo Banca/Credito Romagnolo. For a detailed account of the building programme under Tibaldi see S. Bettini, 'Palazzo Magnani: il testament architettonico di Domenico Tibaldi' in Bettini (ed.), *Palazzo Magnani in Bologna*, pp. 33–89.

20  Samuel Vitali proposes that the fireplace and the fresco cycle were both commissioned immediately after Lorenzo's election to the Senate in May 1590, and that the room was complete before his installation as Gonfaloniere di Giustizia on 1 July 1592. S. Vitali, 'Palazzo Magnani: le decorazioni pittoriche e scultoree del Cinquecento' in Bettini (ed.), *Palazzo Magnani in Bologna*, p. 102.

21  The literature on the Carracci painted frieze in the *sala grande* is vast. See most recently S. Vitali, *Romulus in Bologna: Die Fresken der Carracci im Palazzo Magnani* (Munich: Hirmer Verlag, 2011).

22  Vitali, 'Lorenzo Magnani', pp. 26–7; S. Vitali, 'A New Document for the Carracci and Ruggero Bascapè at the Palazzo Magnani in Bologna', *The Burlington Magazine*, 143:1183 (October 2001), pp. 612–13.

23  Lorenzo married his third wife, Isabella Campeggi, 7 April 1592. Vitali, 'Lorenzo Magnani', pp. 14–15.

24  Vitali, 'A New Document', pp. 612–13; Vitali, 'Palazzo Magnani', pp. 110–12. For an alternative interpretation that takes a biographical approach see A. Stanzani, 'Un committente e tre pittori nella Bologna del 1590' in A. Emiliani (ed.), *Le storie di Romolo e Remo di Ludovico, Agostino, e Annibale Carracci in Palazzo Magnani a Bologna* (Bologna: Nuova Alfa Editoriale, 1989), pp. 167–92.

25  M. Ajmar-Wollheim and F. Dennis (eds), *At Home in Renaissance Italy* (London: V&A Publications, 2006), pp. 37–8.

26  Vitali, 'A New Document', p. 613.

27  P. Thornton, *The Italian Renaissance Interior 1400–1600* (New York: Harry N. Abrams, 1991), p. 285 and note 2 on p. 389.

28  Vitali, 'A New Document', p. 612.

29  *Ibid.*, p. 610.

30  For the fresco, see Vitali, *Romulus in Bologna*, pp. 118–28. It is also referred to as the *Ludi Lupercalia*.

31  No complete or systematic study of fireplaces in Italian Renaissance residences exists. See Tuttle, 'I camini', p. 137.

32  Vitali, 'A New Document', pp. 604–13.

33  The placement of sculptures on the mantel was inspired by examples in the Veneto. The fireplace in the Palazzo Gualdo in Vicenza in the Sala di Carlo V similarly has sculptures of Mars and Minerva on the mantel. See Vitali, *Romulus in Bologna*, p. 80.

34  Plutarch's biography of Romulus in his *Lives* has been suggested as the source for the Carracci frieze – see Vitali, *Romulus in Bologna*, pp. 161–9; Robertson, *Invention of Annibale Carracci*, p. 94. There was a number of editions of Plutarch's *Lives* in the sixteenth century in both Latin and Italian translation. See Vitali, *Romulus in Bologna*, p. 328. For Mars as the father of Romulus and Remus, see Plutarch, 'Romulus' in *Lives*, trans. B. Perrin (Cambridge, MA: Harvard University Press, 2014), vol. 1, p. 99. For the Carracci use of Ovid's *Fasti* in the fresco cycle see Vitali, *Romulus in Bologna*, p. 120. As Vitali notes, a translation was available by mid-century: *I Fasti di Ovidio tratti alla lingua Volgare per Vincenzo Catari*, Venice, 1551 (*ibid.*, note 47 on p. 120). At the opening of the book, when Ovid describes the union of Mars and Rhea Silvia, and the conception of the twins (Ovid, *Fasti*, trans. J. G. Frazer (Cambridge, MA: Harvard University Press, 2014), bk III, p. 121–2), he also introduces Minerva and underscores her warlike nature: 'Thyself dost see that fierce wars are waged by Minerva's hand?' (Ovid, *Fasti*, bk III, p. 121). Later, Ovid refers to her as 'the warlike goddess' who 'delights in drawn swords' (*Ibid.*, bk III, p. 181).

35  Vitali, *Romulus in Bologna*, p. 239.

36  *Ibid*.

37  On domestic harmony as a metaphor for civic harmony, and ultimately universal harmony as expressed in prescriptive writings on the home, see D. Frigo, *Il padre*

*di famiglia: governo della casa e governo civile nella tradizione dell' 'economica' tra Cinque e Seicento* (Rome: Bulzoni Editore, 1985), pp. 75–82, 201–7.

38 Gieryn, 'A Place for Space in Sociology', p. 465.

39 E. Lupton and A. Lipps, *The Senses: Design Beyond Vision* (New York: Cooper Hewitt, Smithsonian Design Museum & Princeton Architectural Press, 2018), pp. 10–11.

40 E. Campbell and O. Vallerand, 'Approaching Home: New Perspectives on the Domestic Interior', *RACAR*, 45:2 (2020), p. 7.

41 H. Lefebvre, *The Production of Space*, trans. D. Nicholson Smith (Malden, MA: Blackwell Publishing, 1991), p. 39.

42 *Ibid.*, pp. 41–2: 'Representational space is alive: it speaks, it has an affective kernel or centre' (p. 42).

43 See Degen, *Sensing Cities*, p. 19. Degen writes that Lefebvre's concept of representational space shows how space is '*lived* through and moulded by everyday actions, memories, experiences and feelings'.

44 D. Howes and C. Classen, *Ways of Sensing: Understanding the Senses in Society* (New York: Routledge, 2014), pp. 66–8; As Marlene Eberhart explains, 'Through our senses, we organize our world and our relations with others.' See 'Sensing Space and Making Publics' in A. Vanhaelen and J. P. Ward (eds), *Making Space Public in Early Modern Europe* (New York: Routledge, 2013), p. 176.

45 Cavallo and Storey, *Healthy Living in Late Renaissance Italy*, pp. 71–2.

46 *Ibid.*, p. 71.

47 *Ibid.*, p. 94.

48 *Ibid.*

49 *Ibid.*

50 *Ibid.*

51 Cavallo and Storey offer the example of a medallion that appears on a fireplace in Palazzo Doria, Genoa which depicts Prometheus. *Ibid.*, p. 95, Figures 3.6a–b.

52 *Ibid.*, p. 95 and Figure 3.7.

53 *Ibid.*, p. 95 and Figure 3.8.

54 Aristotle, *Parts of Animals*, 3.7, trans. by A. L. Peck (Cambridge, MA: Harvard University Press, 1961), p. 265. Cited by P. Simons, 'The Flaming Heart: Pious and Amorous Passion in Early Modern European Medical and Visual Culture' in K. Barclay and B. Reddan (eds), *The Feeling Heart in Medieval and Early Modern Europe* (Berlin and Boston, MA: Walter de Gruyter, 2019), p. 20. I am grateful to Dr Simons for drawing this citation to my attention.

55 Galen, *On the Usefulness of the Parts of the Body*, trans. M. T. May (Ithaca, NY: Cornell University Press, 1968), p. 292. Cited by Simons, 'The Flaming Heart', p. 20. I am grateful to Dr Simons for drawing this citation to my attention.

56 P. Simons, *The Sex of Men in Premodern Europe: A Cultural History* (Cambridge: Cambridge University Press, 2011), pp. 125, 129–34, 142–3.

57 *Ibid.*, p. 30.

58 *Ibid.*, pp. 125, 129, 143.

59 *Ibid.*, p. 129.

60 *Ibid.*

61 *Ibid.*, pp. 129–30.

62 *Ibid.*, p. 130.

63 Simons, *The Sex of Men in Premodern Europe*, pp. 38–45, 112–22.

64 Cavallo and Storey, *Healthy Living in Late Renaissance Italy*, p. 95.

65 Simons, *The Sex of Men in Premodern Europe*, p. 132.

66 *Ibid.*, p. 133.

67 The Carracci drew on the description of the rite in Plutarch's biography of Romulus (Plutarch, 'Romulus', pp. 157–61) and its citation in book II of Ovid's *Fasti*, where it is mentioned in the context of his discussion of the episode of Romulus and Remus and the cattle thieves (bk II, pp. 83–7; see also the appendix, with explanation of

the festival, pp. 389–97). On the Carracci image see Vitali, *Romulus in Bologna*, pp. 121–2 and N. Turner, 'Two Unpublished Drawings by Annibale Carracci in the British Museum', *The Burlington Magazine*, 137:1110 (September 1995), pp. 609–11.

68  Turner, 'Two Unpublished Drawings by Annibale Carracci', p. 610; Vitali, *Romulus in Bologna*, p. 240.
69  Simons, *The Sex of Men in Premodern Europe*, p. 132.
70  Ovid, *Fasti*, bk II, pp. 83–7. Vitali, *Romulus in Bologna*, p. 120.
71  Vitali, *Romulus in Bologna*, pp. 118–28.
72  On the statue of Hercules and some of the proposed identifications of the figures, see Vitali, 'Palazzo Magnani', p. 129.
73  On pneuma see Simons, *The Sex of Men in Premodern Europe*, pp. 138–9, 158–9, 279.
74  *Ibid.*, p. 135.
75  For maiolica childbirth wares see J. Musacchio, *The Art and Ritual of Childbirth in Renaissance Italy* (New Haven, CT and London: Yale University Press, 1999), pp. 91–123. On using art to reconstruct sensory experience, see E. J. Campbell, 'Listening to Objects: An Ecological Approach to the Decorative Arts', *Journal of Art Historiography*, 11 (December 2014), pp. 7, 15–16.
76  Musacchio, *The Art and Ritual of Childbirth in Renaissance Italy*, pp. 112–13 and Figure 101.
77  Simons, *The Sex of Men in Premodern Europe*, p. 287.
78  Ajmar-Wollheim and Dennis (eds), *At Home in Renaissance Italy*, p. 285.
79  Cavallo and Storey, *Healthy Living in Late Renaissance Italy*, pp. 96–7.

# 2

# Sensitive design: Robert de Montesquiou's sensorial installations and their condemnation

*Benoit Beaulieu*

'So sensitive is his soul that a pale green melody will make him swoon with emotion; the touch of a velvet-leafed flower will send him into ecstasies. He must be attuned with vague perfumes, with harmonies of colors.'[1] It is with these words that the French dandy Count Robert de Montesquiou (1855–1921) was described in the newspaper *The North American Philadelphia*. The article highlights the distinctive aspect of the critiques against de Montesquiou: the focus on his hypersensitivity said to be nearing the level of disease. Influential in the artistic scene of *fin-de-siècle* Paris, the dandy became famous precisely because of the sensorial installations of his first apartment that infamously inspired Joris-Karl Huysmans and his novel *Against Nature* (1884). Despite the variety of research on the sensorial aspect of the novel, the specific topic of de Montesquiou's peculiar use of the senses in interior design has never been the focus of scholars. This chapter centres around the ways de Montesquiou transformed the interiors of his first apartment into a work of art through the solicitation of the senses and how this specificity came to be used against him by his detractors.

De Montesquiou occupied his eleven-room apartment in the attic of his parents' *hôtel particulier* for fifteen years (1874–89). Through this specific case study, this chapter aims to offer a better understanding of the role the senses played in the condemnation of queer lifestyles as well as offering a recognition of queer agency and strategies of affirmation. The space was, as soon as 1931, described as queer by artist W. Graham Robertson: 'It was all queer, disturbing, baroque, yet individual and even beautiful, and as a transmutation of a set of unpromising attics into a tiny fairy palace, little short of conjuring trick.'[2] However, queer is more importantly understood in this chapter in all its complexity and its most comprehensive sense as relating to dissidence towards the heteronormative. Theorist David Halperin defines it as '*whatever* is at odds with the normal, the legitimate, the dominant' and therefore 'a positionality vis-à-vis the normative'.[3] Sara Ahmed's queer phenomenology is also taken into account here as it helps to think de Montesquiou's metaphorical and literal positionality towards his family. As she argues: 'To make things queer is certainly to disturb the order of things.'[4] The dandy disturbed the family's straight lines by materializing a queer space inside an unused part of the family's home and by using his inheritance to do so. He thereby quickly rejected the path predestined to him and managed to create an alternative way of living. The queer interior developed by de Montesquiou is here explored through the critiques that it generated in relation to hyperaesthesia, effeminophobia and pathologization. As a strategy of legitimation, de Montesquiou developed an original idea of the interior as artistic, aristocratic and therapeutic.

## Hyperaesthesia

The attic can be understood as a liminal space. Although a part of the familial space it is situated at its margin. Generally inhabited by the domestic workers, the attic became the site of decorative experimentation and identity formation for de Montesquiou. To get to his apartment, one had to go through the familial residences and the clash between both interiors must have been particularly striking. Robertson described the contrast in these words: 'It was curious to leave the stately, almost austere rooms of the old Comte and to climb up a dark stairway, through tunnels of tapestry to the eyrie which Comte Robert had elected to inhabit, and to come into the exotic atmosphere of his extraordinary rooms'.[5] The familial space was likely decorated in the pure French tradition, harmoniously furnished and symmetrically organized, reinforcing the classical decorating ideals of balance and harmony.[6] De Montesquiou's interior, on the other hand, was furnished eclectically and asymmetrically. The contrast of the scale and structural organization of the rooms must have been striking as well. In the family's home, the ceilings were high and the lines were straight. De Montesquiou's apartment was, on the contrary, irregular with the height of the ceilings quite low, and some rooms had vaulted ceilings due to the mansard roof of the building.

De Montesquiou's interior decoration made original use of the senses to engender a specific atmosphere for each room. Each had a specific colour scheme associated with a specific mood or theme. The red parlour was dedicated to the sun and joyous emotions [Figure 2.1]. The assemblage of furniture of different styles and numerous trinkets found cohesion through this colour scheme and the general atmospheric mood. The idea behind the dining room was one of eating in a garden [Figure 2.2]. The general colour scheme was green and William Morris's honeysuckle

**Figure 2.1**    Sun parlour at 41 quai d'Orsay. Bibliothèque nationale de France, Naf. 15037, f. 126.

**Figure 2.2**    Dining room at 41 quai d'Orsay. Photo Credit: © RMN-Grand Palais / Art Resource, NY.

wallpapers participated in the impression of nature. A shelving unit was supposed to imitate an arched trellis. The grey parlour was associated with the moon and more mysterious feelings [Figure 2.3]. When de Montesquiou described this specific room, he invoked every sense to do so: 'A crystal chest contained cloths which made it, when full of them, look like a block of marble with softer veins. A glass cone, the size of a young slave, raised in the air an iris of Suze or a tuft of musk, and an ivory mandora, hung on the wall, seemed to hang there, with itself, in its smooth curve, antiphons in honour of the milky star.'[7] The chaos was ordered here under the perceived exoticism of the arts of Japan and the emblems of the Count, the blue hydrangea and the bat. The bat is, in the case of de Montesquiou, a queer symbol as it represents an animal that does not fit in. Neither a mammal nor a bird, the bat is forced to live in the dark.[8] The animal also represented melancholy through its use by Albrecht Dürer.[9] De Montesquiou was quoted explaining in these words his association with the animal: 'I stand alone – the bat is my symbol – the symbol of melancholy, of solitude. In a crowd of birds the bat is alone.'[10] The blue hydrangea had a queer undertone for de Montesquiou as he liked its singular and artificial look. It was for the dandy a symbol of dissimilarity as it exhibited a colour that was unlike the others.[11]

**Figure 2.3**    Moon parlour at 41 quai d'Orsay. Bibliothèque nationale de France, Naf. 15037, f. 127.

Throughout the apartment, various decorations, like curtains, tinted glass and even glassware, were used to dim or tint the natural light coming from the windows. De Montesquiou's first interiors originated his popularity and can explain how he came to be strongly associated with an excessive sensitivity. Defined as an exacerbated sensitivity of all senses, hyperaesthesia was recognized as a medical condition. The visual chaos created by the presence of many pieces of furniture and clothing, textiles and objects reinforced the hyperstimulation of the senses; a hyperstimulation that concerns not only the eyes but also the touch.

Art historian Michael Hatt informs us of the objections in a large number of decoration handbooks against the different textures and shininess of lacquered furniture deemed as sensuous, vulgar and decadent surfaces.[12] The shininess of surfaces was vilified as excessively exciting to the nerves. Such condemnation of hyperaesthesia and hyperstimulation was theorized by numerous authors including physician Max Nordau (1849–1923), criminologist Cesare Lombroso (1835–1909) and novelist Paul Bourget (1852–1935). Artists were described as particularly prone to this condition. These theorists of decadence feared that the public would be contaminated by their art. In *The Man of Genius* (1891 [1876]), Lombroso describes hyperaesthesia as a sign of higher morality and the root of genius.[13] He depicts the difference between a genius and an ordinary person as 'consist[ing] in very great part in an exquisite, and sometimes perverted, sensibility'.[14] For Bourget, who also tried to understand the roots of artistic talent and genius through biographies of great writers in *Essais de Psychologie Contemporaine* (1883), the quality of the writing of some authors could be explained by a refinement of their senses and a hyperacuity of the sensations that approached the level of a disease.[15] He associated the need for thrills to a strategy to compensate for the void left by a lost and meaningless society. Like Lombroso, Bourget saw some good in sensitivity and even the unhealthiness linked to it, as long as it stayed within the artistic realm and helped to create great works of art.[16] The arts were in part responsible for propagating degeneracy to the rest of the society in Nordau's opinion. He explains in *Degeneration* (1892) that the 'effort of the nervous system' and 'nervous excitement' are causes of decadence.[17] The same effects were true in the domestic realm and in particular the pursuit of sensorial interiors as it was for him a cause of the general degeneracy of society:

> Everything in these houses aims at exciting the nerves and dazzling the senses. The disconnected and antithetical effects in all arrangements, the constant contradiction between form and purpose, the outlandishness of most objects, is intended to be bewildering. There must be no sentiment of repose, such as is felt at any composition, the plan of which is easily taken in, nor of the comfort attending a prompt comprehension of all the details of one's environment. He who enters here must not doze, but be thrilled.[18]

In Bourget's opinion, *bibelots* were the signs of 'a worried time when the weariness of boredom and diseases of nervous sensitivity led man to invent false collector's passions'.[19] The interior full of objects was then a reflection of the loss of guidelines in modern society that witnessed the frantic search for sensorial excitation. De Montesquiou's interior encompassed what these authors abhorred most in modern design and culture.

De Montesquiou was repeatedly criticized for his sensitivity, which was judged to be excessive. His sensitivity was characterised as leading to a physical disorder, as seen in an article in the *Evening World* which reported how the yellow of a glove caused him and his entourage fatigue.[20] The same article related a similarly exaggerated reaction to a gorgeous bouquet of flowers and the impact of its sight and smell. Such hypersensitivity was also caricatured in a follow-up article the next day in which de Montesquiou got sick from an oyster 'not poetically flavored' and further sketches the reaction as 'a dissonance where there is usually harmony in the delicate organs – vulgarly called the stomach –bringing in a confusion of dreams'.[21] His valet is described as trying to soothe his discomfort with a bottle of hot water but is stopped by the possible dissonance of the bottle with the colours of the Count's pyjamas: 'not daring to take any water bag of a shade off the chromatic hue of his master's slumber robes he awakened M. Gabriel'.[22] In these caricatures, a pathologized sensitivity is related to an artistic sensitivity, relating symptoms of discomfort to the fields of poetry, colours and harmonies. The sensitivity is situated in the domestic realm, but the example of the pyjamas reveals that it also concerned the sartorial realm.

The permission granted to professional artists to exhibit the traits of hyperaesthesia was denied to de Montesquiou as he was constantly portrayed as a mere amateur. He had to fight to reclaim the title of artist and thereby gain that permission. In 'Les Snobs', journalist Adolphe Brisson categorized de Montesquiou as an amateur. Brisson recognized some originality and talent on the part of the Count but was worried that he might have a bad influence on 'well-born' young persons and lead them to art and away from their respectable jobs. He added: 'The amateur! Scourge of our decadence!'[23] For his part, art critic Arsène Alexandre presented de Montesquiou in *Le Figaro* as the incarnation of the decadent dilettante and ridiculed his work, criticizing his multiple artistic endeavours, particularly his collaboration on furniture with the designer Émile Gallé (1846–1904), as well as his eccentric clothing.[24] He compared the amateur to a dangerous microbe that infiltrates every aspect of the artistic world, responsible for its decadence. He also criticized the appeal of the artificial against the natural, as he wrote that the amateur prefers blue hydrangeas to roses because the latter's smell is 'unbreathable for his sensitive nostrils'.[25] Overall, it was the impact this could have on France and its perception by other countries that worried Alexandre the most.

De Montesquiou responded in the same newspaper with a letter titled 'Artistes de Profession' in which he rejected the notion of 'professional artists', writing that the word professional is 'bourgeois and mercantile' and 'takes away from [the term artist] all that it has of mysterious and winged, ideal and suprasensible'.[26] He reclaimed the purity of his own approach, detached from any bourgeois mercantile aspects.

The same authors previously quoted who condemned an excessive expression of sensitivity were also highly critical of dilettantism in general. For instance, Bourget associated it with the search for pleasures that resulted in being interested in different activities without fully developing one.[27] Bourget summarized the links between amateurism, interior decoration and sensitivity in the following manner:

> To better grasp how the dilettantism of which he has given such an astonishing example and formulated such a complete apology is in fact in the very blood of this period, consider the manners and society, furnishings and conversation. Is not everything here multiple? Does not everything invite you to turn your soul into a mosaic of complicated sensations?[28]

For Bourget, modern society was responsible for the search for new and complicated sensations and the interior decoration was a symptom of that. The discourse vilifying the amateur and the exhibition of a hypersensitivity outside of the artistic realm was profoundly effeminophobic.

## Performing masculinity

As an aristocrat, bachelor, dandy, poet and interior decorator, de Montesquiou occupied a difficult position: too bohemian for the aristocracy, but not enough for the artistic scene. Regardless, his fields of interest were categorized as feminine. His performance of gender was generally described as effeminate and was swiftly associated with homosexuality, explicitly or not. His effeminacy was highlighted within numerous articles and caricatures emphasizing the popularity of de Montesquiou's lectures among women.[29] This visual corpus portrayed the Count as one of the women, not worthy of the attention of serious-minded men. These caricatures show how de Montesquiou was deemed dangerous to gender norms as he transgressed the clear division between male and female. Fear of the blurring of gender boundaries was also, importantly, at the root of the theories of and fears centred on decadence.[30] De Montesquiou's gender trouble was also evoked through the appeal he had for women. Fear for the possible sexual attraction that women could have towards de Montesquiou was linked to his effeminacy as it was understood as 'an excess of what we would call *heterosexual* as well as homosexual desire'.[31] Caricatures, like the one published by the *Philadelphia Inquirer* in 1903, showed women 'worshipping' the Count at his feet [Figure 2.4]. Looking at them from

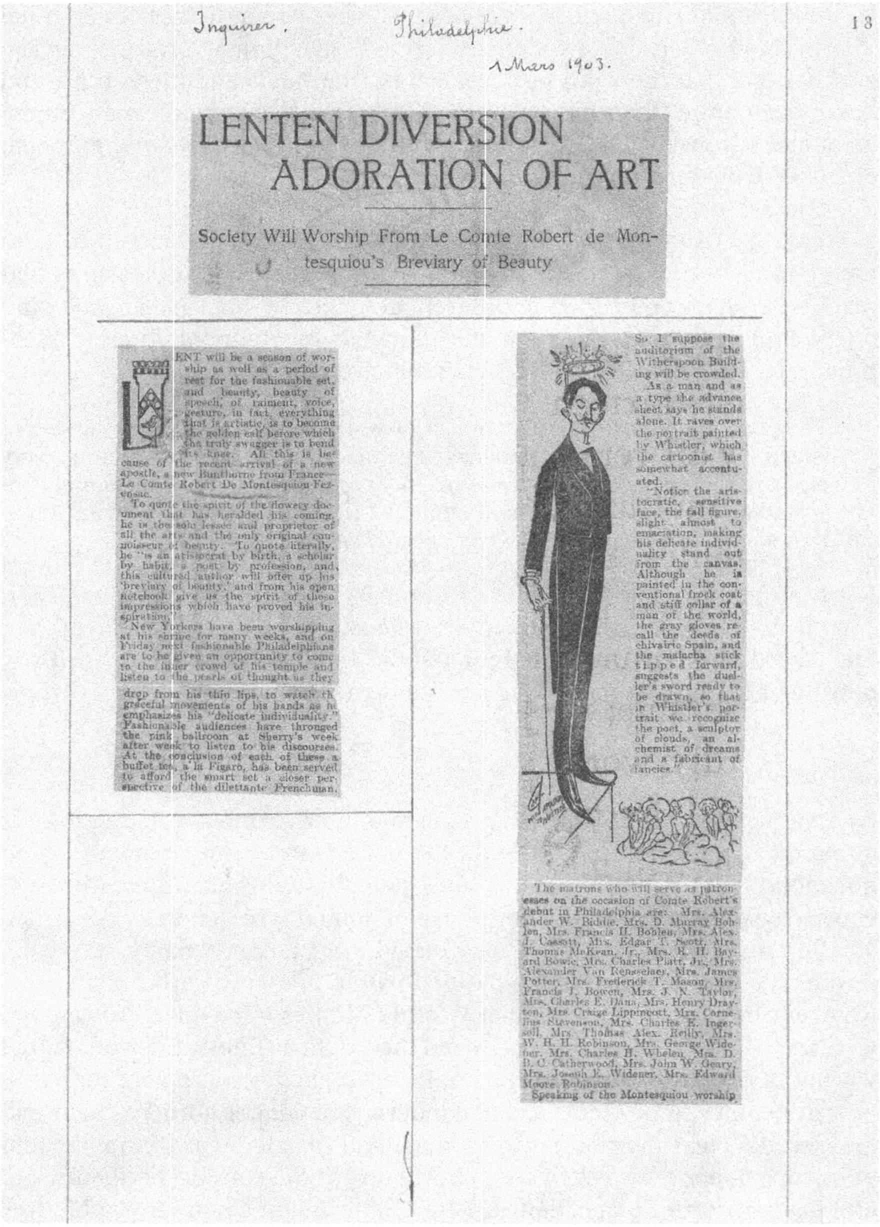

**Figure 2.4** 'Lenten Diversion Adoration of Art', *Philadelphia Inquirer*, 1 March 1903. Bibliothèque nationale de France, Naf. 15061, f. 18.

above with a disdainful stare, de Montesquiou appears as a false prophet with his counterfeit aureole.

Fashion was a prominent stage on which the attacks on effeminacy were waged. A man's extreme care of his image was perceived as superficial and was condemned as effeminate. It was rumoured that de Montesquiou during his trip to the United States had brought thirty trunks of clothes and two barbers, one to take care of his moustache and the other employed to cut his hair. This attention to his appearance was the subject of countless caricatures published in the midst of de Montesquiou's visit to the United States such as the one published in the *Evening World* in which the Count is represented smoking in an armchair while his entourage, consisting of his lover and secretary Gabriel Yturri and his two barbers, are praising him [Figure 2.5]. His gender performance is ridiculed through the use of a ruffled dressing gown that gives him an hourglass shape, flower-patterned trousers and high heels with small ribbons. Music notes are drawn coming out of the clothes, as the caricature illustrated an article mocking the impact of street noises on the harmonies of his clothing.[32] The drawing teases the visual disharmony between the different patterns of his clothes and of the pieces of furniture and decoration, further highlighted by the forced flattery of his entourage. The entourage, also feminized through voluptuous bodies and ruffled cravats, are dressed in all-black costumes and exacerbate de Montesquiou's sartorial eccentricity.

Numerous were the accounts stating that visiting de Montesquiou's home was only a complete experience with the performance of its host, as Philippe Thiébaut has shown.[33] De Montesquiou would animate the rooms through the sound of his voice. The guided tours of his interiors would make sense of the visual chaos as he explained to his guests the hidden rules underlying the decoration – the leitmotifs, as he called them in reference to Richard Wagner (1813–83). In the moon parlour, for instance, the dandy's verbal explanations would reveal the connections between the eclectic mix of artworks, flowers, pieces of furniture and *objets d'art*, all united under the leitmotif of melancholy. These vocal performances were described as 'masterpieces'[34] by journalist Paul Heuzé, while writer Jules Bertaut saw a true spectacle in the way he would host guests: 'He always knew how to dazzle them with the fireworks of his words, a magnificent spectacle of incomparable talker that he offered to himself and to others.'[35] Synaesthetic metaphors were used in descriptions of the sound of his voice, which was equated to a musical instrument: 'the Count's voice is not in the least conversational. It soars musically up the scale and down again'.[36] It was also compared to visual phenomena: 'It has all the tone colors of a rainbow of sound.'[37] Beyond the auditory aspect of the physicality of the tours of his home given by de Montesquiou, the haptic aspect of it is also worth mentioning. A visitor stated that in 'this small museum [...] each objet d'art is understood, changed, caressed by

**Figure 2.5** 'Well, Then, That Fifth Avenue Was So Noisy He Couldn't Hear His Clothes', *Evening World*, 23 January 1903. Bibliothèque nationale de France, Naf. 15059, f. 91.

the one who owns it'.[38] The sense of touch was therefore essential in completing the various atmospheres of each room.

Brisson noted, incorrectly, how de Montesquiou was the first to introduce fragrance into interior decoration.[39] The poet-dandy was believed to have placed a perfume burner in every room to spread sweet odours, each with a particular symbolic meaning. Brisson even stated that the odours would change depending on the nature of conversations. The practice of burning perfumes in the home was not new and although the sophistication of its use is certainly exaggerated, this anecdote highlights, nonetheless, the deep connexion between de Montesquiou and the sense of smell and its importance in conjuring complete sensory atmospheres. Filled with flowers, the rooms were probably heavily scented with perfumes that differed from one room to another in order to accentuate the mood and differentiate further each atmosphere. De Montesquiou reclaimed that association as he was self-titled *le Chef des odeurs suaves* (literally, the leader of sweet odours), despite the attacks that used smell to mock his gender expression. In another satirical article, de Montesquiou was associated with the smell of violets, a description that was coupled with a suggestion that he was not as effeminate as the rumour said: 'There was a disappointing absence of laces and ruffles, and no suggestion of the languorous odor of violets.'[40] Fashion and odour commingled, as both forms of personal adornment were indexical of effeminacy. He was mocked for making an excessive use of perfumes in one article which stated that he had omitted to perfume himself for a fourth time because he was too busy preparing his first lecture in New York.[41] Playing more explicitly with a sexual allusion to his use of sweet perfume, another article reported that during the interludes of his lectures, 'the dear friend M. Gabriel Yturri [...] will spray the throat of this descendant of D'Artagnan with a purple atomizer filled with honey-scented cologne'.[42] Deemed as feminine and ranked at the bottom of the hierarchy of the senses, smell was closely related to the world of flowers and fragrances, all things fleeting and frivolous.[43]

This reference to d'Artagnan points to the frequent evocation by de Montesquiou of his familial relation to Charles Batz de Castelmore (1611–73), the inspiration for the musketeer d'Artagnan in Alexandre Dumas' *The Three Musketeers* (1844) and archetype of virile masculinity. This was a way of historicizing his eccentricities as a distinct family trait. More generally, de Montesquiou reclaimed his sense of belonging to the aristocracy. This strategy justified his high degree of sensitivity as a trait of his social class and naturalized the need for him to stand out. In an article he was quoted as saying: 'I come from a remarkable family, a family unlike other families. I could not be commonplace. I could not be ordinary' and adding that eccentricity was natural to him.[44] In the domestic realm, it justified his idiosyncratic decoration while in terms of fashion it explained his aim to stand out. The evocation of his aristocratic heritage legitimized his multiple artistic endeavours and his self-aestheticization. Inherited pieces of furniture from his family were displayed among his eclectic interior, emphasizing the dandy's noble lineage. In the sun parlour, for instance, an Empire jardinière and a swan-based guéridon were placed next to an eighteenth-century table designed by French cabinetmaker Martin Carlin.

De Montesquiou's kinship was a frequent topic of mockery. A recurring visual strategy of comparing de Montesquiou with the Musketeers accentuated the Count's effeminacy and delicate, slender corporeality. Articles strongly compared de Montesquiou with his famous ancestor on the basis of his physical and mental strength with titles such as 'Scion of the House of D'Artagnan – His Antithesis in Physique and Nerve'.[45] Qualifying him as a 'degenerate descendant', another article summarizes the topics of reproach:

> But the people of New York who hoped to find in D'Artagnan's descendant any of the characteristics that made their hero so fascinating have been disappointed. He is a melancholy aesthete, of the Oscar Wilde type, who composes lugubrious verse in a perfumed room to the strains of voluptuous music, like Mary Maclane, declares himself different from anyone else in the world.
>
> If he chose he might wear the name of his dashing ancestor, but to this modern exquisite so repulsive are the thoughts of his ancestor's strenuous life that he has, because of his sensitive nature, chosen the appellation he now bears [sic].[46]

The description of an interior that overstimulates the senses is instrumentalized to vilify de Montesquiou as weak and decadent. References to Mary Maclane (1881–1929) and Oscar Wilde (1854–1900) are here used to qualify de Montesquiou as homosexual. Known as the 'Wild Woman of Butte', the American writer Maclane was openly bisexual, and her autobiographical novel had recently been published with great controversy. The comparison with de Montesquiou highlights his subversive sexuality but also the fear of strong and free dissidents. The reference to Wilde is even more violent as the British writer had died a few years prior in Paris, ruined after his notable trial of 1895 and subsequent imprisonment. This comparison serves as a reminder of the consequences of being queer. The Count's queerness is correlated to his overtly sensitive nature that therefore explains his lifestyle.

## Pathologization

The discourse that vilified de Montesquiou participated in a more general strategy to pathologize him, relying on his sensitivity and effeminacy as signs of his decadence. As the century was coming to an end, de Montesquiou served as the epitome of the aristocrat *fin de race*, the last and degenerate breed of his kind. Portrayed as overtly sensitive to sounds, odours and even taste and suffering from outside sensorial stimuli, de Montesquiou represented the frail health that was associated with his archetype. Generally presented as a psychological disorder, de Montesquiou's hyperaesthesia was also categorized as a physical disorder or at least as having a significant and apparent impact on his body. The hypersensitivity in the domestic realm is further developed in one of his obituaries which described him as:

> the most meticulous man in Paris. He was to mania, to exasperation. [...] The problem of domesticity, of a satisfactory domesticity, was, moreover, one of the poisons of his existence. A trinket disturbed by a millimetre, a bit of forgotten dust, put him in a mad rage. But apart from these nerves, he was a charming man, extremely meticulous, in every detail of his friendship.[47]

His sensitivity is here linked to his recent passing in claiming that it poisoned his life. Even Anatole France (1844–1924), a champion of de Montesquiou, described his search for the rare and precious as a delicious sickness, but a sickness nonetheless.[48]

De Montesquiou used intersensoriality and multisensoriality as strategies of legitimation, as these strategies participated in his process of reclaiming the artistic label. Sometimes coined as synaesthesia, intersensoriality describes the experience of a stimulus associated with one sense by another sense ('the intermingling of sensations'), while multisensoriality is more about the combination of different media to create a coherent spectacle.[49] Intersensoriality might be the first step leading to multisensorial installations, the wish to materialize a subjective feeling. Intersensoriality and multisensoriality were often combined, like in the case of de Montesquiou's work. His first interior is a prime example of this kind of experiment in decoration as he combined paintings, wallpapers, furniture design, clothing and fabrics, music instruments and *objets d'art* in order to create total sensorial experiences. De Montesquiou went as far as to theorize such sensorial interior decoration in his treatise titled *Les Onze Chambres*, which refers to the eleven rooms that comprised his first apartment. From the still lost text, there remains only the description given by its author: 'This guide, written on assorted papers, included the name of each room, the gem and flower to put in, the animal that might be familiar there, the instrument to be listened to'.[50] The text is nonetheless revealing of the self-awareness and the thought process behind de Montesquiou's decoration and its intersensoriality. The intersensoriality of his practice is particularly manifest in his memoirs, in which he argued that his interior decoration was a form of writing: 'I hold such fantasies pertaining to the walls and furniture, for writings, both literary and musical.'[51] He added that he would organize the different elements of his interior 'like the words of a poem or the notes of a symphony'.[52] Claiming that his decoration was a form of literature or music can also be perceived as a way to elevate decoration to the rank of the fine arts. In so doing, de Montesquiou shared the ideas of the Aesthetes from the other side of the Channel, like his friend and portraitist James McNeill Whistler (1834–1903) and most importantly essayist Walter Pater (1839–94) who famously wrote in *The Renaissance* (1873): 'All art constantly aspires towards the condition of music.'[53] In the conclusion of the same book, Pater further asserted his idea of art for art's sake while promoting an existence devoted to the search for pleasure, mostly the pleasure induced by the stimulation of the sensations through art.[54] The homophobic reception of Pater's conclusion as possibly corrupting the youth exemplifies how de Montesquiou's interiors and his way of life were also received.

The association of the Count with such a practice of mixing and intermingling the arts struck a chord in his critical reception. De Montesquiou was for instance depicted in a caricature as painting a lyre, which can be seen as if he was writing poetry with a paintbrush, as literally combining two forms of art. The Count was also constantly described in synaesthetic terms, as we have seen with his voice and his clothes described in musical or visual terms. Despite the legitimizing aspect of his approach, such practices were often condemned or ridiculed in the visual and literary culture of the time. The numerous treatises on decadence presented inter- and multisensoriality as symptoms of decadence. The differentiated senses were perceived as an evolutionary trait and therefore the combination of senses was associated with a form of regression nearing primeval animals as well as with mental illness.[55] Despite the fact that the literature presenting synaesthesia positively was more prevalent, the literature condemning it was nevertheless influential and used repeatedly against de Montesquiou.[56] Positive views on synaesthesia could also bounce back against the Count, such as *Sexual Inversion* (1897), in which Havelock Ellis (1859–1939) and John Addington Symonds (1840–93) drew a connection between synaesthesia and homosexuality.[57] For them, they were both neurological conditions, not dangerous degeneracies. This example shows that even the most favourable authors saw the combination of senses as abnormal and suspect.

The association between synaesthesia and decadence had been popularized by the novel *Against Nature*. Its main character, Des Esseintes, personified physical decay through illnesses: anorexia, obsessive behaviours, sexual impotence. Des Esseintes' longing for sensations and synaesthesia serve as an additional symptom of his degeneracy. As the epitome of the decadent aristocrat, Des Esseintes was used to further characterize de Montesquiou as part of this cast. This association was constantly made through the story of the gilded turtle taken from *Against Nature*. In the novel, Des Esseintes embellishes the shell of his pet tortoise with precious stones and gold to bring light and animation to his interior. The animal dies under the weight of the excessive adornment of his shell.

This story serves as a metaphor for the morbidity of Des Esseintes' quest.[58] It further participated in blurring the lines between reality and fiction, between Des Esseintes and de Montesquiou, as the latter had made the same experiment with his own tortoise.

De Montesquiou recognized his obsessive attachment to his interior decoration. In his memoirs, he described it as a madness and an intoxication similar to that of hashish consumers and wrote that he felt like he was sometimes possessed by the demon of adornment.[59] He also highlighted the dangerous side of his passion, as it ended up costing him a rather substantial fortune.[60] He later mitigated this affirmation by stating that it prevented him from falling for other passions that could have been even more expensive than decoration.[61] But he also strongly proclaimed the therapeutic virtues of his interior. His memoirs and poems are rich in references to the positive and healthy qualities of his décor, mostly on his mood. He wrote in *Les Pas effacés*: 'few people were allowed to visit these unique premises, of which it seemed to me that the influence, effective for me, to the point that I attributed to them a therapeutic virtue was to be lost and dispersed by the lavishness of their spectacle'.[62] Colours and lights participated deeply in this therapeutic process.

Giving examples of the therapeutic virtue, he wrote that the two golden screens in the sun parlour infused the room with happiness and gave it 'a happy soul'.[63] He added that the coloured glass in the windows of the parlour would protect the interior from the outside sadness by preventing banal lighting, mainly the light of moody days, from entering into the room.[64] It felt like being in a lacquered box, he wrote: 'The sensation it gave was that of believing himself locked in one of those lacquer boxes in different shades of gold.'[65] It was also reminiscent of the poem 'Thérapeutique' in which the poet-dandy emphasized the therapeutic virtue of lacquer: 'And the lacquer, on me, can effect conversions / Which the holiest Zions would demand in vain.'[66] Contrary to the condemnation of shininess and its possible excitation of the nerves, de Montesquiou promoted the same visual elements as a source of calm and happiness. He describes how beautiful *objets d'art* have greater effects on his morale than the strongest cure could ever have.[67] In the poem 'Alluvions', he writes that, when coming home, he finds his interiors have the power of soothing the spleen or the sadness experienced outside of his domestic interior.[68] De Montesquiou used all accessible platforms to promote the healthiness of his practice and try to counter the vehement attacks that disqualified him as decadent.

## Conclusion

The study of Robert de Montesquiou's first apartment and its reception highlights the deep links between the senses and the interior. Belittled as hypersensitive and effeminate, de Montesquiou's care for his interior and its idiosyncratic sensorial installations have made him the archetype of the decadent dilettante. At a time when homosexuality was being theorized with particular attention to the existence of specific characteristics that distinguished it, de Montesquiou became a prime specimen of study. The negative reception of de Montesquiou's persona underlines the proportional impact he has had on culture.

Occupying an uncomfortable place in culture, de Montesquiou managed to legitimize his position through many strategies. His reappropriation of sensitivity as a sign of his artistic and aristocratic excellence and the emphasis he placed on the therapeutic force of his interior authorized behaviours that were pugnaciously condemned. Although the victim of harsh critics and attacks, the Count later managed to become one of the most famous and influential socialites in Paris. The organization of lavish parties dedicated to the advocacy of specific artists came with a turn to more restraint in the expression of his taste, particularly regarding interior decoration. After his death, de Montesquiou left an impressive array of archival documents, including his memoirs in three books and the 369 volumes that compose his archive, the *Papiers Montesquiou*. This archival mania could be seen as a last strategy of legitimation for posterity and an insurance that, despite all the rumours, his truth could be restored.

## Notes

1  *North American Philadelphia*, 'Robert de Montesquiou-Ferzenac [sic], Le Comte, To Sing Sonnet-Songs' (1 March 1903).
2  W. G. Robertson, *Time Was* (London: Hamish Hamilton, 1931), p. 100.
3  D. M. Halperin, *Saint Foucault, Towards a Gay Hagiography* (New York: Oxford University Press, 1995), p. 62.
4  S. Ahmed, 'Orientations: Towards a Queer Phenomenology', *GLQ: A Journal of Gay and Lesbian Studies*, 12:4 (2006), p. 565.
5  Robertson, *Time*, p. 100.
6  The contrast between the decoration of de Montesquiou's apartment and the rest of the familial residences is visually highlighted in the dandy's personal archive by the inclusion, right after the pictures of his first apartment in the dedicated catalogue, of a picture described, incorrectly, as a room at the quai d'Orsay residence. The picture is in fact a parlour in the château de Charnizay, a familial residence in the French department of Indre-et-Loire.
7  R. de Montesquiou, *Les Pas effacés*, 3 vols (Paris: Éditions du Sandre, 2007 [1923]), p. 80; my translation.
8  'The Poet of the Ideal', *The Times* (20 January 1903).
9  E. Munhall, *Whistler and Montesquiou: The Butterfly and the Bat* (New York and Paris: Frick Collection and Flammarion, 1995), p. 36.
10  E. Kemp, 'Are There Any More at Home Like You Count Montesquiou?', *The American* (25 January 1903).
11  De Montesquiou, *Pas*, p. 71.
12  M. Hatt, 'Space, Surface, Self: Homosexuality and the Aesthetic Interior', *Visual Culture in Britain*, 8:1 (2004), p. 113.
13  C. Lombroso, *The Man of Genius* (London: Walter Scott, 1891 [1876]), p. 27.

14  *Ibid.*, p. 26.
15  P. Bourget, *Essais de Psychologie Contemporaine* (Paris: Plon-Nourrit & Cie, 1883), p. 383.
16  *Ibid.*
17  M. Nordau, *Degeneration* (London: William Heinemann, 1898 [1892]), p. 39.
18  *Ibid.*, p. 11.
19  Bourget, *Essais*, p. 380; my translation.
20  *Evening World*, 'Surprising Happening in the Third Day of the Sojourn of the Comte Montesquiou' (20 January 1903).
21  *Evening World*, 'Montesquiou Ill; Ate Bad Oysters' (21 January 1903).
22  *Ibid.*
23  A. Brisson, 'Les Snobs', *La Liberté* (1901); my translation.
24  A. Alexandre, 'Les Amateurs', *Le Figaro* (2 July 1895); my translation.
25  *Ibid.*
26  R. de Montesquiou, 'Artistes de Profession', *Le Figaro* (4 July 1895); my translation.
27  Bourget, *Essais*, p. 59.
28  *Ibid.*, p. 70; my translation.
29  *Evening Journal*, 'Society Goes to See Apostle of Beauty' (6 February 1903). And *New York Press*, 'Count Robert's First Talk: He Lectures on Versailles to a Feminine Audience' (6 February 1903).
30  M. L. Roberts, *Civilization Without Sexes: Reconstructing Gender in Postwar France, 1917–1927* (Chicago and London: University of Chicago Press, 1990), p. 4 in J. Potvin, *Deco Dandy: Designing Masculinity in 1920s Paris* (Manchester: Manchester University Press, 2020), p. 131.
31  D. M. Halperin, 'How to Do the History of Male Homosexuality', *GLQ: The Journal of Lesbian and Gay Studies*, 6:1 (2000), p. 92 in Potvin, *Deco Dandy*, p. 135.
32  *Evening World*, 'Well, Then, That Fifth Avenue Was So Noisy He Couldn't Hear His Clothes' (23 January 1903).
33  P. Thiébaut, *Robert de Montesquiou ou l'art de paraître* (Paris: Réunion des musées nationaux, 1999), p. 14.
34  P. Heuzé, 'Sur Robert de Montesquiou', *L'Opinion* (24 December 1921); my translation.
35  J. Bertaut, 'Une Aventure de M. de Montesquiou', *Le Paris-Journal* (25 December 1921); my translation.
36  Kemp, 'Are There Any More at Home Like You Count Montesquiou?'.
37  J. Montague, 'Beauty Count Talks to Society Women', *Evening Journal* (6 February 1903).
38  Thiébaut, *Robert de Montesquiou*, p. 15; my translation.
39  Brisson, 'Les Snobs'.
40  *Philadelphia Inquirer*, 'Æsthetic Count Was Disappointing' (7 March 1903).
41  *Denver's Post*, 'Poetry for Cold Feet' (23 January 1903).
42  *Evening World*, 'Count Robert's Thrills To-Day' (6 February 1903).
43  C. Classen, 'Engendering Perception: Gender Ideologies and Sensory Hierarchies in Western History', *Body & Society*, 3:2 (1997), p. 4.
44  Kemp, 'Are There Any More at Home Like You Count Montesquiou?'.
45  *Saint-Louis Star*, 'Scion of the House of D'Artagnan – His Antithesis in Physique and Nerve' (1 March 1903).
46  *Detroit News Tribune*, 'True Story of the Three Musketeers Told by a Descendant of the Hero, D'Artagnan' (1 March 1903).
47  H. de Forge, 'Le Poète méticuleux', *Le Courrier du Soir* (20 December 1921); my translation.
48  A. France, 'Le Comte Robert de Montesquiou', *Le Temps* (13 November 1892).
49  D. Howes and C. Classen, *Ways of Sensing: Understanding the Senses in Society* (London and New York: Routledge, 2014), p. 11.

50 Sales Catalogue Hôtel Drouot, *Bibliothèque de Robert de Montesquiou* (Paris: M. Escoffier, 23–26 April 1923), p. 76; my translation.

51 De Montesquiou, *Pas*, pp. 76–7; my translation.

52 *Ibid.*

53 W. Pater, *The Renaissance: Studies in Art and Poetry* (London: MacMillan and Co., 1902 [1873]), pp. 135 and 237.

54 *Ibid.*, p. 237.

55 Nordau, *Degeneration*, p. 142.

56 J. Jewanski, J. Simner, S. A. Day, N. Rothen and J. Ward, 'The "Golden Age" of Synaesthesia Inquiry in the Late Nineteenth Century (1876–1895)', *Journal of the History of the Neurosciences*, 29:2 (2020), p. 21.

57 M. L. R. Poueymirou, 'The Sixth Sense: Synaesthesia and British Aestheticism 1860–1900' (PhD diss., St Andrews, 2009), p. 4.

58 W. Klee, 'Incarnating Decadence: Reading Des Esseintes's Bodies', *Paroles gelées*, 17:2 (1999), p. 61.

59 De Montesquiou, *Pas*, pp. 65 and 82.

60 *Ibid.*, p. 61.

61 *Ibid.*, p. 63.

62 *Ibid.*, p. 83; my translation.

63 *Ibid.*, p. 79.

64 *Ibid.*, p. 77.

65 *Ibid.*

66 De Montesquiou, *Les Hortensias bleus* (Paris: G. Charpentier and E. Fasquelle, 1896), p. 149; my translation.

67 *Ibid.*

68 *Ibid.*, pp. 140–1.

# 3

# Reassessing Pierre Legrain's 'Black Deco': sensual luxury, primitivism and the French bourgeois interior

*John Potvin*

Primitivism is a highly contested term and forms part of a volatile lexicon rooted in colonial ambitions and an imperialist world view. In the early twentieth century the term served as a cipher for aesthetic initiatives that would become the hallmark of modern art, design and Western cultural identity itself. Countless are the texts exploring the so-called 'heroic' work of Pablo Picasso whose avant-garde cubist pictures were the outcome of his own well-documented study and collection of African masks. Despite the vast, influential scholarship exposing the relationship between modern art and primitivism, inspired by MoMA's controversial exhibition *'Primitivism' in 20th Century Art: Affinity of the Tribal and the Modern* from 1984–85, no comparable study has yet to be undertaken exploring the impact, influence and tensions primitivism has had on the interior design of the early twentieth century. Much scholarly attention has been paid specifically to African sculpture and masks as sources of inspiration, yet what about the African furniture and domestic objects that served as design blueprints and were transformed into *objets de luxe* for the French bourgeois home? As influential art dealer and collector Paul Guillaume (1891–1934) famously asserted, not only was the *style moderne* (or art deco) seen as a critical path toward recovery following the devastation wrought by World War I, primitivism specifically was *the* path to the renewal of design and modern existence itself. In fact, Guillaume posited that at the celebrated, though controversial, Exposition Internationale des Arts Décoratifs et Industriels Modernes of 1925 *'the predominance of the negro motif was obvious among the really new and distinctive notes in interior decoration. [...] The most important lines of influence were [...] the possibility of applying negro sculpture principles to a resurrection of artistic traditions that had been considered dead'.*[1] Guillaume, however, was not alone in suggesting that primitivism would be a vital conduit to aesthetic as much as economic and cultural rejuvenation.

To claim that the haptic is critical to practices, production and uses of design is indeed axiomatic. However, as it concerns historically distanced objects in general and more precisely art deco, much of our attention has been paid to the 'look' – or even the visual feel – of the objects that populated the domestic interior. A significant feature of the success, attention paid to and enormous sums paid at auction for art deco furniture remains the haptic; the attention paid to detail and the heightened sense of glamour and luxury that could only have been read and understood through one's touch. In turn, I claim this largely overlooked haptic economy of art deco had a tacit racial dimension. This chapter, then, attempts to reposition the centrality of the senses, more specifically the haptic, and their association with African and African-inspired design within the complicated and fraught landscape of *style moderne* interior design. To do so, I turn to two unique chairs designed by *ensemblier* Pierre Legrain (1889–1929)[2] that were integral to his larger interior design programmes for two fashionable, wealthy French patrons, *couturier* Jacques Doucet (1853–1929) and *modiste* Jeanne Tachard (1870–1963). Decoration, or ornamentation, and the lower senses (the haptic especially) have too often been deployed as ciphers of (sexual) degeneracy, the feminine and colonized peoples. Yet, collectors like Guillaume and *ensembliers* like Legrain unabashedly celebrated decorative abandon as much as the sensory potential of African material culture. The coupling of the haptic and the primitive here firmly underscores a cultural contest and tension and resides at the centre of the chapter's investigation of the use of so-called 'Black Deco' within interwar *haute bourgeois* interior design.

Within the restrictions and limitations of this chapter, there is little room to fully elaborate on the histories, differences between and linguistic and sociopolitical pitfalls of historical uses of *l'art nègre, l'art primitif* and *l'art africain*. However, while each term emerged at different junctures of French colonial history, the first two of these terms were often collapsed and conflated, one meant to stand in for the other as seen in Guillaume's writing briefly outlined above. Gradually over the course of the 1920s *l'art primitif* began to slowly replace *l'art nègre*, as a stand-in not only for the arts of Africa but for all colonized regions.[3] While remaining sensitive to the colonial and racist agenda, conscious or otherwise, imbedded in such terminology, classifications and aesthetic designations, as an overarching term, though deeply inadequate and not without problem and limitations, I deploy primitivism in the spirit of Sieglinde Lemke's important suggestion that 'wittingly or unwittingly, Euro-American modernism's identity has always been hyphenated, has always been hybrid, has always been biracial'.[4] Both individual and official responses to primitivism are intimately bound up with the way the so-called primitive was mobilized through the global flow of objects which entered into France, expropriated through a distinct 'colonial matrix of power'.[5] Colonialism and modern design were so inextricably linked they gave form to material practices of an elaborate 'colonial matrix of power' that affected the sensory dimension of such objects. As my title suggests, I borrow art historian Rosalind Krauss's notional 'Black Deco' that she insinuates, even if in passing, signifies a 'stylizing attitude that allows for the resultant playful recombination and transmutation of the original examples'. Krauss avers that designers, like Pierre Legrain specifically, were successful precisely because they managed to conjure a purported 'Africanity' (to borrow from Roland Barthes as Krauss does), 'without preserving the structural integrity of the models'.[6] Perhaps more significantly for my purposes are the so-called aesthetic qualities to which 'Black Deco' refers. Legrain's furniture, the outcome of a seemingly alchemical transformation of African original objects, is notable precisely because of its 'smoothed out' quality, which renders it shiny, slick and hence sufficiently bourgeois and, more importantly, sensuously luxurious. This transformative act is also enabled through the legitimated, authorial agency of the designer. Here, the white, Western solitary artist-designer translates the so-called primitive, colonial objects produced by unidentified artisans into cosmopolitan objects of consumption.

## Pictures of some lovely chairs

There is a lingering perception, among enough people, that Design History is nothing more than the study of 'pretty' or 'interesting' historical chairs. With no small hint of irony and despite this frustrating, misinformed ignorance, I humbly wish, nevertheless, to make a case for the critical dimension of chairs within the complicated, intersecting histories and cultures of race, colonialism and design within the *moderne* French home. Pierre Legrain, perhaps better known today for his lavish art deco leather bookbindings, most notably for the private collection of Jacques Doucet, also created some of the 1920s' most iconic furniture and interiors for an elite, fashionable clientele. Like most *ensembliers* from the period, he took inspiration from countless historical and global sources. However, Legrain himself confessed to Léon Rosenthal in 1923 that his own study of African art had 'modified his sensibilities'.[7] Indeed, numerous are the examples of Legrain transforming Western domestic seating into African-inspired stools or *tabourets* as they were referred to. In one notable instance, Legrain pairs black (Japanese) lacquer with shagreen (sharkskin stingray) to construct a simple yet deeply luxurious decorative object [Figure 3.1]. The U-shaped seat is supported by four polygonal columns lacquered in black in addition to a central column also covered in sharkskin. This narrow central column at the seat's centre rests on a flat square base covered with gold leaf adding to its preciousness, uniqueness and sense of luxury. Gold leaf is also reintroduced for the middle step of the tri-stepped lacquered base. In this example, Legrain conjures a cosmopolitan transcultural

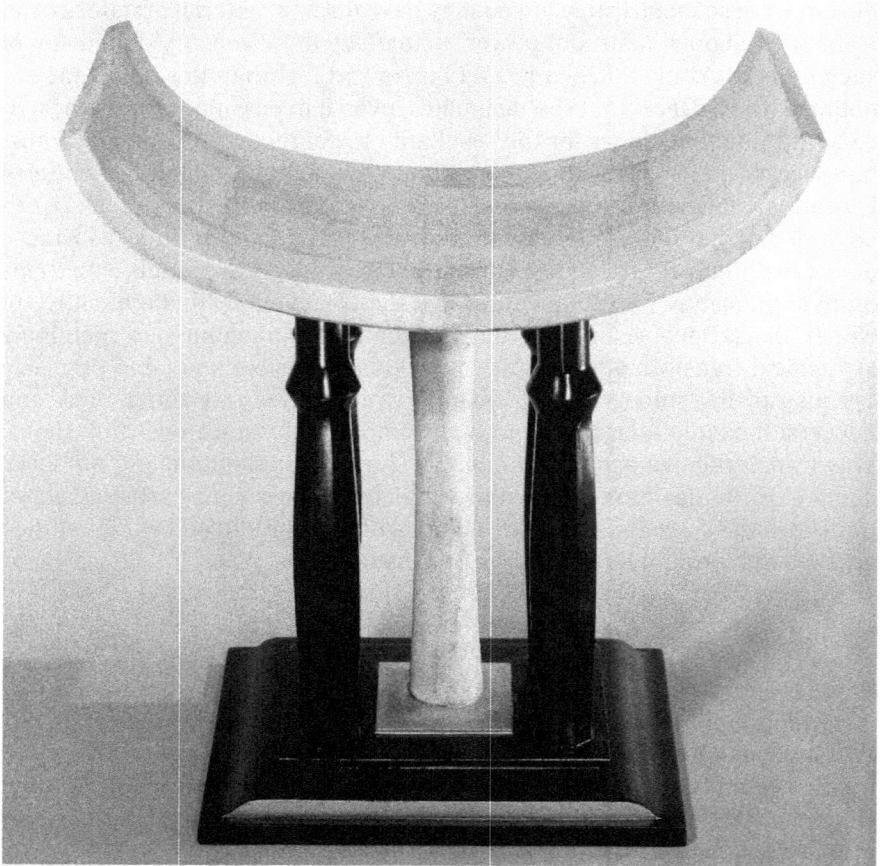

**Figure 3.1**    Pierre Legrain, stool (*tabouret*), *c.*1923. Wood, shagreen (likely stingray skin), lacquer, gilding, 55.9 x 53.3 x 30.5 cm.

object synthesized by adopting and adapting copies of African original furniture (*tabouret*) with Asian materials (shagreen) and Japanese techniques (black lacquer) transformed into an object of luxury for a European consumer. Here the raw materials themselves form an integral component and facilitate the colonial matrix of power. The coloniality of the object is not simply a product of inspiration and admiration but a direct result of global trade structured through colonial networks and labour. These natural and human resources formed an integral part of how France understood and represented itself.[8]

The *tabouret* was originally designed for Doucet as part of a complete refurbishment and modernization project of his studio-home at 33 rue Saint-James in the Paris suburb of Neuilly-sur-Seine for which Doucet had commissioned Legrain [see cover]. It took direct and unabashed inspiration from the well-documented royal thrones from present-day Benin. In one photograph from 1928 we see the former king of the Dahomey's throne surrounded by his last remaining closest relatives. Erected on the skulls of his defeated enemies, the tallest throne placed in the centre is that of King Gezo (1818–58) [Figure 3.2]. Here Legrain recasts a ceremonial and regal throne, transforming it into a precious quotidian object devoid of regal or religious significance. Initially presented at the 1923 *Salon des artistes décorateurs*, Legrain produced a number of these one-of-a-kind *tabourets* for patrons like Doucet.

In a second example designed for Jeanne Tachard's salon in her Villa La Celle Saint-Cloud (in Yvelines, France), Legrain set out to carve a larger and seemingly more restful *tabouret* out of one impressive piece of hardwood supported by four legs [Figure 3.3]. Tachard, who had purchased milliner and fashion house Suzanne Talbot from its creator Juliette Mathieu-Lévy in 1917, was well known in fashionable circles and recognized as an avid collector. A near exact copy of a Ngombe (today part of the Democratic Republic of Congo) original, the cantilevered backrest curves away from the rear legs creating a restful surface for repose. Unlike in the original, Legrain's materials and ornamentation keep within abstracted *moderne* dictates that emphasized the slick lacquered surfaces and repetitive carved-out pyramidal geometric pattern. By varnishing the reclined seat with a translucent, deep red lacquer, Legrain enhanced the rich brown colour of the wood underneath. In the original chair, the unidentified Ngombe craftsmen used wood, brass and iron tacks to allow for a different form of slick and yet repetitively bumpy surface [Figure 3.4]. Likely the property of a tribal chief, the chair in many ways mimics the scarification preferred by the Ngombe peoples [Figure 3.5].

Within this sensory landscape, the body and the object on which the body rests share a common, though differing visual and haptic expression and experience. Like tattoos, the mass image in the West of African bodies displaying techniques of scarification and even laterally similar techniques in furniture design mark the site of a commodity to be seen and transformed into a surface more palatable for the Western bourgeois body. At the same time, it is crucial to recognize that within 'a racist society, for example, one's skin is objectified as a signifier of racial difference (and deviance) rather than an active feeling organ'.[9] The facial and bodily scarification of Ngombe men and women, commonly understood as 'strange' and 'grotesque' in the West, is equated with fearful, suspicious and mystical people [see Figure 3.6]. The racial othering of meaningful practices, understood as grotesque decorative practices, becomes a site of a double negation, in which the primitive and the decorative are subsumed within the colonial matrix of meaning-making and power. As Dimeji Onafuwa has argued, '[e]rasure tactics are revealed in the totalitarianism seen in Western-centric design, where designers make clear

**Figure 3.2**  Former King of Dahomey's last closest relatives around the throne of Behanzin, in Dahomey, 1928.

**Figure 3.3**  Pierre Legrain (1889–1929), *tabouret* (stool), *c.*1923. Lacquered wood, horn, gilding, L. 64.1 cm (25¼ in.).

**Figure 3.4**    Ngombe Peoples, Democratic Republic of the Congo, Chief's stool (Tabouret Ngombe), late nineteenth century. Lacquered wood, brass and iron tacks, 23⅝ × 8⅗ × 18½ in. (60 × 22 × 47 cm).

judgments about what they include as valid, as well as what they decide to exclude as Other'.[10] Legrain transforms a so-called savage, fleshly surface into modern, geometric decorative patterning rendering the copy just different enough from its original.

The significance here is not merely at the material level but occurs at the epidermal and haptic levels as well. For, as Constance Classen reminds us, '[t]he European Man was associated with vision, while at the lowest end of the hierarchy established as early as the nineteenth century, the African was referred to as the "skin-man"'.[11] In the West, ornament and the haptic have long been associated with feminine and primitive impulses within society. As Classen further elaborates, '[t]he social consequences of this gendering of the senses were multifold. The fact that the "male" senses of sight and hearing were classified as "distance" senses and the "female" senses of smell, taste and touch were characterized as "proximity" senses, was interpreted to mean that men were suited for "distance activities," such as travelling and governing, while women were made to stay at home'.[12] However, the interwar period

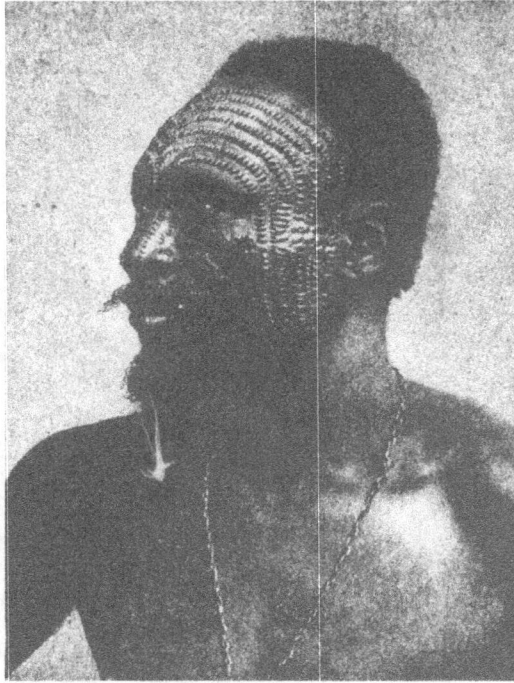

**Figure 3.5**  'This Ngombe chief displays a strange scar arrangement; more interesting is the man himself, with strong face, alien master of Congo country, famous for initiative'. Taken from *The Secret Museum of Mankind*. Five Volumes in One, 1935.

in particular witnessed what Adam Jolles asserts was a 'tactile turn'. For according to him the avant-garde celebrated the haptic dimension of their largely two-dimensional work: 'Any cursory survey of the work produced by the French avant-garde in the early 1930s brings to light the sudden privileging of the tactile'.[13] Legrain has exchanged distance for proximity, bringing the colonies 'home' and emphasizing the purportedly haptic nature of primitive sources.

The relationship between materiality, the senses and identity took on decided importance for contemporary figures like surrealist poet and author Tristan Tzara who also famously housed a vast array of African *objets* in his office and home in Montmartre, a flat designed by Adolf Loos. He contended that 'materials hard in appearance but easily transformable, softening materials in dark colors, those evoking sensations of warmth and wetness, nocturnal materials, wood, coal, semiprecious stones (with lunar symbolic function), ivory, velvety fabrics, skins, gold, pottery, straw, etc., all appear to me to be indicated for representation of prenatal memory'.[14] For Tzara, these material facets took on decidedly corporeal, phenomenological and sensory dimensions that had the

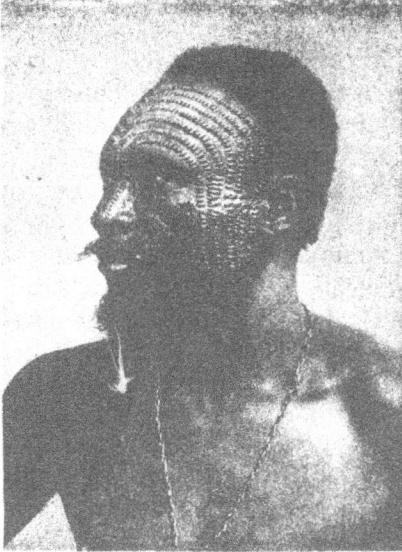

This Ngombe chief displays a strange scar arrangement; more interesting is the man himself, with strong face, alien master of Congo country, famous for initiative

This grotesque face pattern in ridged flesh is known as a "full rasp." The man could only be photographed asleep; he fled the camera as witchcraft

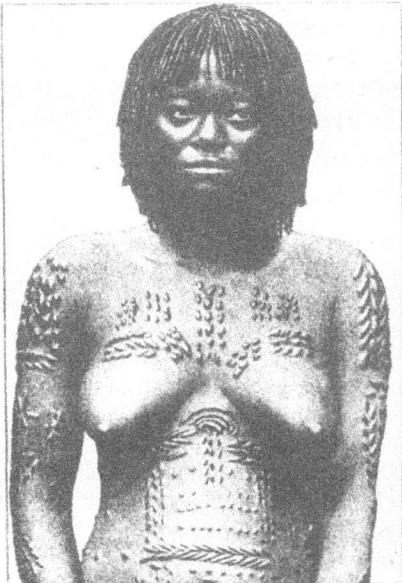

She is a perfect Congo beauty. Each scar has been made by wounding with a knife and inserting irritating stuff to make the flesh swell up

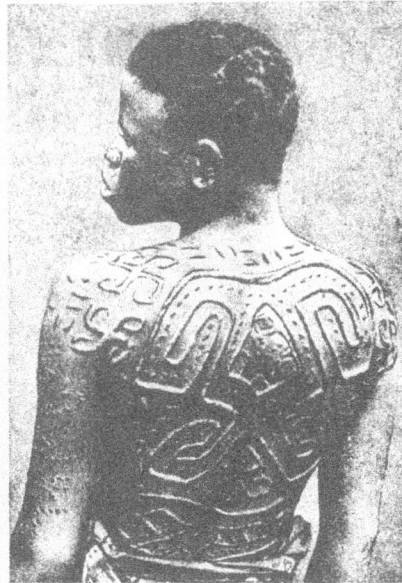

The ancient cross, known as the swastika, scarred upon this woman's back, seems to be sole evidence of Congo negro knowledge of the mystic sign

**Figure 3.6**    Page devoted to Ngombe scarification practices. Taken from *The Secret Museum of Mankind. Five Volumes in One*, 1935.

potential for future renewal: 'Olfactory, gustatory, and auditory sensations must also serve to determine the diurnal or nocturnal character of objects; along with degrees of polish, roughness, etc., they will create the new criteria of an aesthetic issuing more precisely from man and capable at last of being truly useful to him'.[15] Sensory and material affect held particularly powerful sway in Tzara's ideals of utility and function, through the inspiration of African objects, which, as we will see in the section that follows, was decidedly contrapuntal to advocates of international modernism including his own architect-designer Loos. Yet Loos too valued the haptic facet of his own designs within the interior, arguing against photographing interiors. In his 1924 article 'On Thrift', he insisted that 'precisely what I want is for people in my rooms to feel the material around them, I want it to have its effect on them, I want them to be aware of the enclosing room, to feel the material, the wood, to see it, touch it, to perceive it sensually, to sit comfortably and feel the contact between the chair and a large area of their peripheral sense of touch, and say: this is sitting as it should be'.[16]

One of the earliest authors to write about Legrain's designs, Philippe Garner noted in 1975 how 'Legrain had an undeniable flair for exploiting the visual and tactile qualities of the most unusual material, often in incongruous relationship with one another'. He particularly noted the designer's repeated use of lacquer in numerous colours. In the 1920s lacquer had been popularized in Paris by designers Eileen Gray (1878–1976) and Jean Dunand (1877–1942) who both studied the technique under the tutelage of Japanese master Seizo Sougawara (1884–1937). Worth quoting at length is Garner's description of Legrain's use of rough textures, primitivism and the unusual exoticism that infused his work:

> Palm was one of several unusual woods used regularly by Legrain. Its coarse open grain was in keeping with the African-inspired pieces for which he often used this or similar woods – typical is his bench seat for Doucet with its primitive flavour and aggressive motifs, though its lacquered gold seat and the finesse of its execution give it an air of luxury that keeps it within the best tradition of French furniture. Dark, heavy patterned palisander veneers gave a similarly primitive character, as in Legrain's African-style drum-table for Doucet. Dark, highly glossed ebony was another favourite, as in the desk and matching stool for Doucet. […] Legrain's pursuit of novelty was keen, but seldom at the cost of logic or elegance. He showed great refinement in his use of exotic fabrics and animal skins. Most usually he employed soft hides, off-white vellum or fashionable, pale-tinted sharkskin, or galuchat.[17]

The luxurious effect of these objects and various techniques elicited a symbiotic sensory connection between vision and the haptic. African or tribal-inspired designs and objects were the site of a cultural contest and were emblematic of either primitive practices or as a liberation that renewed modern Western culture. '[R]ace is felt and sensed into being.

Multiple senses are engaged to *feel* race and racial differences, and such embodied multisensory feelings are integral to the social, political, and ideological construction of race'.[18] In fact, I argue that the commingling of decorative luxury and Africanity lay at the heart of a contest to define and design modern French domesticity itself. The fraught and tense relationship between modernism and the *style moderne* has conjured a series of mostly artificial oppositional forces that coalesce around the *liaison dangereuse* between the decorative, the sensory and the primitive within the colonial metropole.

## Contested terrain

Both the *style moderne* and discourse around race revolved around deep-seated fears of degeneracy and decorative excesses that have their roots in the nineteenth century. Within the walls of the domestic interior, the interiority of the private citizen was initiated through the phenomenological impressions elicited by the countless objects that populated its landscape forming a sort of intersensory perception of, in and through space. If the word luxury derives its meaning from the old French root of *luxurie* and from the Latin *luxuria* and *luxus*, then luxury, as seen through the prism of the interwar period, certainly refers to what we might describe as a sort of colonial material and sensory culture of abundance. As Walter Benjamin claimed:

> [t]he collector proves to be the true resident of the interior. He makes his concern the idealization of objects [...] The collector delights in evoking a world that is not just distant and long gone but also better – a world in which, to be sure, human beings are no better provided with what they need than in the real world, but in which things are freed from the drudgery of being useful.[19]

However, not all were positively convinced by the role played by private collections or by the *bibelots* that seemingly overpopulated the home. In the previous century, Edmond de Goncourt coined the term *bricabra-comania* in his much-referenced *La Maison d'un artiste* (1881) wherein he defined the condition as a 'psychology of accumulation', one he also classified as a contagious disease. For his part, de Goncourt's contemporary Paul Bourget claimed it was 'the diseases of the nervous sensibility [that] led man to invent the factitious passion for collecting because his interior complexities made him incapable of appreciating the grand and simple sanity of things in the world around him'. For yet another critic, '[s]ociety disintegrates under the corrosive action of a deliquescent civilization [weighed down by] refinement of appetites, of sensations, of taste, of luxury, of pleasures; neurosis, hysteria, hypnotism'.[20] However, no critic was more aware of the relationship between certain types of homes and the sensuous or more vociferous in his attacks on the decadent or aesthetic modern interior than physician Max Nordau when he claimed that '[e]verything in these houses aims at exciting the nerves and dazzling the senses. The disconnected and antithetical effects in all arrangements, the constant contradiction between form and purpose, the outlandishness of most objects, is intended to be bewildering [...] He who enters here must not doze, but be thrilled'.[21] Indeed, the *fin-de-siècle* home was the site for a new war being waged, in which health and morality were increasingly important concerns as the new century was dawning.

Taken up by heroic figures from the new century, nineteenth-century eclecticism, with its penchant for accumulation and overabundance within the interior, warned against the feminizing affects of *luxuria*. At the turn of the new century, pathology and the decoration of the modern interior became a point of connection as much as contention. For Paul Souriau, the decorator took 'pleasure in multiplying ornaments so as to distort form. [In the] modern apartment, [one sees] artifices [*mensonges*] of form and color every-where [*sic*]'.[22] Visions such as these are described in psychiatric studies by Dr Gatian de Clérambault who, along with Dr Charcot, believed that hysteria *particularly* predisposes one to these visual experiences. Yet, for his part Clarence Cook, the sardonic New York critic of the *Tribune*, extolled the virtues of decoration and the role it performed within the interior when he posited that '[o]ur senses are educated more by these slight impressions than we are apt to think; and *bric-à-brac*, so much despised by certain people, and often justly so, may have a use that they themselves might not be willing to admit'.[23] For art historian Susan Sidlauskas, the *fin-de-siècle* 'psychologised interior' constitutes the mature expression of a longer cultural interest in the interior as a 'metaphorical vessel for the self that coincided with the development and decline of modern bourgeois identity'.[24] As feminist art historian Griselda Pollock has argued, '[p]henomenological space is not orchestrated for sight alone but by means of visual cues refers to other sensations and relations of bodies and objects in a lived world'.[25]

For Emile de Laveleye, however, 'luxury is entirely relative'.[26] In 1912 de Laveleye suggested that '[w]hen all is said, his needs are but limited. It is possible without excessive spending to afford the senses all real satisfaction, and a man who aims at real comfort will not be ruined. What costs so much is ostentation, the desire to shine. To this, in fact there is no limit'.[27] Referring to M. Baudrillart, de Laveleye outlined what he identified as the three sentiments which 'give rise to luxury'. These sentiments, both 'natural and universal' were, according to Baudrillart and de Laveleye 'vanity, sensuality and the instinct of adornment', characterized as fundamental social ills.[28] For his part, influential German economist Werner Sombart assigned a sexual dimension to the desire for fine crafted luxury objects. Luxury, according to him, satisfied a base desire for sensual pleasure and averred that

[a]ll personal luxury springs from purely sensual pleasure. Anything that charms the eye, the ear, the nose, the palate, or the touch, tends to find an ever more perfect expression in objects of daily use [...]. In the last analysis it is our sexual life that lies at the root of the desire to refine and multiply the means of stimulating our senses, for sensuous pleasure and erotic pleasure are essentially the same. Indubitably the primary cause of the development of any kind of luxury is most often to be sought in consciously or unconsciously operative sex impulses.[29]

In short, the desire for luxury objects, for Sombart among others, was quite simply emasculating. For him, luxury increased not only where 'wealth begins to accumulate', but also, perhaps more intriguingly, where 'the sexuality of the nation is freely expressed'.[30]

However, within the design landscape of interwar France, more was at play in the creation and consumption of luxury design. Bridget Elliott proposes the *style moderne* as a site of hybridity precisely because of its supposedly 'stylistically impure, superficial and commercially contaminated' designs.[31] Mimicry and hybridity were essential within 'colonialism's institutions and systems'[32] and, I argue, were endemic to the (Black) Deco project that became an essential component of the reinvigoration of national industries that Guillaume, among others, prognosticated.[33] As John Wayne Monroe elaborates:

> In the years immediately after World War I, Guillaume engaged in a wildly successful campaign to publicize African sculpture, and in the process, helped touch off what French cultural historians call the *vogue nègre*, a widespread fascination with things black – from African folktales to American jazz – that lasted into the 1930s.[34]

In tandem with this rise in interest in all things African, the West also witnessed 'the rise of global markets and the growing social influence of the bourgeoisie [that] predetermined ideas of luxury gave way to a taste culture meant to give pleasure by exciting the senses'.[35] Yet, this expanded consumer landscape was not only enabled through the colonial programme, but also instigated fears around the nature and detrimental effects of luxury on society. Originally presented in 1908, Vienna-based architect-designer Adolf Loos' 'Ornament and Crime' specified a clear moral and ethical dimension for interior design and fervently warned against the primitivizing, degenerative and criminal nature he saw as inherent in excessive decoration. According to Loos, who lived in Paris from 1922 to 1927, a clear connection could be made between what a man wore and where a man lived. More exactly, the measure of ornamentation was symptomatic of the degree of an entire civilization, people or race for, according to him: 'The evolution of culture is synonymous with the removal of ornament from utilitarian objects'.[36] However, he underscored the primitive nature of ornament when he boldly theorized that

[w]hen man is born, his sensory impressions are like those of a newborn puppy. His childhood takes him through all the metamorphoses of human history. At 2 he sees with the eyes of a Papuan, at 4 with those of an ancient Teuton, at 6 with those of Socrates, at 8 with those of Voltaire. [...] The child is amoral. To our eyes, the Papuan is too. The Papuan kills his enemies and eats them. He is not a criminal. But when modern man kills someone and eats him he is either a criminal or a degenerate. The Papuan tattoos his skin, his boat, his paddles, in short everything he can lay hands on. He is not a criminal. The modern man who tattoos himself is either a criminal or a degenerate.[37]

For Loos, criminality, degeneracy and the primitive were synonymous and legibly revealed equally on the surface of bodies as well as objects. Loos was not alone and in fact took his cues from influential writers like physician Max Nordau and Charles Darwin. The latter, for example, claimed how, '[j]udging from the hideous ornaments and the equally hideous music admired by most savages, it might be urged that their æsthetic faculty was not so highly developed as in certain animals, for instance, in birds'.[38] The problem with the *style moderne* was that it flirted too loosely not only with ornamentation but with countless sources of inspiration. It also freely indulged in an exoticism that at once reinforced French style and taste while also celebrating the country's colonial material reach. It is worth noting that Loos' much-cited treatise 'Crime and Ornament' was significantly first published not in German but in French in *Les Cahiers d'aujourd'hui* (June 1913) and then reprinted in Le Corbusier's magazine *L'Esprit Nouveau* (15 November 1920).

Men like Hermann Muthesius, Loos and even Henry van de Velde advocated the virtues of simplicity, authenticity and integrity, contrasting these sober and 'virile' qualities with the sentimentality, ornamentation and ostentatious pretensions associated with eclecticism and ornamentation. Taking his cue from Loos, Le Corbusier further racialized decoration by dismissing it as the 'charming entertainment of the savage'.[39] The Swiss-born architect advocated a novel design for the interior, one more adequately suited to the 'men of vigour in an age of heroic reawakening' who could no longer 'lounge on ottomans and divans among orchids in the scented atmosphere of a seraglio and behave like so many ornamental animals or humming-birds in impeccable evening dress'.[40] I have argued elsewhere in regard to the erasure of sexuality and its presence within Le Corbusier's work. However, here I wish to draw attention to the ways in which Le Corbusier's both literal and symbolic whitewashing signalled a purposeful attack on otherness more broadly, and race more specifically through an Orientalist-engendered fear of masculine effeminacy.[41] The policing of the interior through the use of ribbon windows and Ripolin was a purposeful attack on and fears of the domestication of otherness within the French interior, and within the French Republic. Moreover, it symbolized Le Corbusier's repeated and vociferous attack on art deco and its perceived decadence and degeneracy. Fears around and hostility toward the decorative arts were aligned with a moral concern for purity and health understood along lines of sexuality as much as race. As Le Corbusier proclaimed: 'Whitewash is extremely moral. Suppose there were a decree requiring all rooms in Paris to be given a coat of whitewash. I maintain that that would be a police task of real stature and a manifestation of high morality, the sign of a great people'.[42] As Sachi Sekimoto and Christopher Brown have argued '[r]acism, at its core, is powerful not because of the *meaning* ascribed to racialized bodies, but because it denies or subordinates the sensuous materiality of lived bodies of color'.[43] Indeed, Loos and Le Corbusier's theories on the modern interior at once denied the sensory expressions and experience of the Other, racial bodies, but also attempted to cut off the potential for similar experiences within the colonial metropolis.

Figures like Tzara did not share in Le Corbusier's 'machine for living in' idealized whitewashed interior design and domestic homogeneity. According to him,

> [a]s hygienic and stripped of ornament as it wishes to appear, 'modern' architecture has no chance of survival – it will continue to limp along thanks only to the transitory perversities that a generation thinks itself entitled to formulate while inflicting on itself the punishment for who knows how many unconscious sins (bad conscience due perhaps to capitalist oppression) – for it is the complete negation of the image of the dwelling.[44]

In the interwar period, interior decorators like Jean Dunand, Jacques-Émile Ruhlmann, Eyre de Lanux, Jean-Michel Frank and Eileen Gray and Pierre Legrain developed a new, though not unproblematic, vocabulary that sought to wed so-called modern/e/ism with luxurious, exotic objects and materials from around the world meant to celebrate, activate and enliven the sensuous, sensory dimension of modern life. Objects amassed for and within these interiors were less about a collection and more about the corporeal and sensual possibilities of the occupant, their needs in the quotidian, their experience of 'being' modern, of performing modern, unique identities. The bourgeois interior as *the* site of the middle-class value of respectability, which, since the revolution of 1789, stood as the hallmark of masculinist civic governance and virtue,[45] inflected itself into the codes of proper and moral design. To possess these African objects and *moderne* copies was to signify a degree of wealth and luxury made possible through colonial acquisition and the matrix of colonial power. Yet, on the other hand, it also designated an attack, in numerous instances, on the notions of respectability and (racial) homogeneity. Blackness and the primitivized Other became a conduit for individual designers to 'craft very different living spaces for […] very different bodies',[46] despite the fact that 'engaging with the "primitive" [stylistically] ran the risk of appearing

degenerate'.[47] Through their exotic collections and Legrain-designed furniture, elite collectors like Tachard and Doucet seemingly risked their
reputations through their domestication of the primitive within the private
domain of the home. In contradistinction to painting and sculpture, furniture facilitates specific modes of orientation through quotidian bodily acts.
What then do we make of Tachard's home, in particular, which housed
both African original and Legrain copy? What sort of orientation would
this have elicited for herself and her guests? Here by way of answer I
simply reassert the importance of the haptic and the critical role it played
as a conduit between the *style moderne* and the so-called primitivism of
African objects as a site of continuous and unresolved tension.

## Primitive by design

Despite continued and more recent calls to return the original Dahomey
throne to Benin,[48] its curated presence in Paris remains essential for a
Western audience whose gaze is predicated on how the throne signifies its importance as 'source material' and 'inspiration' for the 'genius'
of Legrain. Its existence and significance within the metropole today
are guaranteed through its colonial legacy and link to French avant-garde
cultural production within the empire of interior design. Luxury, while the
domain of privilege, is also, more importantly an act of resistance in
the *moderne*–modernist hybridity of Legrain's design as a colonizer's
act of self-care; that is, an act against industrialist modernism and its
'machine for living in' that collectors like Tzara, Doucet and Tachard, for
example, turned their backs on. A sense of luxury within the modern interior as truly, deeply and even madly felt was indeed the truest experience
and expression of modern living. That this had to be materialized through
the use and appropriation of African objects, textures and colonial woods
in many instances speaks to what Hal Foster argues 'is this *currency* of
the primitive among the moderns – its currency as sign, its circulation
as commodity – that allows the modern/tribal affinity-effect in the first
place'.[49] Skin as haptic surface and sight of difference services in the
West as an expanded corporeal and racial landscape through which the
colonial project could be performed and literally, metaphorically and sensorially mapped out: surfaces (landscapes, skin and seating) were the site/
sight of colonial expansion. Discursive as much as they are material and
embodied, the intersecting histories of luxury, primitivism, the senses
and interior design are largely absent in the histories of the *style moderne*. Nevertheless, the colonial gaze activated through a relationship with
touch, and enabled and promoted through consumption, transgresses
hearth and home within the purifying ethos established by figures like
Loos and Le Corbusier. These decorative objects, regardless of their origins, become a form of colonial contamination. I assert that Legrain's

Africanist *tabourets* at once trouble and yet reinforce the relationship marking out the boundaries between proximity and distance, absence and presence and finally Self and Other.

## Notes

1 P. Guillaume, 'La sculpture nègre et l'art moderne' in *Les écrits de Paul Guillaume. Une esthétique nouvelle. L'art négre. Ma visite à la Fondation Barnes* (Neuchâtel: Idées et Calendes, 1993), p. 80, original emphasis.

2 The *ensembliers*, or *artist-décorateurs*, as they were referred to within the distinct French context, was a term that gained currency in the 1920s. It did not simply refer to a decorator or designer, but rather emphasized an overall vision or ensemble for a designed interior.

3 For more on this change see J. W. Monroe, *Metropolitan Fetish: African Sculpture and the Imperial French Invention of Primitive Art* (Ithaca, NY: Cornell University Press, 2019).

4 S. Lemke, *Primitivist Modernism: Black Culture and the Origins of Black Transatlantic Modernism* (Oxford: Oxford University Press, 1998), p. 9.

5 D. Onafuwa, 'Allies and Decoloniality: A Review of the Intersectional Perspectives on Design, Politics, and Power Symposium', *Design and Culture*, 10:1 (2018), p. 8.

6 R. Krauss in W. Rubin (ed.), *'Primitivism' in 20ᵗʰ Century Art: Affinity of the Tribal and the Modern* (New York: Museum of Modern Art, 1984), p. 507.

7 L. Rosenthal, 'Pierre Legrain, Relieur', *Arts et Décoration*, Vol. I (1923), p. 68.

8 J. Méniaud, *Nos Bois Coloniaux* (Paris: Commission de Synthèse et Comité Économique Colonial, 1931).

9 S. Sekimoto and C. Brown, *Race and the Senses: The Felt Politics of Racial Embodiment* (London: Bloomsbury Academic, 2020), pp. 14–15.

10 Onafuwa, 'Allies and Decoloniality', p. 8.

11 C. Classen, 'Engendering Perception: Gender Ideologies and Sensory Hierarchies in Western History', *Body & Society*, 3:2 (1997), p. 6.

12 *Ibid.*, p. 4.

13 A. Jolles, 'The Tactile Turn: Envisioning a Postcolonial Aesthetic in France', *Yale French Studies*, 109 (2006), p. 18.

14 T. Tzara, 'Concerning a Certain Automatism of Taste: The Pasted Paper or the Proverb in Painting' in P. Hulten (ed.), *The Surrealists Look at Art: Eluard, Aragon, Soupault, Breton, Tzara* (Venice, CA: Lapis Press, 1990), p. 210.

15 Tzara, 'Concerning a Certain Automatism of Taste', p. 211.

16 A. Loos, 'On Thrift' in *On Architecture* (Riverside, CA: Adragne Press, [1924] 2002), pp. 179–80.

17 P. Garner, 'Pierre Legrain – Décorateur', *The Connoisseur*, 189 (1975), p. 134.

18 Sekimoto and Brown, *Race and the Senses*, p. 1.

19 W. Benjamin, *The Arcades Project* (Cambridge, MA, and London: The Belknap Press of Harvard University, 1999), p. 19.

20 'Le Decadent' (1886) in D. Pick, *Faces of Degeneration: A European Disorder* (Cambridge: Cambridge University Press, 1989), pp. 41–2.

21 M. Nordau, *Degeneration* (New York: D. Appleton and Company, 1905), p. 11.

22 P. Souriau, *L'Imagination de l'artiste* (Paris: Alcan, 1886), p. 24.

23 C. Cook, *The House Beautiful: Essays on Beds and Tables, Stools and Candlesticks* (New York: Scribner, Armstrong and Company, 1878), p. 103.

24 Susan Sidlauskas, *Body, Place and Self in Nineteenth-Century Painting* (Cambridge: Cambridge University Press, 2000), p. x.

25 G. Pollock, *Vision and Difference: Femininity, Feminism and the Histories of Art* (London and New York: Routledge, 1988), p. 65.

26  E. de Laveleye, *Luxury* (London: George Allen and Company, 1912), p. 5.

27  *Ibid.*, p. 15.

28  *Ibid.*, p. 7.

29  W. Sombart, *Luxury and Capitalism* (Ann Arbor, MI: The University of Michigan Press [German 1913; English 1922], 1967), pp. 60–1.

30  *Ibid.*, p. 61.

31  B. Elliott, 'Art Deco Hybridity, Interior Design and Sexuality between the Wars: Two Double Acts: Phyllis Barron and Dorothy Larcher/Eyre de Lanux and Evelyn Wyld' in L. Doan and J. Garrity (eds), *Sapphic Modernities: Sexuality, Women and National Culture* (New York: Palgrave Macmillan, 2006), p. 110.

32  P. Morton, *Hybrid Modernities: Architecture and Representation at the 1931 Colonial Exposition, Paris* (Cambridge, MA: MIT Press, 2000), p. 13.

33  See T. Gronberg, *Designers on Modernity: Exhibiting the City in 1920s Paris* (Manchester: Manchester University Press, 1998); J. Potvin, *Deco Dandy: Designing Masculinity in 1920s Paris* (Manchester: Manchester University Press, 2020).

34  Monroe, *Metropolitan Fetish*, p. 16.

35  J. Merwood-Salisbury, 'On Luxury', *AA Files*, 58 (2009), p. 21.

36  A. Loos, 'Crime and Ornament' in M. Ward and B. Miller (eds), *Crime and Ornament: The Arts and Popular Culture in the Shadow of Adolf Loos* (Toronto: YYZ Books, [1908] 2002), p. 20. Italics in original.

37  *Ibid.*, p. 19.

38  C. Darwin, *The Descent of Man, and Selection in Relation to Sex* (New Jersey: Princeton University Press, 1981 [1871]), p. 64.

39  Le Corbusier, *The Decorative Art of Today* (Cambridge, MA: MIT Press, 1987 [1925]), p. 85.

40  *Ibid.*, p. 192.

41  J. Potvin., 'A Bathroom of One's Own: Hygiene, Sexuality and Creative Communities beyond the Public/Private Divide, c. 1880–1940' in M. Cook and A. Gorman-Murray (eds), *Queering the Interior* (London and New York: Bloomsbury Publishing, 2017), pp. 161–71.

42  Le Corbusier, *The Decorative Art of Today* p. 192.

43  Sekimoto and Brown, *Race and the Senses*, p. 10.

44  Tzara, 'Concerning a Certain Automatism of Taste', p. 212.

45  G. L. Mosse, *Nationalism and Sexuality: Respectability and Abnormal Sexuality in Modern Europe* (New York: Howard Fertig, 1985).

46  J. Rault, 'Losing Feelings: Elizabeth Eyre de Lanux and her Affective of Sapphic Modernity', *Archives of American Art Journal*, 48:1/2 (2009), p. 61.

47  Elliott, 'Art Deco Hybridity, Interior Design and Sexuality between the Wars', p. 122.

48  See for example, D. B. Sawa, 'Watch the Throne: Why Artist Thierry Oussu Faked an Archaeological Dig', *Guardian* (10 July 2018) www.theguardian.com/artandde sign/2018/jul/09/thierry-oussou-faked-archaeological-dig-african-art-colonial-loot ing (accessed 1 December 2021).

49  H. Foster in W. Rubin (ed.), *'Primitivism' in 20ᵗʰ Century Art: Affinity of the Tribal and the Modern* (New York: Museum of Modern Art, 1984), p. 52.

# 4

# 'Brother and I in bed': queer photography at home in New York, 1925–35

*Alice T. Friedman*

For the men and women of New York's tight-knit avant-garde in the 1920s and 1930s, the boundaries between the senses were remarkably porous and fluid: no doubt this was heightened by the combination of their passionate curiosity about sexuality and the arts – both as a matter of personal experience and as a topic of salon conversations – and the pervasive homophobia and repressive social values imposed on them by American society overall. Thus, in the works of well-known figures like the bisexual writer Carl Van Vechten (1880–1964) or the unmarried painter and poet Florine Stettheimer (1871–1944), as for other members of their circle, including the queer, young photographer and composer Max Ewing (1903–1934), the sounds of music, talk and urban life, and the sight of colours, textures and especially human bodies were often exuberantly celebrated and enjoyed, while touch, and particularly eroticized touch, was repressed or displaced to other sense experiences. Writing in a draft of *Crystal Flowers*, the collection she compiled between 1917 and 1944, Stettheimer described this deeply felt physicality as an inspiration for her painting:

> For a long time
> I gave myself
> To the arrested moment
> To the unfulfilled moment
> To the moment of quiet expectation
> I painted the trance moment
> The promised moment
> The moment in the balance
> In mellow golden tones ...
> Then I saw
> Time
> Noise
> Color

Outside me
Around me
Knocking me
Jarring me
Hurting me
Smiling
Singing
Forcing me in joy to paint them.[1]

Living at home on New York's respectable West Side with her sisters and mother, Stettheimer had to be cautious, using the eye and the ear in particular as surrogates for the 'knocking', 'jarring', 'hurting' sensations that she felt, just as Van Vechten or Ewing learned to channel their queer eroticism – real and imagined – into collecting images and objects, talking, going to parties, bodybuilding (and looking at bodybuilders) and, most of all, into making, possessing and studying photographs, particularly of men. Moreover, all three used their homes as studio spaces, galleries and above all as places of entertainment. Thus, for all three, the domestic sphere had a fluid multivalency that reflected the complex displacements that helped them navigate their world.[2]

In the winter of 1934, the bodybuilder and model Bill Ritter wrote to Max Ewing, a good friend who had recently left town to try his hand as a screenwriter in Hollywood. Ritter's letter, one of a series exchanged by the two men between the spring of 1933 and the winter of 1934, is full of vivid details about the queer scene in New York that Ewing was missing out on because of his exile from the city:

> Fred and I [are] spending most of my time in dear old Harlem – it is very gay there this season. Clinton Moore's cocktail hours have been pretty good lately a new crowd of English boys are taking the place by storm. Met George Lynes the other night at some awful dizzy party, you can imagine how these partys [sic] effect me, out all night and then work the next day, some fun. You remember the pictures George took of us he claims they were in a French magizine [sic] he wants us to come up and then at the same time take more pictures. We recently went to some of the bigger partys [sic] in town, started the season with a drag, as usual then came the Bowery Ball, the Mad Hatters etc. Fred and I crashed the gayest of society's balls this year, the Peacock and the Packard Motor Ball they were really gala affairs and we met plenty of different people. Despite everything I still manage to keep in fair condition, intend taking some new pictures soon if any come out OK will send you copies.[3]

Ritter and his brother Fred had met Ewing and George Platt Lynes (1907–55) around 1930, either at Coney Island, where Ewing and Lynes went to meet and photograph bodybuilders at the outdoor gyms and swimming pools, or at one of the many Harlem drag balls (judged on at least one occasion by their friends Carl Van Vechten and Muriel Draper, whose homes were favourite gathering places for young men), or at one or another of the queer-themed events that Ritter alludes to in his letter.[4]

The beautiful Ritter brothers proved to be not only amusing companions but also talented male models who were more than willing to pose in staged scenarios in artists' and photographers' homes. In 1932, for example, Ewing regularly photographed Fred Ritter in his apartment on West 31st Street, both nude and in assorted costumes, including an elegant dressing gown that Ewing had acquired in France [Figure 4.1]. That same year, Ewing created a series of portraits entitled *The Carnival of Venice* in which celebrities and friends, including both Ritter brothers, posed in front of a backdrop printed with a view of the Piazza San Marco [Figure 4.2]. Fred Ritter alludes to the Venice series a number of times in his letters: in July 1933, for example, he writes that he missed Ewing's little studio, adding that 'I shall always remember it as [I] have numerous pictures which you took of me in about every corner of it, including Venice which you made so famous'. He wrote to Ewing again on 12 February 1934 to report that 'Geo Lynes [...] is planning on getting a fifteen room apartment near the east river and using it for something, he is also going to photograph brother and I in bed, quite a contrast from the canals of Venice, also Geo had a picture of brother and I he took placed in the Photographie some French publication.'[5]

Lynes's well-known photograph of the two men, *Untitled (The Ritter Brothers)* [Figure 4.3], does indeed show the two brothers in bed; it was one of a series that established the artist's successful professional career. By contrast, Ewing's amateur efforts, like the man himself, faded into obscurity soon after his death. In these years, however, Lynes, Ewing and Carl Van Vechten (a married bisexual and an impresario of the bohemian scene) were all beginning to experiment with cameras, props and scenography on more or less the same footing, using their homes as studios in which to stage, produce and share queer images, including male nudes and erotica.

A number of themes emerge from Ewing's correspondence with the Ritter brothers, not least of which is the importance of domestic interiors as sites of queer sociability, avant-garde networking and artistic production. These carefully composed and curated spaces served not only as private stages on which queer identities could be invented and performed but also as sites of cultural exchange and belonging that emerged through the unfolding of sensory experiences, sequenced and enhanced for the pleasure of a select group. Here the role of the senses was foregrounded both through the making, sorting and viewing of photographs of private (and often illicit and sexualized) images and through participation in extended conversations about photography and visual pleasure that took place among members of this group. These conversations were not simply a by-product, but an essential component in the development of a coherent, queer subculture, not least because of the homophobic exclusion of these men by mainstream society. Talking and sharing stories, jokes and

**Figure 4.1**    Max Ewing, *Fred Ritter in Max's Dressing Gown, c.*1932.

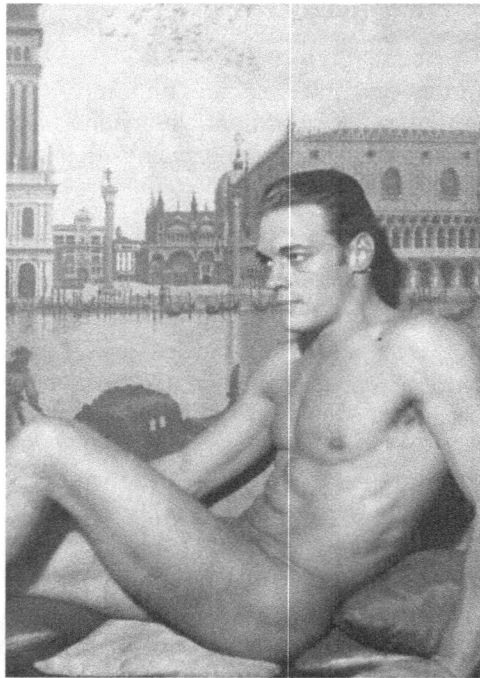

**Figure 4.2**    Max Ewing, *Portrait of Fred Ritter,* from *The Carnival of Venice* series, 1932.

**Figure 4.3**   George Platt Lynes, *Untitled (The Ritter Brothers)*, c.1934.

social or sexual fantasies reinforced the coherence of a queer subculture and alleviated the shame that too often distorted identity and demonized the very sensations that these men recuperated through their scopophilia, their collecting and their shared enjoyment of fashion, gesture and physical beauty.

Moreover, as a composer and musician, Max Ewing placed a particular emphasis on sound and its imaginative and emotional effects: his small studio apartment was dominated by a grand piano on which he practised his craft and entertained his friends with both serious and light music and songs. Moreover, members of his circle – including performers, singers, stage designers and composers – also used their home studios and salons as incubators of ideas for productions, which were talked through, sketched out and performed on the piano and other instruments: among the most significant were the productions of the *Grand Street Follies*, an annual revue for which Ewing wrote the music in 1928 and 1929, and *Four Saints in Three Acts*, the well-known opera by Gertrude Stein, with music by Virgil Thomson, that was workshopped in the homes of Ewing and his friends.[6] By curating and staging visual and other sensory experiences in his private interior, Ewing used interior design to create a complex, synaesthetic self-portrait animated by mechanisms of projection and displacement – in short, by fantasy and imagination – endemic to the pursuit of theatre, celebrity and glamour.[7]

The pivotal role played by private salons for New York's bohemia has, of course, been well documented, but here it is worth highlighting the special significance of private drawing rooms, libraries and studio interiors as part of the 'archipelago' of queer-friendly venues, a chain of safe spaces, loosely connected in the imaginative psycho-geography of the community, that included the 'buffet flats', speakeasies and nightclubs of Harlem where queer and sexually curious men and women gathered, flirted, danced and drank.[8] As a number of scholars have noted, particularly those who have grappled with the problematic status of Van Vechten in the Harlem Renaissance, the New York avant-garde thrived within a highly specialized social, cultural and geographic milieu that was, to quote the historian Henry Louis Gates, 'surely as gay as it was black'.[9] Though each venue had its own character and rules, private and semi-private interior spaces throughout the city served as performative *mise-en-scènes*, framing devices and incubating environments in which the queer visual arts flourished. This is especially evident in the production and reception of photographs, but it is true of sensory experience in general. That these salons were often crowded, loud, pungent with the smell of alcohol and cigarettes, and swirling with an ever-changing parade of bodies, gestures and fashions, heightened both the physical and emotional experiences of participants. As such, understanding the design and skilful 'choreography' of such places takes on new significance, since these spaces served as both glamorous and recuperative responses to homophobic exclusion, and as three-dimensional self-portraits, which pushed back on homophobia and shame by using intimacy, secrecy and a newly encoded language of sensory experience to perform and celebrate queer identity in the 1920s and 1930s.

Max Ewing (1903–34) was a star-struck young man who moved to New York City from the tiny farming town of Pioneer, Ohio in the Fall 1923, a few weeks before the start of his senior year at the University of Michigan.[10] Impatient to get on with his training as a concert pianist, and ready to begin a new life in the glamorous world that he knew – or thought he knew – as an avid fan of opera and movies, Ewing was like a character in a story by F. Scott Fitzgerald, anxious to experience firsthand the elegant exhibitions, brilliant concerts and alcohol-fuelled parties of his imagination. He dreamed of a life in the city, complete with the tinkling sound of ice in cocktail glasses and the animated voices of bohemian New Yorkers, and he imagined himself fully immersed in that world long before he arrived.

From an early age, Ewing crafted his experience through a series of stage sets, fashion ensembles and accessories, often inflected by humour and by a camp sensibility that knowingly referenced international travel and the elite culture of New York, Paris and Venice. As his teenage diary from 1917 makes clear, by the age of fourteen, Ewing was already building the knowledge that would provide him with an entrée into that world, using a storeroom above his parents' dry goods store to produce reenactments of film and opera roles played by his favourite stars, including Marguerite Namara, Mary Garden and Geraldine Farrar. He stuffed his scrapbooks with photos and clippings, collected records, attended the opera in Toledo and Detroit with his father, tried his hand at fashion design and went to the movies as often as possible, noting the titles in his diary.[11] Through these activities, Ewing honed the skills in design and curation that he would later use in the interior of his own New York apartment, a space that deployed images, music, performance and intimate scale to create a vivid, glamorous and decidedly queer self-portrait of the young man as an artist, photographer and man about town.

Arriving in New York in 1923, one of Ewing's first stops was the home of Carl Van Vechten, not yet a photographer at this stage but well known as an outspoken proponent of literary and artistic modernism and greatly admired by Ewing and his friends. Indeed, Ewing's meeting with Van Vechten was an event that Ewing had long prepared for, studying the role of Peter Whiffle, the title character in Van Vechten's recently published novel, and writing a breathless appreciation of Van Vechten's work for the Michigan student newspaper. The young man's visit to Van Vechten's New York apartment marks the beginning of a long and intimate friendship between the two men, one founded on a queer sensibility that they shared and, in large part, invented: a love of the city, theatre, books and music, a zeal for collecting objects and images, and a hunger for immersion in the glamorous social whirl of downtown parties, literary salons and all-night bar crawls through Harlem.[12] Van Vechten, whom his friends called 'Carlo', introduced Max to his circle, and he proved to be a popular addition to the tight-knit world of bohemian New York: handsome, charming and worldly. As Max described it in a letter to his mother on 9 October 1923,

> Last evening I spent with Carl Van Vechten, alone, in his rooms on E. 19th st. [...] He wants me to come often. He goes out little. He has heard all the music, seen all the plays, known all the artists, read all the books, seen all the pictures, visited all the capitals, & now he's tired of it all. He would rather spend a night talking with me than go out, he says. His cat was lovely. We talked music, books, & pictures. He likes me. He can introduce me to anyone I want to know

The following day he sent another letter about the experience, noting that

> the young man who spent last Monday evening with Carl Van Vechten in a red & yellow silk-lined room in 'Fairfax Arms' was a creature I can't recognize today at all. My body was there, yes. But where on earth was I? ... You must take me as I am, and overlook my craziness-es [sic]. Van Vechten says I'm 'fascinating.'[13]

Ewing quickly emerged as a regular at Van Vechten's parties and a welcome companion on his nightly round of entertainments.[14] His packed social calendar soon left him little time to practise the piano, and as a result of an injury to his finger sustained at a boisterous rehearsal for the New York production of George Antheil's *Ballet Mécanique* in 1927 – one of the many eye-popping connections between the young Max Ewing and the major figures of American modernism – it was difficult for him to play serious music in any case. He composed songs for off-Broadway shows, wrote light fiction and left town in 1933 to try his hand at writing film scripts in Hollywood. None of this would prove as satisfying as his pursuit of pleasure and celebrity, his love of photography and his zeal for collecting images and ephemera, sustained by his friendship with Van Vechten.[15]

Sharing images and stories, and creating the domestic interiors in which they could be appreciated and experienced to greatest advantage, not only reinforced the pleasures of friendship but also enriched a rarefied, private and decidedly queer language of belonging that had long been Ewing's dream. These activities, like the ceaseless whirl of parties and events that threatened to overwhelm the elite in the 1920s so brilliantly captured by their friend F. Scott Fitzgerald in *The Great Gatsby* (1925), often took on a frenzied pace, rooted in the increasingly pervasive imaginary of Hollywood glamour and the seductive mechanisms of consumer culture. The cultivation and performance of these fantasy experiences through enhanced sensory experiences, shared in private interior spaces though cautiously tempered in public, became a hallmark of the queer culture these men created, documented and preserved: in this, as in most things, Ewing followed Van Vechten's lead.

Indeed, it is only thanks to Van Vechten that we know of Ewing's life and work at all. In June 1934, Ewing suffered a breakdown and took his own life, deeply depressed by the death of his mother and isolated in Pioneer, Ohio, to which he had been forced to relocate just months after moving to Hollywood. Though shocked and saddened by Ewing's death, Van Vechten – ever the collector – immediately began amassing and shaping an archive of his letters, books, photographs and scrapbooks, which he donated to the Yale library in 1943 – for the benefit of future researchers and 'as a slight memorial to his charming soul', as he explained to the family soon after his death.[16] As is well known, Van Vechten also donated his own enormous archive of papers, books and photographs to Yale, including a collection of eighteen private scrapbooks of queer ephemera and erotica – closed to both librarians and researchers at his request for the twenty-five years following his death. Among these previously sealed materials is a handful of Ewing's photographs of male nudes, and a number of items he presented to Van Vechten, including a programme from the Egyptian Theater in Hollywood showing the '4 The Marx Sisters' in drag, inscribed: 'Dear Carl, For one or another of your collections of Amatory Curiosa'.[17]

Given the extreme homophobia and secrecy surrounding such activities, it goes without saying that queer socializing, collecting and performance were conducted in private interior spaces as a matter of necessity.[18] Homosexual acts between men were not only illegal in the United States for much of the twentieth century but increasingly policed throughout the late 1920s and 1930s.[19] Queer-friendly salons such as those hosted by Van Vechten, Muriel Draper (1886–1952), the Stettheimer sisters, the Askews or the Harlem-based heiress A'lelia Walker (1885–1931) – all frequented by Ewing – proved to be significant places of social and intellectual exchange.[20] Yet even in avant-garde circles, flirting, dating and overt references to queer sexuality were frowned upon. As the historian Steven Watson put it, 'once a man made a pass at another man, the butler brought him his coat. The rule was, we do not camp in public.'[21]

A case in point is the weekly salon hosted by Kirk and Constance Askew at their East 61st Street brownstone, where Ewing and Van Vechten were frequent visitors. These gatherings attracted many intellectuals from the art world but were known to be the most conservative in terms of social behaviour and interracial mixing. As the gallery owner Julien Levy recalled in his memoir, the group that gathered there included such luminaries as Alfred Barr and his wife; Muriel Draper, sometimes in the company of Ewing and at other times escorted by a very young Lincoln Kirstein; Esther Murphy, sister of the expatriate painter Gerald Murphy and friend of both Edmund Wilson and the F. Scott Fitzgeralds; Philip Johnson and his sister Theodate; and the Stettheimer sisters, among many others.[22] Here as elsewhere, the etiquette of the avant-garde was complicated: while queer people were always careful to modulate and encode their private identities and attachments, expressions of individual eccentricity and personal style were highly valued – though clearly within limits that varied according to gender and sexual orientation.

The salon maintained by the painter Robert Chanler (1872–1930) at his home on East 19th Street, known as the 'House of Fantasy', attracted a more diverse and hard-partying crowd. With his booming voice and eccentric manners, Chanler performed a sort of hypermasculinity that set the tone at the House of Fantasy and encouraged his guests' spirited explorations of all the senses. The house was known for its displays of his exotic paintings and animals, for its multifloor entertainment spaces and book-filled library.[23] Chanler's parties were famous for their size and drunken theatrics: Ewing's letters describe drinking, dancing and sexual rivalries which not infrequently erupted in loud arguments and even fist-fights among the guests, or between Chanler and his hot-tempered consort, Louise Hellstrom.[24]

By contrast, the salon held at the sprawling apartment of the three Stettheimer sisters – Florine, Carrie and Ettie – and their mother at Alwyn Court on West 69th Street was more intellectually ambitious, decorous and exaggeratedly feminine.[25] Art world luminaries, including Marcel Duchamp and Gaston Lachaise, gathered there with the Stettheimers' trusted friends, including Max Ewing himself.[26] The salon was well known for the performative quality of the sisters' dress and etiquette, and for the highly ornamented décor that characterized both the family apartment and Florine's Bryant Park studio. Surviving photographs show the hanging lace and fringe, the carved white and gold furniture, and the 'billowing cellophane curtains hanging between rooms' that historian Cecile Whiting has characterized as 'interior décor taken to its fantastical, whimsical, and feminine extreme'.[27] Here the pleasures of touch and of the eye were simultaneously stimulated and deflected by veils of reflective materials, just as the elaborate social rituals of the salon highlighted intimacy and the body, yet insisted on physical and emotional distance.

Florine Stettheimer – who depicted the dapper Ewing standing with Muriel Draper in her *Cathedrals of Fifth Avenue* (1931) – was a particular friend of queer artists and clearly fluent in the language of encoded performance. Her paintings, in particular her portraits of queer men, often included details only legible to those 'in the know'. For example, she painted a large purple pansy in one corner of her portrait of the queer composer Virgil Thomson; although he was concerned that viewers would 'get' the reference, his friends assured him that the 'unknowing never would and the knowing knew already'.[28] At Stettheimer's salon, one learned to see and hear through codes, and things were not always as they seemed.

Muriel Draper's salon in the East '40s was known for the sounds of people talking.[29] Like Chanler, Draper was a performer, well known for her stories, her unusual fashion sense and her imperviousness to age. She was not only a *saloniste* and a mentor of young men (including Ewing, Lincoln Kirstein, who became her lover, and the African American singer Taylor Gordon) but also a devoted follower of the spiritualist Gurdjieff who often hosted international guests and fellow travellers: her home had the character of a private club, decorated with silk drapes, silver candlesticks and gilded baroque-revival furniture, where the pleasures of the mind and the senses seemed always to be on offer.

These examples help us to view Van Vechten's West 55th Street apartment (from 1924 on) and the parties he hosted there in the context of queer culture, interior design and sensory experience: his home was a fastidiously curated stage set on which he performed and, like Draper's, it was well known as the site of large gatherings and interracial parties where people sang, danced and crowded together in a suite of noisy rooms. Ewing and other friends, including Virgil Thomson, were often to be found at the piano and on one occasion Bessie Smith performed.[30] In mixed company, Van Vechten and his closest friends were generally careful to stay within the bounds of accepted etiquette, making good use of camp sophistication, irony and a literary style that the critic Kristin MacLeod has termed 'arched-brow' modernism.[31] Private gatherings of queer men, on the other hand, could be more relaxed, as we know from Van Vechten's photographs and day books, which often refer to late-night visitors and after-parties.[32]

Ewing clearly modelled his home and his weekly social gatherings on those of his prominent friends, albeit on a smaller scale.[33] He moved into his West 31st Street studio in 1927, decorating the small space with furniture donated by Muriel Draper and works of art by friends. As Ewing explained to his mother, he wanted to host a weekly salon both to entertain and to show off his collections, particularly his photographs and a series of sculptures he created depicting his beloved Muriel Draper in a variety of poses.[34] The details of his guest lists, his menus and the entertainers he hired were all carefully chosen and recorded.

It was through his home, and literally inside his walk-in closet, that Max Ewing expressed his true passions [Figure 4.4]. Here he created his *Gallery of Extraordinary Portraits*, a sort of three-dimensional scrapbook of 300 meticulously arranged and numbered images. The gallery featured portraits of queer cultural heroes, including Marcel Proust, Radcliffe Hall and Oscar Wilde, as well as actors and actresses, bodybuilders and boxers – some scantily clad – and artists and entertainers, both Black and white. The well-known Paris *saloniste* Natalie Barney and her partner, the painter Romaine Brooks – with whom Ewing had travelled to the south of France and on to Venice in the summer of 1927 – were shown in Ewing's own snapshots. There were also portraits of Jean Cocteau, Margaret Anderson and Jane Heap (the couple who had edited the *Little Review* and become good friends in Paris) and of the French aristocrat Princesse Eugénie Murat, all created by his friend Berenice Abbott, who would later photograph Ewing himself for the dust jacket of his novel, *Going Somewhere,* published in 1933.

Photographs of the interior of the *Gallery* taken over time show that the display was constantly changing: in 1932, Ewing added his movie-star hero Gary Cooper, pinned high up on the wall, and the popular Harlem nightclub entertainer Paul Meeres, whose portrait by Van Vechten was also exhibited. Thanks to a contact sheet preserved among Van Vechten's meticulous cataloguing, we can date the Meeres portrait to 1 April 1932; while it is not clear when the portrait was acquired by Ewing, we know from letters that he had befriended the handsome dancer in 1928 and even entertained him in his own home.[35] We also know that Ewing often used his closet *Gallery* as a lure, inviting famous people to view his collection – catalogues in hand – and to pose for him. The display thus became a sort of interactive self-portrait, one that pushed the boundaries of propriety and personal disclosure with its artfully arranged images of celebrities, queer icons and beautiful men. The cramped, windowless closet space no doubt enhanced the feelings of physical presence and sensation, from visual

**Figure 4.4**   Anon., *Max Ewing in His Gallery of Extraordinary Portraits*, 1932.

pleasure to the sound of animated voices, the smell and touch of bodies and fabric, and the taste of food and alcohol served to guests.

Beginning in 1932, Ewing experimented with staged art photography of his own making, creating the extraordinary *Carnival of Venice* mentioned above. He worked with a Kodak camera and used the same backdrop of Venice for all his portraits, staging friends like Paul Robeson and Muriel Draper in theatrical costumes and holding props. The list of sitters is extraordinary: Ewing's idol, the singer Marguerite Namara, makes an appearance, as do Agnes de Mille, Lincoln Kirstein, Julien Levy, Isamu Noguchi, Miguel Covarrubias and E. E. Cummings, among others.

Berenice Abbott posed for Ewing, as did George Platt Lynes. Ewing had written to Van Vechten in 1932 to explain that he began the *Carnival of Venice* series in order to supplement the images in his closet gallery, but the difference between the two collections shows how far he had come: he knew all of these famous and fascinating people personally, and he photographed them in his home. That these stars performed in costume or hammed it up for his camera and pleasure made Ewing's fantasy complete. That some of these men and women posed nude or partially clad was even better.

The complex fate of Ewing's portraits of the Bahamian entertainer Paul Meeres from *The Carnival of Venice* suggests the challenges faced by queer photographers when images were circulated beyond the confines of the home. Ewing photographed Meeres for the series in a number of poses, wearing either a dapper suit or nothing at all. His full-length nudes were cropped for display at a one-day exhibition and party held at the Julien Levy Gallery on 26 January 1933, but they reappear, uncropped, in Van Vechten's scrapbooks, with jokey captions clipped from newspapers and magazines collaged onto the page.[36] Some images appear twice with different captions, which sometimes include the casual racism for which Van Vechten is known; indeed, for both Ewing and Van Vechten, creating images of Meeres and celebrating his beauty became part of a racialized, scophophilic fantasy of possession and control.[37] Similarly, many variants showing the Ritter brothers are here as well, together with pictures of other athletic young men, some of which appear in the 'official' *Carnival of Venice* series. Clearly Van Vechten had been very strategic in his role as archivist: letters show that Ewing's family had asked to have any nude images removed from the collection at Yale, but Van Vechten – whose own efforts to create such images are well documented – simply moved them into his own scrapbooks.[38]

We know that Van Vechten also began staging and producing his own images early in 1932 because he wrote to his brother-in-law in January to say that he had become obsessed with photography.[39] He wanted to focus on 'Harlem' and 'Celebrated Sitters', he told Ewing, and began by taking pictures of friends – including Prentiss Taylor and Bill Robinson, Gladys Bentley and Nora Holt – on the streets of Harlem.[40] By March he was exclusively photographing in his home, using backdrops of books, posters or cloth hangings to create individual portraits in his characteristic style. Sometimes, however, Van Vechten photographed a group in a more intimate and relaxed mode: one such image from a series taken in his library on 5 March offers a rare glimpse of the private expressions, gestures and dapper attire of his intimate circle [Figure 4.5]. He shows the African American singer and dancer Jimmie Daniels, who would later form a long-term relationship with the architect Philip Johnson, Donald Angus (Van Vechten's lover), Prentiss Taylor and the actor Tonio Selwart:

**Figure 4.5**   Carl Van Vechten, *Donald Angus, Jimmie Daniels, Tonio Selwart, and Prentiss Taylor, March 5, 1932.*

these men sit close together and touch, gazing at one another adoringly. In another image from the series, Daniels and Selwart are nude from the waist up, exchanging a loving look as though in bed. Here, and in bare-chested portraits of the actor Paul Robeson and the poet Langston Hughes, he staged private scenarios (inflected by his own queer and racialized visual erotics) for his own pleasure. Like many queer artists, Van Vechten was fascinated by the ways in which identities were constructed to reveal and conceal; indeed, a few days after the shoot with Hughes, Van Vechten took a number of self-portraits in his pyjamas, sitting at his desk and posed in front of the open door of his shoe closet. These reveal not only the characteristic awkwardness of his early work, but also his preoccupation with the codes of gender and sexuality, dress and gesture, through which individual identity was performed.

By the time these images were made – and certainly by the time that Ewing was called back to Pioneer, Ohio to attend to his mother in January 1934 – this glamorous world was already beginning to fade. People died, or moved, or lost their fortunes in the Crash of 1929, new laws were passed to outlaw homosexuality, and the curtain slowly came down on the marvellous show that had been New York in the 1920s. Even the *House of Fantasy* was empty and abandoned, following Chanler's death in 1930. As Ewing told his mother, 'Bob Chanler's house stands gray and gloomy in 19th St. All the curtains and furnishings are out of it and you can look in the front windows and out the back ones. FOR SALE signs are all over it, and there are no buyers … The whole neighborhood throws out an air of violence and disintegration.'[41]

Ewing suffered greatly from these changes. His confidence – and, it seems, his very survival – depended on the vibrant, queer, urban culture of which he had become such an integral part, and without it he lost all hope. Perhaps Van Vechten knew all along that this would happen: of all of Ewing's friends, he was the only one who refused to have his picture taken for *The Carnival of Venice*; both men knew well the shame that came with being gay in twentieth-century America.[42] Even Carl's wife, Fania, sat for Max, but Van Vechten kept his distance, preferring instead to stand apart, ever the mentor, the archivist and the photographer who controlled the narrative from behind the camera. The queer boy with the breathless enthusiasms, a talent for interior design and a taste for naked bodybuilders had perhaps become a liability that Van Vechten would leave for future generations to decode.

## Notes

1  Florine Stettheimer, Ms. of *Crystal Flowers*, Florine and Ettie Stettheimer Papers, YCAL MS 20, Box 8, Folder 138. The poems were privately printed in 1949. See Irene Gammel and Suzanne Zelazo (eds), *Florine Stettheimer: New Directions in Multimodal Modernism* (Toronto: Book Hug Press, 2019).

2  See E. Lupton and A. Lipps, *The Senses: Design Beyond Vision* (New York: Princeton Architectural Press and Cooper Hewitt National Design Museum, 2018).

3  Bill Ritter to Max Ewing (hereafter as ME), no date, Max Ewing Collection, Yale Collection of American Literature, Beinecke Rare Book and Manuscript Library, YCAL MSS 656 (hereafter as MEC), Box 9, Folder 68. The letter clearly relates to another from 12 February 1934 (note 3). For Clinton Moore's Harlem 'buffet flat' and its entertainments, see C. Heap, *Slumming: Sexual and Racial Encounters in American Nightlife, 1885–1940* (Chicago: University of Chicago Press, 2010), pp. 258–9. For gay Harlem, see T. H. Wirth (ed.), *Gay Rebel of the Harlem Renaissance: Selections from the Work of Richard Bruce Nugent*, foreword by Henry Louis Gates (Durham, NC and London: Duke University Press, 2002).

4  For Lynes, see T. Waugh, *Hard to Imagine: Gay Male Eroticism in Photography and Film from Their Beginnings to Stonewall* (New York: Columbia University Press, 1993), pp. 102–32, and E. Brown, *Work!* (Durham, NC: Duke University Press, 2017), Chapter 3. See also S. Watson, *The Harlem Renaissance: Hub of African-American Culture, 1920–1930* (New York: Pantheon Books, 1995), pp. 98–163.

5  *Ibid.*

6  See note 25 below.

7  For an overview of glamour, see A. T. Friedman, *American Glamour and the Evolution of Modern Architecture* (New Haven, CT: Yale University Press, 2010); and N. Thrift, 'Understanding the Material Practices of Glamour', in M. Gregg and G. J. Seigworth (eds), *The Affect Theory Reader* (Durham, NC: Duke University Press, 2010), pp. 289–308.

8  S. Watson, *Strange Bedfellows* (New York: Abbeville Press, 2003).

9  J. Smalls, *The Homoerotic Photography of Carl Van Vechten: Public Face, Private Thoughts* (Philadelphia: Temple University Press, 2006), p. 38; see also S. Herring, *Queering the Underworld: Slumming, Literature, and the Undoing of Gay and Lesbian History* (Chicago: University of Chicago Press, 2007), Chapter 3.

10  For Ewing's biography, see W. K. Ewing, *Genius Denied: The Life and Death of Max Ewing* (Grand Rapids, MI: W. K. Ewing, 2012); and A. T. Friedman, 'Max Ewing's Closet and Queer Architectural History', Pts 1 and 2, *Platform* (8 and 21 October 2019), www.platformspace.net/home/max-ewings-closet-and-queer-ar chitectural-history-part-1-1 and www.platformspace.net/home/max-ewings-clos et-and-queer-architectural-history\part-2 (accessed 30 October 2019).

11  Max Ewing's Diary, 1917, MEC, Box 30, Folder 225.

12  E. White, *The Tastemaker: Carl Van Vechten and the Birth of Modern America* (New York: Farrar, Straus and Giroux, 2014); K. MacLeod, 'Introduction: The Blind Bow-Boy: "A Great Forgotten American Novel of the 1920s"' in K. MacLeod (ed.), *Carl Van Vechten, The Blind Bow-Boy* (Cambridge: Modern Humanities Research Association, 2018), pp. vii–xxii.

13  ME to Clara Ewing, 9–10 October 1923, MEC, Box 1, Folder 6.

14  White, *Tastemaker*, pp. 169–78, and B. Kellner (ed.), *The Splendid Drunken Twenties: Selections from the Day Books 1922–30* (Urbana, IL: University of Illinois Press, 2003).

15  K. MacLeod, 'The Librarian's Dream Prince: Carl Van Vechten and America's Modernist Cultural Archives Industry', *Libraries & the Cultural Record*, 46:4 (2011), pp. 360–87.

16  CVV to A. J. Ewing, 16 July 1934, MEC, Box 9, Folder 70.

17  Undated (after September 1933), Carl Van Vechten Papers, YCAL MSS 1050 (here-after as CVVP), Box 213, Vol. 8.

18  For queer domesticity and material culture, see J. Potvin, *Bachelors of a Different Sort: Queer Aesthetics, Material Culture and the Modern Interior in Britain* (Manchester: Manchester University Press, 2015) and *Deco Dandy: Designing Masculinity in the 1920s* (Manchester: Manchester University Press, 2020).

19  See G. Chauncey, *Gay New York: Gender, Urban Culture and the Making of the Gay World 1890–1940* (New York: Basic Books, 1994); and K. J. Mumford, *Interzones: Black/White Districts in Chicago and New York in the Early Twentieth Century* (New York: Columbia University Press, 1997), Chapter 6.

20  For the Stettheimers, see L. Nochlin, 'Florine Stettheimer: Rococo Subversive' in M. Reilly (ed.), *Women Artists: The Linda Nochlin Reader* (London: Thames and Hudson, 2015); for Walker, see A. Bundles, *Self Made* (New York: Scribner, 2019), Watson, *Harlem Renaissance*, pp. 108–10, and M. K. Johnson, *Can't Stand Still: Taylor Gordon and the Harlem Renaissance* (Jackson, MI: University of Mississippi Press, 2019); see also T. Dudley, 'Seeking the Ideal African-American Interior: The Walker Residences and Salon in New York', *Studies in the Decorative Arts*, 14:1 (Fall–Winter 2006–7), pp. 80–112.

21  Watson, *Strange Bedfellows*, quoted in R. Stitton, *Lady in the Dark: Iris Barry and the Art of Film* (New York: Columbia University Press, 2014), pp. 157–8. See also S. Watson, *Prepare for Saints: Gertrude Stein, Virgil Thomson and the Mainstreaming of American Modernism* (New York: Random House, 1998). The exception was A'lelia Walker's home at 80 Edgecombe Avenue, where people of all persuasions were free to indulge their tastes: see 'Mabel Hampton Interviews', 13 January 1983, *Lesbian Herstory Archives*, http://herstories.prattinfoschool.nyc/omeka/exhibits/show/mabel-hampton-oral-history/item/74.

22  J. Levy, *Memoir of An Art Gallery* (New York: Putnam, 1977), pp. 104–6. For Murphy, see L. Cohen, *All We Know: Three Lives* (New York: Farrar, Straus, and Giroux, 2012), pp. 7–147. For Kirstein, see S. Friedman et al. (eds), *Lincoln Kirstein's Modern* (New York: MoMA, 2019).

23  B. Fahlman, 'Reclaiming an American Modernist' and L. Drapala, 'Building the House of Fantasy' in G. Wouters and A. Gollin (eds), *Robert Winthrop Chanler: Discovering the Fantastic* (New York: Monacellli, 2016), pp. 21–49 and 51–79.

24  20 May 1930, MEC, Box 4, Folder 25.

25  C. Whiting, 'Decorating with Stettheimer and the Boys', *American Art*, 14:1 (Spring 2000), pp. 24–49; and C. Breward, 'Styling *Four Saints in Three Acts:* Scene, Costume, Fashion and the Queer Modern Movement' in P. Allmer and J. Sears (eds), *4 Saints in 3 Acts: A Snapshot of the American Avant-Garde in the 1930s* (Manchester: Manchester University Press, 2017), pp. 82–102.

26  2 September 1930, MEC, Box 4, Folder 27; 6 April 1930; 23 May 1930, etc., Box 5, Folder 28. In July 1932, Ewing accompanied Florine Stettheimer to the top of the Empire State Building: MEC, Box 5, Folder 32. On 3 December 1932, the Stettheimers showed Max the photos that Van Vechten had taken of them, 'and said [he] was the only person alive they would show them to, they were so bad', MEC, Box 5, Folder 33.

27  Whiting, 'Stettheimer', p. 36.

28  A. C. Tommasini, *Virgil Thomson: Composer on the Aisle* (New York: W.W. Norton, 1997), p. 229, cited by L. Barg, 'Modernism in Tableaux: Race and Desire in *Four Saints in Three Acts*', in Allmer and Sears, *4 Saints*, pp. 64–81.

29  B. Fahlman, 'That Great Draper Woman: Muriel Draper and the Art of the Salon', *Woman's Art Journal*, 26:2 (Autumn 2005–Winter 2006), pp. 33–7, and C. Beaton, *The Glass of Fashion: A Personal History of Fifty Years of Changing Taste* (London: Weidenfeld and Nicholson, 1954), no page numbers.

30  White, *Tastemaker*, pp. 177–81, and C. Albertson, *Bessie* (New Haven, CT: Yale University Press, 2003), pp. 172–4.

31  MacLeod, *The Blind Bow-Boy*, p. xiii.

32  For example, Kellner, *Splendid Drunken*, pp. 160–2.

33  C. Breward, 'The Closet' in Cook and Gorman-Murray (eds), *Queering the Interior*, pp. 187–97.

34  April 1928, MEC, Box 4, Folder 21, and passim.

35  ME to CE, 28 October 1928, MEC, Box 4, Folder 22.

36  The scrapbooks are in the CVVP, Boxes 205–223; the images of Meeres are from Box 211, Volume 6.

37  E. Bernard (ed.), *Remember Me to Harlem: The Letters of Langston Hughes and Carl Van Vechten, 1925–1964* (New York: Knopf, 2001), introduction, and Smalls, *Homoerotic*, Chapters 2–4.

38  CVV to Doris Ewing, CVVP, Box 43, Folder 587. For Van Vechten's male nudes, see Smalls, *Homoerotic*, and J. Weinberg, '"Boy Crazy": Carl Van Vechten's Queer Collection', *The Yale Journal of Criticism* (1 January 1994), pp. 25–49.

39  *Ibid*, p. 23.

40  Real-photo postcard 'The View from Carl Van Vechten's Apartment', CVV to ME, 7 February 1932, MEC, Box 8, Folder 60.

41  ME to CE, 26 April 1933, quoted in Ewing, *Genius Denied*, p. 130.

42  There were exceptions, of course: the Stettheimers are not shown in the series, perhaps for the reasons suggested in Whiting, as in note 25.

# · 5

# Conquering the home front: Nazi propaganda and sensory experiences in the German domestic interior, 1933–45

*Serena Newmark*

> The Nuremberg tribunal should have ordered Richard Wagner to be beaten in effigy once a year in the streets of every German town.[1]

On New Year's Day 1933, Germans were citizens of a democracy, but by summer 1933, they were living in a dictatorship. After years of existing as an obscure party with few constituents and little publicity, the Nazi party received nearly a third of parliamentary votes in late 1932, and Adolf Hitler (1889–1945) was installed as Chancellor on 30 January 1933. Using myriad violent tactics against rival political candidates and their supporters, the Nazi party secured almost half of the votes cast in the March 1933 parliamentary election, formed a coalition government, quickly made all other political parties illegal, and allowed Hitler to bypass parliament and rule by decree. However, even at their most successful, and then only with the use of harassment and physical violence, the National Socialists never won the support of more than 45 per cent of the electorate. To solidify their authority over the citizenry, the majority of whom did not originally want them in power, Nazi leadership swiftly began a campaign of inserting propaganda into virtually all aspects of German life, and Hitler appointed Joseph Goebbels (1897–1945) as Minister of the newly created Ministry of Public Enlightenment and Propaganda.

By bombarding the German public with sensory experiences, propagandists created a new National Socialist (NS) aesthetic that was applied to decorative arts, music and the spoken word, and printed texts, as well as food and drink. As even the grandest event at the mammoth Nuremberg rally grounds designed by infamous Nazi architect Albert Speer (1905–81) could only host a small section of the population for a few hours, the Third Reich forced the Nazi aesthetic into the German household to cement control over the citizenry daily, and virtually no aspect of domestic life was deemed too minute to exist beyond the reach of the propagandist. This chapter focuses on only a few of the most intimate aspects of this purpose-fully manufactured aesthetic and the NS influence on sensory experiences in the German civilian home, with particular emphasis on the daily propaganda directed at women and children.

During the rigorous process of de-Nazification after the Second World War, overt Nazi symbols and propaganda were removed from German daily life as Germans and occupying allies redirected their energy towards building a post-war Europe. Thus, scholars can find it challenging to convey accurately how thoroughly the sensory experiences of regular German citizens were dominated by Nazi propaganda from 1933 until 1945. As seeing the time-bleached monochrome white stone of the Elgin Marbles has given generations of art lovers an incorrect impression of the once brightly polychrome ancient Acropolis, so too have the black and white photographs of the 1930s and 1940s failed to provide an adequate portrayal of the Nazi use of colourful propaganda and the striking visual impact it had on those who witnessed it firsthand. By the time war began, Nazi propagandists had already spent years deftly creating a new aesthetic and manipulating the population using what they allowed the public to hear, to see, to smell and eat, what their hands and bodies could feel, and their perception of time and space.

Nazi propaganda entered the German home and civilian sensory experiences via a variety of methods. Media outlets, civic groups, and institutions of formal education were either brought under government control or disbanded and replaced with National Socialist alternatives.

> Since the advent of the National Socialists the power of the agencies of propaganda has been intensified and coordinated so that all avenues of communication – press, school, radio, motion picture, and even the church – must carry but one propaganda to the public mind, must express one will, one voice, one opinion. Hence the Hitler regime has, in common with other fascist countries, established a system wherein authority flows from the top down; and from the people comes blind, instant, unquestioning obedience.[2]

From 1933 to 1945, the German home was not a refuge from politics or the conflicts of the outside world, as some of the smallest and seemingly insignificant parts of family life were dominated by the totalitarian government. Even a letter to a friend would require the use of a Nazi postage stamp, the image on which would have been purposefully selected to encourage enthusiasm for the Third Reich.[3] Propaganda in the domestic interior was typically not confined to manipulation of one sense at a time. In many cases, it is impossible to distinguish between the influence of the senses. Taste and smell are intimately linked. Music only penetrates the ears until it compels the listener to clap their hands in applause or dance and feel the floor beneath their feet. Reading a newspaper is not only a visual experience, as the sound of its arrival on the doorstep, the smell of fresh newsprint, and the physical presence of an object that takes up space and then must be disposed of also leave their imprint on the user and within the home environment.

The purpose of Nazi propaganda in the domestic interior was not only to galvanize support among the citizenry for the new dictatorship but also to convince the population, via Hitler's Four-Year Plan, to prepare for total war by turning Germany into a completely independent autarky. Nazi propagandists developed an aesthetic that used a fictionalized Teutonic history coupled with a worship of the German soil and a fascination with a pre-Christian past to create a Germany myth, a country that was self-reliant and required no imported raw materials. This mythic Germany was at once firmly established throughout the ages, while simultaneously one that ignored much of German history, as any form of authority that might challenge Nazi authority, such as Weimar Democracy, the Christian Church, or the former Royal Family, need not be mentioned.

## Striving for the impossible

Nazi propaganda, as it entered and dominated the domestic interior via the five senses, both encouraged racism and focused on persuading civilians to make any changes and sacrifices necessary to attain a non-specific goal of German grandeur and world dominance that was simultaneously inevitable and yet always just out of reach. From 1933 to 1945, German civilians were asked to do something that was literally impossible. Australian historian Stephen H. Roberts described this process as he observed it while researching in Germany well before the start of the war.

> There are thirty-four vital materials without which a nation cannot live, and unfortunately, Germany is worse off than any other great State in so far as these are concerned. Whereas the British Empire is largely dependent on out-side sources for only nine of these, Germany has only two in ample quantities – potash and coal. That means that she must turn to the foreigner for all of her supplies of twenty-six of these and for part of six more. Yet this is the Power that sees fit to launch a plan for complete self-sufficiency. It is ludicrous [...] Yet the mass of Germans are so inflamed by official propaganda that they believe Hitler when he says that Germany must, and can, stand alone.[4]

The overarching Nazi aesthetic that invaded the family home was one that used music, food, clothing, toys, furniture, and home textiles to convince the public that it was possible to achieve two wildly divergent goals: the return to a pre-industrial, pre-Christian, agrarian, self-sufficient past and the creation of a modern and prosperous consumer society where every household had a new refrigerator, and the government was able to support a technologically advanced military.[5] Sound and the visual impact of contemporary industrial design were able to transmit these divergent concepts simultaneously. The appearance of a new, streamlined radio on a living room table was evidence of the wonders of modern technology available to the many, while the tune of a rediscovered old German folk song emanating from it reinforced notions of a return to an idealized pre-modern past.

In the 1920s, German radio stations mostly played entertainment, educational and apolitical local news programmes.[6] As Hitler and his allies gained power, they also seized control of radio broadcasting, which would become a primary method for disseminating the NS aesthetic as well as the Führer's speeches.

> After Hitler's appointment as chancellor, between February 1 and the parliamentary elections of March 5, the Nazis launched a daily radio political campaign. During this five-week campaign, Hitler, who had never been given access to radio before, spoke 16 times on the radio. The total number of appearances of the Nazi officials on the radio during the March 1933 election campaign was 28, compared to a total of 4 appearances during the entire period for 1923 to January 29, 1933. The Nazis also blocked access to radio of all other parties and minimized airtime of its coalition partner.[7]

Access to radio programmes in Germany did not only require listeners to own a radio but also to pay a modest radio subscription fee. In his capacity as Minister of Propaganda, Goebbels requested the engineer Otto Griessing (1897–1958) design an inexpensive and fashionably modern radio that most Germans could afford. The Volksempfänger, a pared-down and sleek bakelite radio, was introduced to the public at the Große Deutsche Funkausstellung in August 1933. An even less expensive and smaller radio, the Deutscher Kleinempfänger, was introduced in 1938. In addition to supporting the manufacturing of a financially accessible radio, the Third Reich exempted an increasing number of households from having to pay the radio subscription fee, and radio listenership consequently skyrocketed. In 1934, only around a third of German households had a radio, while nearly two-thirds owned a radio in 1938.[8] The home itself became a location of group broadcasting, as some would open their windows and turn up the radio volume when the Führer was speaking.[9] Manipulation of the citizenry via the radio was very consciously and purposefully part of the Nazi propaganda machine, and listening to foreign radio stations was strictly forbidden. Having spent the Nazi era creating built environments purposefully designed to deliver Hitler's words to a captive audience, architect Albert Speer included the following statement in his final words when on trial in Nuremberg after the war: 'Through technical devices such as radio and loudspeaker, 80 million people were deprived of independent thought. It was thereby possible to subject them to the will of one man'.[10]

While overt political speeches were, quite reasonably, the broadcast type of greatest interest during the Nuremberg Trials, Nazi propaganda and anti-Semitic philosophies were communicated through musical programming as well. Upon coming to power in 1933, the Nazis began removing Jews and virtually anyone deemed unfit by the Third Reich from intellectual or cultural life. Through a purge of the universities, all non-Aryans, Jews, and individuals suspected of being communists were fired without recourse. Those purged included twenty past or future Nobel Prize winners, including Albert Einstein (1879–1955). In some institutions of higher learning, the staff removed from the workplace accounted for a third of the academic faculty. Those who remained employed after the purge were required to take an indoctrination course and pledge an oath to the Reich.[11] By the summer of 1933, Jews were no longer allowed to teach in music conservatoires or work in state opera houses.[12] The dead were treated no better than the living. Music by the great nineteenth-century German composer Felix Mendelssohn (1809–47) was banned because, although he was a baptized Lutheran, his father had been a non-observant Jew. The composer Johann Strauss II (1825–99), an Austrian contemporary of Mendelssohn's, was spared the same treatment, as he only had one Jewish great-grandparent, the maximum amount of Jewish heritage considered to be acceptable.[13] The Reich Chamber of Music, a division within Goebbels' Ministry of Public Enlightenment and Propaganda, was in charge of using music to encourage the *Gleichschaltung*, incorporating all German society into one ideologically and culturally homogenous society with full support of Hitler's regime. Richard Wagner (1813–83) was notoriously the composer most associated with Hitler's ideologies. Not only were members of the late composer's family part of Hitler's social circle and his frequent guests, but several of Wagner's operas included Nordic and pagan themes that were considered well within the Nazi aesthetic, and Hitler made Wagner's custom-designed opera house in Bayreuth into a national shrine.[14]

Music history and musicology, like all other academic subjects, were redirected towards service of the Nazi government. Needing to fill airtime and attract a wide variety of musical tastes, NS propaganda music, by necessity, needed to reach beyond the confines of nineteenth-century grand opera and Hitler's beloved Wagner. The government encouraged the writing of new 'folk' songs, even granting prize money for those deemed the best. Marches and folk music of ages past were rediscovered and used as evidence of German ethnic superiority. 'Equipped with racial and folk norms, the musicologists were to comb through the past and present music cultures to verify Nazi truths, to weed out alien and decadent components and to establish the folk-related art in confirmation of the Nazi myth of "blood and soil".'[15] A representative day of midweek radio offerings in the early years of the Nazi regime included the sounds of the local church bells followed by a children's programme and an afternoon devoted to an interview with the Propaganda Minister,[16] thus bringing National Socialist directives into the home alongside lighthearted family entertainment and the familiar and comforting soundscape of the local churchyard. Despite repeated attempts, Nazi approaches to music were not tremendously successful in creating Aryan alternatives to jazz or Christmas music. Jazz, as made famous by Black Americans, was always condemned by the Nazi party as being deviant, but to boost morale after Germany's heavy military losses in early 1942, recordings of Duke Ellington and Louis Armstrong were allowed on the radio, albeit without their names.[17] For centuries, Germans had incorporated pagan rituals into Christian holidays,[18] but Christmas and its associated church music could not be removed completely from the local culture.

> While hostile Nazi functionaries tried to replace the Christian Christmas for the armed forces with a neopagan celebration of the winter solstice, chaplains advised one another to remain calm. The men would not tolerate Christmas without 'Stille Nacht' ('Silent Night'), they told themselves. And they were right. Even SS men, infamous for their aggressively anti-Christian paganism, were known to mark 25 December in what they considered unique German ways: by singing Christmas hymns familiar from their childhood.[19]

Although traditional carols were never successfully erased by the NS, Nazi publications presented the public with alternative holiday music to sing, often featuring text that referenced current sensory discomfort caused by wartime scarcity. A Christmas song published on the cover of the late year 1944 edition of the *NS Frauen-Warte*, the National Socialist newspaper for women, included lyrics instructing children not to ask why the bread is hard and the house is cold, telling them instead that it will eventually become clear why all the current deprivation will have been necessary. Written in the 4:4 time signature and with the rhythm of a military march, the newly composed Nazi Christmas carol is clearly designed to turn children into little soldiers for the Reich [Figure 5.1].[20]

By Christmas 1944, when specially written military marches disguised as Christmas carols were instructing children to ignore the lack of suitable food and heat in their homes, the Nazi regime had already spent a decade dictating how German children should experience Christmas. During the 1935 Christmas season, a foreign journalist remarked on the abundance of Third Reich-themed Christmas gifts for children, which included phonograph records of military marches and child-sized trench helmets. Feeling the hard metal of the helmet resting on his head while presenting the image of small, uniformed soldier to the members of his household, a German child could then wage mock battles with toy soldiers dressed in colourful Nazi uniforms and armed with an extraordinary variety of toy weapons [Figure 5.2].

> Under the spreading Christmas trees these 'Made in the New Germany' lead soldiers – Brown Shirts, Black Guards and World War frontline fighters

**Figure 5.1**   H. Baumann, 'Trotz Kampf, Krieg und Tod bleibe uns Weihnachten das Fest der Liebe und der gläubigen Herzen' (Through Battle, War and Death, Let Us Keep Christmas as the Festival of Love and True Hearts), *NS Frauen-Warte* (second half of the year 1944), p. 25.

**Figure 5.2**   National Socialist toy soldiers, manufactured by Hans Frömter, 1935–43.

of all armies [...] front-line settings include miniature fighters in German, British, French and American uniforms in every posture of clubbing and bayoneting [...] All kinds of weapons are depicted in lethal operation – including even miniature batteries of flamethrowers [...] In the background, surveying the troubled fields, there is usually a figure of Hindenburg – or even of Hitler.[21]

Well into advanced age, those who were children during the Second World War could recall receiving war-themed gifts for Christmas.[22]

## Women within the Nazi home

Although German women and girls had experienced a time of relative liberation in the 1920s, the Nazi government demanded that they largely leave public life and devote themselves to the domestic sphere, with exceptions made for women particularly skilled in creating propaganda. 'A special privilege is given to Leni Riefenstahl, the former film star, who is now allowed to earn a million marks a year as virtual dictator of the German film industry. For the others, there are *Kinder, Kirche, und Küche'*.[23] Teenage girls found themselves taken out of maths and foreign languages classes to be taught needlework, and embroidering one's household linens with swastikas was encouraged.[24] Subsequently, the number of female students at German universities fell by over two-thirds from 1932 to 1939. Married women in the civil service were removed from their positions, and national health insurance policies no longer provided payment to married women physicians.[25]

As housewives and mothers were expected to be responsible for the family housekeeping budget, the Ministry of Propaganda set up organizations and published materials that encouraged women to make domestic choices allied with Nazi government objectives. The Deutsche Frauenwerk Abteilung Volkswirtschaft-Hauswerkschaft, a government agency focusing on home economics, published newspapers and pamphlets, opened advice centres, and provided free classes to teach women how to make do with less. Housewives could consult their copy of the *NS Frauen-Warte* to find advice on how to feed their families using plants and animals that were found on the German soil or in German waterways. The most highly encouraged meal for properly dedicated NS housewives was the *Eintopf*, or one-pot meal. Considered the meal of sacrifice for the Reich,[26] the *Eintopf* was not just a dish but a domestic ritual. Instead of enjoying an elaborate meal of roast chicken or beef on Sunday evenings, as was the established custom, German families were asked to eat a simple stew consisting of scraps of local meat and vegetables cooked in broth so that they could donate the extra food to the less fortunate. While the image associated with the *Eintopf* meal is that of a single stewpot, in practice the concept of the *Eintopf* meal also included the *Auflauf*, a baked casserole. Women were encouraged to use vegetables that grow well in Germany, such as celery (both greens and root), carrots, and asparagus, as well as German potatoes. Consuming eggs and meat from backyard chickens was encouraged as was eating local fish, a practice that was less common, particularly among the wealthy, before 1933. At first glance, these diet recommendations do not appear vastly different from what households were asked in Allied Nations, where Victory Gardens were encouraged and ration cards required. However, the scale of sacrifice expected of German households was far greater, and the ultimate goal, turning Germany into an autarky, was completely impossible. Additionally, Nazi propagandists began dictating what food, and subsequently what tastes and smells, were permitted in German households well before the war began, not only to conserve resources but to solidify German soil worship and, by extension, solidify feelings of distrust towards anyone considered not sufficiently Teutonic.

For decades, German home economists and leaders of housewives groups had urged German women (especially working-class women) to pursue more rational, self-disciplined styles of housekeeping. But under the Nazi Four-Year Plan they were being asked to become almost surreally efficient and self-sufficient, renouncing both free time and any weakness for butter. And now, they were to make 'martyrs' of themselves not for their families but rather for the state. In some ways, these sacrifices resembled those that were asked of American or British women during the two World Wars (e.g., the 'meatless' or 'wheatless' days in the United States in 1917–1918), but German housewives were being asked to retool their menus and households during peacetime.[27]

While NS menu planners and recipes, printed alongside jaunty illustrations of elves making *Eintopf* stews, are presented as practical advice for feeding a family with rationed resources, the intention may have been more nuanced [Figure 5.3]. By 1933, most adult German women had already lived through the difficult times of the First World War and the economic depression and, except those of particularly fortunate means, they were well versed in preparing meals from a modest amount of ingredients. Recipes from the *NS Frauen-Warte* newspaper focus on the use of local ingredients and are designed to stretch quantities of dairy products and meat, which would have been in short supply. The real-world practice of cooking *NS Frauen-Warte* recipes and then serving them reveals that appearance and smell seem to take precedence over taste and even nutrition. Recipes often feature a mix of ingredients that would be better served separately than combined. Many people, particularly growing children, would be fine eating plain macaroni, mashed celeriac, or meatballs made with tomato paste and a splash of milk. However, once those ingredients are mixed and baked together in an *Auflauf*, the result is an almost inedible dish, albeit one that smells good while baking in the oven and gives the appearance of a substantial meal when placed on the kitchen table.[28]

**Figure 5.3** 'Eintopf Geister' February meal planner including 'Eintopf Elves' cut paper silhouette by Dagmar von Bentheim. *NS Frauen-Warte* (January 1936), p. 528.

## Design books as an instrument of propaganda

As the war progressed and conditions on the home front became increasingly dire, Nazi publications focused on quaint sensory experiences in the domestic realm. A slim paperback volume with a quote from German Romantic painter Caspar David Friedrich, 'The Only True Source of Art is Our Heart', as its title, takes the reader on a tour of an idealized yet presumably universal German home. Starting with a message from Heinrich Himmler (1900–45) warning that a country is only successful so long as its citizens remember their ancestors, the author then presents the reader with photographs of household objects alongside individual descriptions of the sensory experiences associated with each object, all attempting to invoke feelings of invented racist nostalgia. Not only are the appearance and usability of objects remarked upon but also the associated smells and relationship to environmental temperature. For instance, a coffee bean grinder is a totem of Aryan German family life, as it was used by previous generations but is currently clasped between the daughter's knees, who grinds coffee as she cheerfully describes adventures among local German garden plants and dreams of how the warm coffee will feel on her tongue during cold winter days.[29] The author is careful, as NS propagandists typically were, to avoid any mention of potentially competing sources of authority, such as the Kaiser or the Church. The last image in the book, a gravestone, was undoubtedly chosen because it depicts local flora and has text celebrating the deceased as the mother of eleven children but omits any use of Christian imagery, such as angels or a cross.[30]

Propagandists were tremendously interested in how German civilians furnished their homes, wanted to make sure that the worship of products of German soil would be carried into domestic space, and sought to influence how furniture looked and interacted with the human body. The notorious propagandist Johann von Leers (1902–65), a professor and frequent freelance author for Nazi publishers, wrote books on the history of rural German dwellings and German domestic furniture and handcrafts. As academic reviewers noted at the time of their publication, von Leers' books were thinly disguised NS propaganda with zero academic value, and their only purpose seems to have been to provide an attractively bound presence on the bookshelf.[31] Like most printed Nazi propaganda of the 1930s and early 1940s, von Leers' books on German domestic objects were typically published with text in Fraktur.[32] A blackletter font that has been associated with Germanic languages since the medieval period, Fraktur stands in sharp visual contrast to the Latin alphabet historically associated with Romance languages.[33] Although the text was in Latin, the Gutenberg Bible was published in a blackletter font similar to Fraktur, as was the German language Luther Bible. Initially eager to associate their government with an old German aesthetic rather than any twentieth-century streamlined text, the Nazis declared that all official printed materials, including newspapers and schoolbooks, should be printed in Fraktur. Private publishers were in danger of losing their government subsidies, thus becoming insolvent, if they did not change their typeface to Fraktur.[34] Visual representations of Germany's supposedly superior past entered the family home via books and newspapers and the visual experience of reading a distinctively Germanic script, until practical considerations made the use of Fraktur unsustainable. Shortly after France surrendered to Nazi Germany, the NS leadership realized that the exclusive use of Fraktur would make materials difficult to read, particularly in the newly occupied nations, and that it would be costly and difficult, if not impossible, to replace all Latin-script typewriters with Fraktur versions. Thus, on the third of January 1941, the Third Reich officially announced (falsely) that blackletter fonts were created by Jews[35] and were no longer to be used; only Latin script was permitted. The official internal party memo on the subject was typed with a Latin-script typewriter on a piece of National Socialist letterhead, which had been printed earlier in Fraktur.[36] As in all aspects, Nazi edicts on the aesthetics of books and printed materials were not about admiration for the visual culture of eras past or even providing a consistent message but were instead centred on consolidating political power.

Despite official encouragement, not all Nazi-era home advice manuals printed before 1941 were published in Fraktur or other blackletter fonts. Some adapted the popular, streamlined, and practical aesthetic of the modern art movement and the Bauhaus into the service of the NS government in a subtle way. *Der Heim-Berater: Gutes und Böses in der Wohnung* was first published in 1933, the year the Nazis closed the official Bauhaus school, and again in 1937.[37] Sometimes mistaken for an early modernist furniture guide, *Der Heim-Berater* was printed with a striking geometric cover design and simplified Latin typeface that would appear alien next to the Luther Bible. Promising few words, many pictures, and lots of recommendations for where to go shopping, *Der Heim-Berater* explains the new Nazi autarkic aesthetic for the home without overt Nazi references, such as swastikas or quotes from high-ranking Nazi officials. Instead, domestic furniture, textiles, cutlery, ceramics, and even household appliances are seen as either within or outside the Nazi aesthetic and are considered purely in terms of good and bad, with accompanying illustrative pictures. Much of the advice is similar to that espoused by design reformers and modernists. Simplicity and cleanliness are valued, as is truth to materials, particularly if the material was sourced locally. However, *Der Heim-Berater* describes a consumer's purchasing choice in furniture and home accessories in absolute moral terms, with German autarky being correct and with foreign or luxurious being sinful. The sparing use of plain, geometrically patterned textiles is considered virtuous while lavish bed hangings are an abomination. A table made of plain German wood is to be praised, as the touch of hand to a local timber solidified the user's connection to the products of German soil, while any table with a hint of French or Chinese materials or stylistic influence is deviant. Household goods could be virtuous only if they were plain and newly created by German handworkers out of German materials, and family heirlooms were only acceptable if they were simple, practical objects created in a rural setting. The utility of a household object was secondary to its purpose of advancing the objectives of the Third Reich.[38]

Propaganda images of domestic objects often reappear in several different kinds of printed materials. Photographs from *Der Heim-Berater* were published in a monthly supplement to the *NS Kurier*, a National Socialist newspaper. The accompanying article states that readers can only be assured of having worthwhile furniture if they buy from local craftsmen who use German woods and work exclusively in old German styles because, as the article plainly states, to be German is to be true. A series of mocking cartoons includes an image of a man so enraged by the presence of an art deco sideboard that he takes an axe to destroy it [Figure 5.4]. The caption reads, 'The best solution'. Although the image is intended to be comical, it is nonetheless encouraging an attitude of physical violence against household objects that were created during the Weimar period in favour of something deemed to be authentically German, and thus within the Nazi worldview. A baby elephant is pictured nuzzling an art deco glass cabinet over the insulting description, 'He sought and found something like himself.'[39]

The baby elephant and art deco glass cabinet show up again in *Das deutsche Möbel*, published in 1942. The book presents several detailed

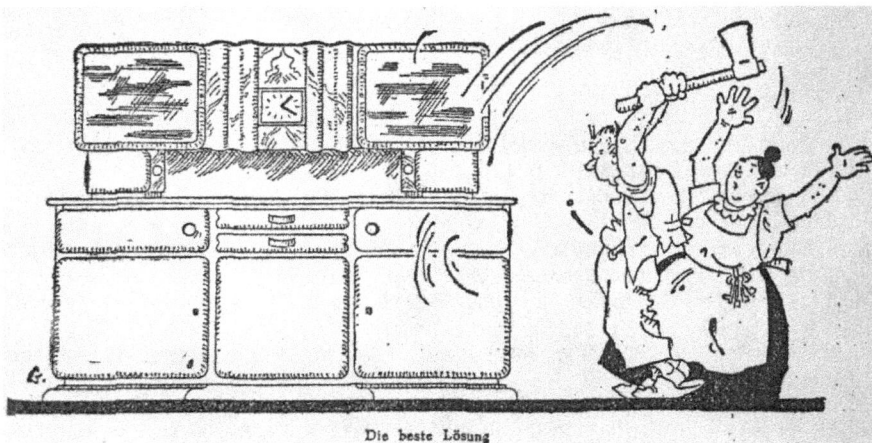

Die beste Lösung

**Figure 5.4**    Unnamed author, 'Die beste Lösung' (The best solution), Kennen Sie Bubinga oder Sapeli. *Technik: Monatsbeilage Zum NS Kurier* (October 1934), p. 1.

drawings of furniture of ages past, but it is immediately identifiable as being a tool of the Nazi state and designed to encourage hatred of Jews and foreigners as communicated through a text on household furniture, past and present. The Third Reich-appointed Minister of the Furniture Makers Guild wrote the introduction, and the text begins with a quote from Adolf Hitler. The following history of European furniture includes referring to art deco as 'the Jewish style' and ends with photographs of the Third Reich's preferred interiors, those furnished with simple farmhouse furniture made of German wood. The last page of text ends with a drawing of an agrarian domestic scene of a father, mother, and two children with their farmhouse in the background. The accompanying caption describes the image as a picture of the future, a promise that the men currently on the battlefield would one day return and form loving families that would be bound to the German soil.[40]

Nazi propagandists used all five human senses to bring Third Reich indoctrination into the domestic interior, but the invasion of the home was, for many, never entirely complete. Some Germans continued to cook foreign recipes, eat at art deco dining tables, and even, although it was forbidden, listen to the BBC's German Service.[41] Although domestic habits did not change immediately or entirely in every German household, the presence of Nazi propaganda in the domestic interior and its influence over daily sensory experiences cannot be overstated. In many cases, wartime scarcity ended up being the unintentional enforcer of Nazi aesthetics, since those on the home front were compelled, by necessity, to eat what they could grow or scavenge and make do with grandmother's long-forgotten dishware. Nazi propaganda, like the propaganda of all violent totalitarian regimes, used selected aspects of the nation's culture to convince the public that absolute and magnificent victory would be achieved only with their extreme and constant personal sacrifice.

## Notes

1 P. Quignard, *The Hatred of Music*, trans. M. Amos and F. Rönnbäck (New Haven, CT: Yale University Press, 2016), p. 148.
2 J. Yourman, 'Propaganda Techniques within Nazi Germany', *The Journal of Educational Sociology*, 13:3 (1939), p. 148.
3 F. Lauritzen, 'Propaganda Art in the Postage Stamps of the Third Reich', *The Journal of Decorative and Propaganda Arts*, 10 (1988), pp. 62–79.
4 S. H. Roberts, *The House that Hitler Built* (London: Methuen Publishers, 1938), p. 173.
5 N. R. Reagin, *Sweeping the German Nation: Domesticity and National Identity in Germany, 1870–1945* (Cambridge: Cambridge University Press, 2007), p. 171.
6 M. Adena, et al. 'Radio and the Rise of the Nazis in Prewar Germany', *Quarterly Journal of Economics*, 130:4 (2015), p. 1893.
7 Adena, et al. 'Radio and the Rise', p. 1897.
8 *Ibid.*, pp. 1898, 1900.

9  H. Rosenbaum, *'Und Trotzdem War's 'ne Schöne Zeit': Kinderalltag im Nationalsozialismus* (Frankfurt: Campus Frankfurt, 2014), p. 508.

10  *Nuremberg Trial Proceedings*, 22 (31 August 1946), The Avalon Project, Lillian Goldman Law Library, Yale University Law School, https://avalon.law.yale.edu/imt/10-01-46.asp (accessed 20 May 2021).

11  C. M. Hutton, *Linguists and the Third Reich: Mother-Tongue Fascism, Race and the Science of Language* (London: Routledge, 2014), pp. 58–9.

12  D. Neuschwander, 'Music in the Third Reich', *Musical Offerings*, 3:2 (2012), p. 101.

13  L. E. Moller, 'Music in Germany during the Third Reich: The Use of Music for Propaganda', *Music Educators Journal*, 67:3 (1980), p. 41.

14  M. Meyer, 'The Nazi Musicologist as Myth Maker in the Third Reich', *Journal of Contemporary History*, 10:4 (1975), p. 661.

15  *Ibid.*, p. 653.

16  H. Pohle, *Der Rundfunk als Instrument der Politik* (Hamburg: Hans Bredow Institut, 1955), p. 411.

17  Moller, 'Music in Germany', p. 42.

18  While the practice of decorating an evergreen tree at Christmas has generally been adopted in the Anglophone world largely thanks to the efforts of German-born British Royal Consorts Queen Charlotte (1744–1818) and Prince Albert (1819–61), other practices, such as having a mammoth bonfire at Easter, have largely not been adopted internationally.

19  D. L. Bergen, 'Hosanna or "Hilf, O Herr Uns": National Identity, the German Christian Movement, and the "Dejudaization" of Sacred Music in the Third Reich' in C. Applegate and P. Potter (eds), *Music & German National Identity* (Chicago: University of Chicago Press, 2002), p. 143.

20  H. Baumann, 'Trotz Kampf, Krieg und Tod bleibe uns Weihnachten das Fest der Liebe und der gläubigen Herzen', *NS Frauen-Warte* (second half of the year 1944), p. 25.

21  R. Thurston, 'Under the Nazi Christmas Tree', *The New Republic* (25 December 1935), p. 193.

22  Rosenbaum, *'Und Trotzdem'*, p. 466.

23  Roberts, *The House*, p. 231.

24  H. S. Müller-Landau, 'Für die Frau von der Frau', *NS Frauen-Warte* (June 1936), p. 842.

25  M. Mouton, 'From Adventure and Advancement to Derailment and Demotion: Effects of Nazi Gender Policies on Women's Careers and Lives', *Journal of Social History*, 43:4 (2010), pp. 948–9.

26  G. L. Mosse, *Nazi Culture: Intellectual, Cultural and Social Life in the Third Reich*, trans. S. Attanasio, et al. (Madison, WI: University of Wisconsin Press, 1966), p. xv.

27  Reagin, *Sweeping the German Nation*, p. 170.

28  All recipes recreated in the author's home kitchen were published in a Nazi party propaganda newspaper for women, *NS Frauen Warte: die einzige parteiamtliche Frauenzeitschrift*. Heidelberg Open Access Publications of the University of Heidelberg Digital Library. https://digi.ub.uni-heidelberg.de/diglit/frauenwarte (accessed 1 December 2020).

29  S. Lehmann, *Die einzig wahre Quelle der Kunst ist unser Herz* (Berlin: Ahnenerbe Stiftung, 1943), pp. 34–5.

30  Lehmann, *Die einzig wahre*, pp. 44–5. While floral and maritime, rather than Christian, motifs are common on nineteenth-century gravestones in the area where this gravestone is found, the island of Wyk auf Föhr, they are uncommon among German nineteenth-century gravestones generally.

31  R. S. F, 'Das Lebensbild des deutschen Handwerks', *Books Abroad*, 16:4 (1942), p. 417.

32  J. Von Leers, *Die Geschichte des deutschen Handwerks* (Berlin: Hans Holzmann Verlagshaus, 1940).
33  P. Th. Bertheau, 'The German Language and the Two Faces of Its Script: A Genuine Expression of European Culture?' in P. Bain and P. Shaw (eds), *Blackletter: Type and National Identity* (New York: The Cooper Union, 1998), p. 22.
34  H. P. Willberg, 'Fraktur and Nationalism' in Bain and Shaw (eds), *Blackletter*, p. 44.
35  This statement was objectively false: Jewish-owned printing houses were not responsible for the development of hundreds of years of Blackletter font usage. H. P. Willberg, 'Fraktur and Nationalism' in Bain and Shaw (eds), *Blackletter*, pp. 48–9.
36  *Ibid.*, p. 48.
37  H. Glenewinkel, *Der Heim-Berater: Gutes und Böses in der Wohnung* (Leipzig: Verlag Otto Beyer, 1937).
38  *Ibid.*, pp. 41, 66–9, 72, 76–9.
39  'Kennen Sie Bubinga oder Sapeli', *Technik: Monatsbeilage zum NS-Kurier* (October 1934) pp. 1–2.
40  E. Augst, *Das deutsche Möbel: Grundzüge seiner stilgeschichtlichen Entwicklung und zeitgemässen Gestaltung* (Augsburg: Verlag von Hans Rösler, 1942), pp. 5, 8, 118, 128, 153–76. The book was republished in 1950 with overt Nazi language removed and was published again in 1984 without photographs under the title *Deutsche Möbelgeschichte*. Both the 1950 and 1984 versions include a family in 1930s era farm clothing described as 'A Picture of the Future'.
41  The BBC started its German Service in 1938 with the goal of convincing Germans that Hitler's regime would fail and they were better served by aligning with Britain and Britain's Allies. The German Service featured news on the war, educational and entertainment programmes featuring German and Austrian intellectuals and actors living in exile, and the names and physical condition of German prisoners of war in Allied custody. V. Plock, 'Broadcasting to the Enemy: The BBC German Service during the Second World War', *BBC History Research Blog*, 22 April 2019, www.bbc.co.uk/blogs/bbchistoryresearch/entries/49d858be-5db0-4111-8e07-dc59e67ee217 (accessed 15 June 2021). British Broadcasting Corporation, *Overseas Programming*, www.bbc.com/historyofthebbc/research/bbc-at-war/overseas-programming/ (accessed 15 June 2021). Rosenbaum, *'Und Trotzdem'*, pp. 256–7.

# PART II

# Aesthetic entanglements

# 6

# Into the sensorium: scenes from the dressing room

*Louisa Iarocci*

In the medical sciences the sensorium is defined as the 'seat of sensation', that part of the brain that receives and coordinates all the external stimuli received by the body. It can also refer to the sensory system itself, not simply as five autonomous receptors of information but as the totality of the perceptual apparatus including all cognitive, emotional and intellectual functions.[1] This meaning of the sensorium has been taken up in the humanities and social sciences to expand the understanding of human perception beyond the sensory mechanics of the individual subject to consider how experience is shaped by a person's ever-changing social and cultural position in the world.[2] Explorations into different forms of media by scholars across a wide range of disciplines have challenged the focus on the dominant senses, especially sight, in order to explore the complex and dynamic nature of human perception.[3] The understanding of this embodied experience of space is amplified in the confines of the domestic interior that provides a close-up view of the dynamic relationship between the actions of the human subject and their external environment.[4] The interaction between the mind and body is highlighted in the dressing room, the small private chamber for a transformation that is both physical, in the protective act of covering, and social, in the expression of personal identity.[5]

In this chapter I examine the representation of the dressing room in the stereoscopic photograph or stereograph that reached the height of popularity in the mid-nineteenth century.[6] These images produce an illusion of three-dimensionality when seen through a viewer, engaging the spectator and the subject in an interactive experience. Going beyond sight to solicit the tactile and even aural dimensions, these stereographs of the dressing room act as a kind of spatial sensorium,[7] amplifying the intimate exchanges between the human subject and the outside world.[8]

## Enclosure: the contained body

The basic function of the dressing room as a private place dedicated to the acts of dressing and undressing involves a close relationship between the body and its surroundings. This specialized domestic space emerges in the Victorian era as an architectural form for an occupant that is clearly marked by class and gender.[9] The earliest evidence of a room specifically designated for the purposes of dressing in an Anglo-American context can be found in the floor plans of elite English country houses of the mid-eighteenth century.[10] As seen at Norfolk House, built in London in 1756, the dressing room is typically part of a suite of private spaces associated with the bedchamber that was devoted to sleeping and resting.[11] The provision of separate adjoining rooms for each gender to bathe and don clothing was a mark of distinction, especially in England where married couples commonly shared the same bedchamber.[12] In his guide to the design of English residences of 1865 Robert Kerr states that the ideal arrangement of the bedroom itself is reliant on the proper size and location of the dressing room – particularly of that for the lady of the house.[13] He notes that the room should be entered through an 'out of the way door' in the bedroom along with another from the corridor, to achieve a layout of graduated privacy that would keep separate the movement of couples and that of their servants. Kerr provides further recommendations for such 'primary features' as the placement of a window with south-east orientation, showing consideration of light and ventilation along with the most desired paths of sight and movement. The heightened awareness of the room's connection to the exterior world is further evident in the provision for a 'comfortable fireside' to ensure a comfortable climatic environment for the individual who spends considerable time within this chamber.

This close connection between the character of the architectural envelope and the nature of the activities performed in it is evident across the various guises the dressing room takes on. In its most basic form as a cabinet or closet the chamber served the basic function of sequestering the body during intimate acts of bathing and dressing. While sometimes used interchangeably, other names like sitting room and boudoir often referred to a room with a more formal and public function for men and women of means.[14] Derived from the French *bouder* or 'to pout', the boudoir in eighteenth-century France was originally defined as a dedicated space or corner of the bedroom for a lady to retire to when requiring privacy.[15] Owing to frequent changes of dress, elite women devoted a great deal of time to their toilette, which began to function as 'a site for sociability' where guests were invited to serve as a private audience.[16] In their book *The Decoration of Houses* of 1897, Edith Wharton and Ogden Codman identify the boudoir as a sitting room where the lady of the house conducts daily household business, which should be located off an ante-chamber that separates the

bedroom from the main corridor. The authors devote considerable attention to the decoration of this 'modern boudoir' in terms of the treatment of
the walls with delicate styles of painting, stucco ornamentation and wood
carving that sought to simplify the excesses of eighteenth-century French
prototypes.[17] But the authors are less interested in such visual effects in the
more utilitarian dressing room, beyond the provision of practical furnishings for the bathing and robing of the body. Instead it is the location of the
dressing room relative to the lady's movement through the house that is of
upmost importance – the chamber is given an even more secluded location
adjacent to the bathroom to achieve the privacy of interior space described
'as one of the first requisites of civilized life'.[18]

## Object: room as body

Other interior decorating manuals of the period reinforce the sense that
the dressing room was the domain of an embodied occupant, one situated
in this enclosed space as both a corporeal and social entity. The activities
that took place within it were inherently multisensory in nature involving
close exchanges between the visual and tactile, and between living bodies
and inanimate objects. The essential furnishings of this chamber for dressing were identified as a dressing or toilet table, a chiffonier or chest of
drawers for storage and, whenever possible, a long cheval mirror (to supplement one that might be a part of the dressing table). Where space is at a
premium, fixtures related to bathing, which ideally would take place in the
adjoining lavatory or bathroom, could even be included, like a washstand,
basin or tub and one or two commodes containing a concealed chamber
pot.[19] In 1903 Lillie French provides detailed specifications for the defining piece of furniture, a 'table to dress by', taking into consideration the
position of the user who could be either sitting or standing, and their easy
access to toilet accessories.[20] French states that 'the dressing-table must
be first of all in spotless order, and then be pretty', observing that only
framed photographs and brushes and combs 'made for display' should be
found on its outer surface, with other small toilet articles stored in drawers. 'The surface of the table – and the mirror – should also be protected
by a fabric wash cover laid across the top, readily removed to be shaken
or washed'.[21] The physical nature of the act of handling and arranging the
toilet articles is evident in this preoccupation with cleanliness and order,
which conveys the tactile nature of the rituals conducted on the horizontal
surface of this 'altar' of self-preparation.

The designated furnishings of the dressing room serve to map out
the stages of the preparation of the corporeal body, from washing and
grooming to the storing and laying out of clothing and accessories.[22]
The specific pieces of furniture can be seen as acting as stand-ins for the
human occupant and for the room itself. Jennifer Van Horn has argued that

the eighteenth-century dressing table in the United States was a physical object that embodied meanings beyond its primary function of enabling the physical manipulation of personal goods by acting as an inert marker of social status. She observes that this object is the site of a 'tactile inter-action between the woman's body and the material goods of adornment' that represents the symbiotic relationship between the occupant and their surroundings.[23] In 1906 Emily Burbank also observed this close connec-tion, noting that the dressing room is the most 'personal of rooms, we take it for granted that its decoration is eloquent with the individuality and taste of its owner'.[24] In her argument for dressing as an art, she observes that 'the woman who takes her personal appearance seriously just as any artist takes her art [...] can have her dressing-room so arranged with mirrors, black walls and strong cleverly reflected electric lights that she stands out with a clean cut outline, like a cameo, the minutest detail of her toilet dis-closed'.[25] The dressing room itself is thus presented as a kind of viewing apparatus through which the occupant is framed and extended – as Van Horn argues, 'the living body unfold[ing] onto the material objects around her'.[26]

## Frame: 'embodied vision'

The intimate sensory connection between the female occupant and the dressing room is further evident in its popular representation in the nineteenth century. The lady's toilette had been a frequent subject in European art and literature since the late seventeenth century.[27] Derived from the French *toile* for cloth, the toilette was defined as the elaborate process of preparation that could include washing and grooming along with donning attire.[28] Scenes in the dressing room represented in paint-ings and prints typically depicted attractive women sitting or standing in front of their mirrored dressing table or a full-length mirror in a domestic interior.[29] Despite the simple premise, the narrative varied widely, pre-senting various stages of the toilette from an early moment of decision to a later stage of inspection and display. The main figure could either be alone in the room or accompanied by a wide range of characters from a lone attendant to multiple companions and admirers participating in a lively social gathering. Throughout the eighteenth century this type of genre scene provided artists and their patrons with the opportunity to celebrate or ridicule the ideals of female beauty. The partially exposed body was put on display for the pleasure of a voyeuristic audience, presented variously as a sanctified work of art or as a degenerate, erotic object for consump-tion. Scenes ranged from the sentimental and sensual to the erotic and satirical that exposed the female body and human vanity in the fruitless efforts to combat the ravages of time.[30] The architectural environment provided the material enclosure that conveyed the weight of the physical body, supporting it in geometric space. In its decoration and furnishing the room was often 'dressed' to reflect the time and place of the scene – taking on the persona of its occupant in terms of their appearance and social standing.

The rise in the popularity of the stereoview or stereograph at the end of the nineteenth century offered a distinctive new medium for genre scenes of domestic life for popular consumption. Melody Davis has argued convincingly for the transformative effect of this widely available optical device that produced the illusion of depth through the presentation of two side-by-side images in a stereo viewer.[31] By combining the realism of photography with the illusion of three-dimensionality the stereoscope proved a highly effective instrument for the dual purposes of entertainment and instruction.[32] Writing in the *Atlantic* in 1859 Oliver Wendell Holmes celebrated the democratic potential of the stereoview, which could capture any aspect of the world and bring it into the space of the home. Along with other contemporary observers he was particularly interested in what this 'triumph of human ingenuity' revealed about the workings of human perception.[33] Holmes observed that if photography had fixed our fleeting illusions, the stereoscope had 'produced an appearance of reality which cheats the senses of its seeming truth'. This nineteenth-century optical device might basically operate in a way that, like other devices before it including the camera obscura and still camera, seemed to prioritize sight. However, Holmes argued that it proved 'that everything is seen only as a superficial extension, until the other senses have taught the eye to recognize depth, or the third dimension, which gives solidity, by converging outlines, distribution of light and shade, change of size, and of the texture of surfaces'.[34] Other contemporary observers agreed that 'human perception had to be understood through the concept of the sensorium or all the senses operating as one sensory apparatus.'[35] Stereoscopic images might be carried through the 'dark chamber of the eye' but relied on activating all the bodily faculties that roused sensation, especially touch, in order to produce a dynamic phenomenological experience that linked the mind and body to the world around it.[36]

The depiction of the dressing room scene in stereoscopic space was thus bound up in this activation of the dialogue between the visual and tactile in the translation between planar and volumetric space. The narratives set in this domestic space drew upon long-established models of popular genre scenes to entertain the popular audience in the home by providing a glimpse of an upper-class life [Figure 6.1].[37] In *Before the Ball* published by Underwood and Underwood in 1897 the lady sits in her dressing room, in ready anticipation of the impending festivities, costumed in a floor-length ball gown complete with jewellery and hair accessories. Her formal attire is echoed in the rich decoration of the room with multiple rugs on the floors and patterned wallpapers and draped wall treatments. The framed

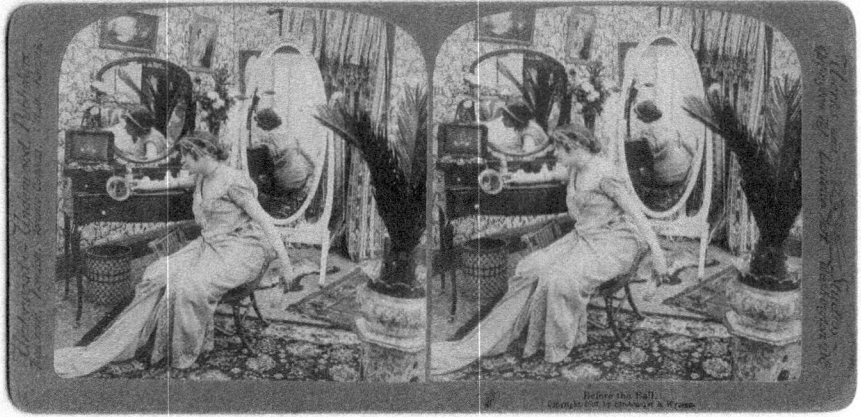

**Figure 6.1**    Joseph John Elliott, *Before the Ball*, published by London Stereoscopic Company, 1897.

pictures, curtained window and potted plant in the foreground reinforce the sense of enclosure around the draped figure. The requisite furnishings of a well-appointed dressing room such as the dressing table and cheval mirror complete the recreation of an upper-class private interior. The dressed domestic interior provides a protective enclosure for the intimate act unfolding, but at the same time offers an opening for the male spectator to look in. The viewer is led into the interior through the careful placement of a series of objects from the foreground to the background that take on three-dimensional form through the stereoscope. With her arm resting upon the surface of the dressing table, and her reflection in its mirrored surface, the main figure is physically linked to her surroundings in appearance and touch. The multiple mirrors – from that in her hand to the dressing table and the large cheval on the floor – set off a volley of reflections that reveal multiple points of contact. Her resting arm on the table, her foot on the floor and her body settled into the stool convey her solidity as an object and her tactile connection to the textured surfaces of the room.

The illusion of depth produced by the stereoscopic device relies on sensory connections between the eye and brain that were recognized at the time as both visual and tactile in nature. In 1909 Albert Underwood, founder of one of the main producers of stereoviews at the time, observed that: 'By means of these two different views of an object, the mind, as it were, feels around it and gets an idea of its solidity.'[38] This sculptural quality is made manifest in these dressing room scenes where the female body is featured as a kind of living work of art – evoking the past history of the 'toilette' portrait as 'a social performance of the rituals of taste and consumption'.[39] A related category of stereoviews that offered a glimpse of the dressing scenes as a 'potent status symbol' were those

**Figure 6.2**    *Dressing the Bride*, copyrighted by C. H. Graves (The Universal Photo Art, no. 3272).

featuring brides. Melody Davis observes that multiple companies in the United States produced series of wedding views that began with the proposal and ended with the newly married couple, 'alone at last'. In views like *Dressing the Bride*, the second in the series by C. H. Graves published in 1901, the bride is shown preparing for her big day with the assistance of several female attendants [Figure 6.2]. The empty chairs and human figures are positioned to lead the viewer's eye into the depths of the room and encircle the shapely form of the main character as she is adorned like the objects displayed on the wall behind her. While their gazes seem mostly averted and their poses stilted, the attending women are all actively touching something – the bride, each other, the room's surfaces and/or the crisp white garments. The atmosphere of solemnity and ceremony of this momentous event before the big day is amplified by the silent play of tactile gestures that physically connects all the figures while keeping the focus on the main act of transformation.

The ability of the stereoscope to create the illusion of volumetric space enabled a glimpse of the body as a sensing entity but also of its sensuous qualities. A type of scene described by Melody Davis as 'dressing room erotica' featured the female subject (un)dressing and unconsciously (or consciously) exposing her ankles or a leg to the viewer.[40] The dressing of 'volumetric' space in its decorated surfaces and ornate furnishings provides a thin veil of respectability and familiarity to the otherwise risqué events. In *Reflections* by William Rau of 1903 an attractive woman is seated in a lavishly decorated room that contains the basic elements of dressing table, mirrors and chairs, rugs and prints and plants and flowers [Figure 6.3]. The addition of other personal articles makes clear the

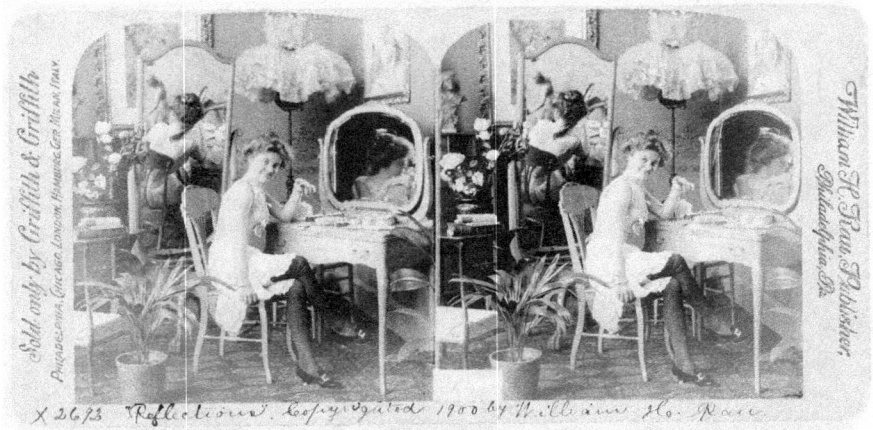

**Figure 6.3**    *Reflections*, published by William Rau, Philadelphia, 1903.

lady is in her private chambers ready to perform her toilette. But the now more spare furnishings evident in the stencilled walls quickly reveal the illusion of the staged tableau. The lone female figure looks directly at the viewer, amusedly aware of the multiple reflections of her exposed body that echoes the nude statuette in the background. In her relaxed pose and direct gaze, she challenges her objectification by engaging the intruding viewer as if challenging them to enter her private interior. The odd frilly floor lamp behind her that may just be her missing petticoat on a stand exposes the illusion of a domestic interior – and acts as a kind of surrogate for her body.[41] The title, *Reflections*, hints at both the visual and the mental replications taking part in this stereoscopic scene, where the main subject and viewer are engaged in exchanges that are optical and tactile in nature.

This physical play of the senses between viewer and the subject in the stereoview becomes evident in other more crowded versions of the dressing room scenes. A popular variation evident in the view *Taking in a Reef* subverts the role of early toilette scenes as symbols of social status to offer a more bawdy and humorous interpretation that shows a woman being tightly laced into her corset by her male partner [Figure 6.4].[42] The physical exertion in this tug of war is expressed in the facial expression and dynamic pose of the muscular man who heavily braces himself against the leaning form of his much smaller wife. Despite the painful procedure she acknowledges the viewer and lightens the atmosphere with a knowing smile, captured in the mirror.[43] The combative nature of this physical encounter is reflected in the disordered state of the room with cushions and garments scattered about the floor. These foreground objects lead the viewer into the spatial box where human figures also tumble about, bouncing off each other. The bare wall surfaces of the room reflect their

**Figure 6.4**    *Taking in a Reef*, published by Underwood and Underwood, 1900.

working-class life but enable an even more exaggerated impression of the recession of space that becomes visible in the stereoscope. Paralleling the shaping of the woman's figure, the spatial volume moulds itself around the figures and objects it contains, highlighting the haptic dimension of the encounter. Other examples of 'corset tightening' scenes even added an aural dimension to the stereoscopic experience with humorous titles like 'You're a Peach', providing a line of dialogue exchanged between the couple.[44]

Other versions of these novelty interpretations of the dressing room scene further activate this dynamic, embodied quality of space by engaging the senses and emotions of the viewer and the subjects. Different variations of *Curiosity Punished* depict a group of women who appear to have been unexpectedly caught in various stages of dress in the midst of their bedtime or morning rituals [Figure 6.5]. The setting is now a clearly a working-class interior that is crowded with figures and furnishings including a bed on the left and a dresser on the right that functions as makeshift dressing table. An unwelcome male intruder has managed to wedge his upper body through the door but two of the women have joined forces to prevent his entry. The standing woman braces herself against the dresser with one arm and pushes against the door with the other, while keeping her body forward to display her hourglass silhouette. Her barefooted companion kneels on the floor, pressing her weight forward to aid her companion. The seated woman in the foreground clutches her garments in modest dismay, but at the same time reveals her bare crossed legs that extend forward in space. The curving limbs and bodies of the women form a ribbon of movement of flesh and fabric that leads the viewer's eye through the three-dimensional space to land on the outstretched, nearly touching hands of the two main combatants. In other versions of *Curiosity*

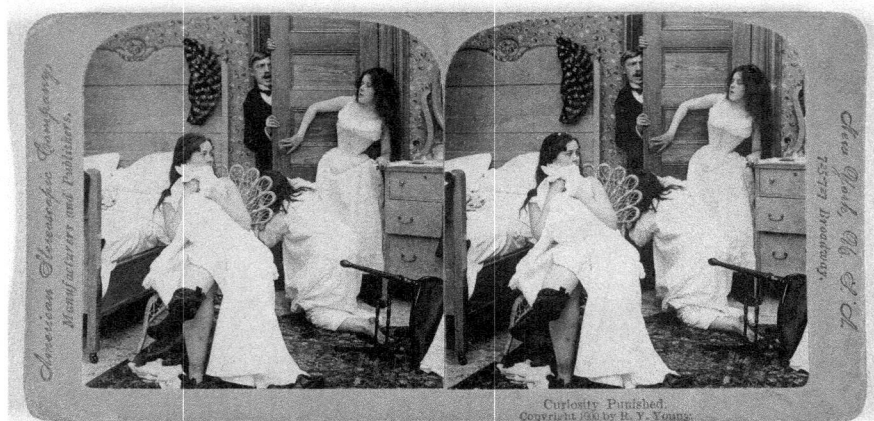

**Figure 6.5**  *Curiosity Punished*, R. Y. Young, American Stereoscopic Company, New York, *c.*1900.

*Punished* the physicality of the scene is even more evident – in the dynamic poses of the combatants who interact with each other and the objects and space around them, evident in upended furniture and scattered clothing. Other versions of this type of scene reveal that the mood can veer fluidly between humour and drama – with the comical but forceful act of trapping the intruder before he can physically assault the exposed women. This dynamic action scene has an almost cinematic quality, capturing a moment of suspense in time and engaging the viewer emotionally in a morality tale with an uncertain ending.

## Conclusion

John Plunkett observes that the principal attraction of stereoscopy was its tangibility, which 'marked a changed relationship between the senses' and brought about a 'haptic, sensuous, sculptural mode of viewing that was as much the forceful assimilation of touch by sight'.[45] His argument that the stereoview was 'a refiguring of the Victorian sensorium' can be extended to the represented space of the domestic interiors that this photographic medium captured. The illusion of three-dimensional space in these dressing room scenes reinforced the connection between the body as a sensing entity and the interior as a spatial device, activating a fluid exchange of visual and tactile contacts between them. The illusion of depth closed the distance between the human subject and the material objects around them – fluidly extending bodies into space and space into bodies.[46] The haptic dimension of this way of looking made possible an experience of 'embodied realism' that through its demonstration of depth perception offered the viewer the illusion of taking part in the scene in a visceral way. The physical surfaces of the room and its furnishings offered the viewer a means to support and contain its occupants, but in its weight and tactility the corporeal body pushes back and resists. These domestic scenes in private interiors offered a glimpse of the way the human subject interacts with the corporeal world through the external senses as well as through the 'senses of the soul'.[47] The sentient body expands out and contracts as it changes in real and imagined space through the sensorium of the represented dressing room.[48]

## Notes

1 A. Clements, 'Senses, Ancient Conceptions of' in S. Hornblower, A. Spawforth and E. Eidinow (eds), *The Oxford Classical Dictionary*, 4 edn (Oxford: Oxford University Press, 2012), https://doi.org/10.1093/acref/9780199545568.001.0001. Walter J. Ong has defined the human sensorium as 'the entire sensory apparatus as an operational complex'. W. Ong, 'The Shifting Sensorium' in D. Howes (ed.), *The Varieties of Sensory Experience* (Toronto: University of Toronto Press, 1991), p. 28.
2 M. Bull, P. Gilroy, D. Howes and D. Kahn, 'Introducing Sensory Studies', *The Senses and Society*, 1:1 (2006), pp. 5–7.
3 In art see F. Bacci and D. Melcher (eds), *Art and the Senses* (Oxford: Oxford University Press, 2011) and C. Jones (ed.), *Sensorium: Embodied Experience, Technology, and Contemporary Art* (Cambridge, MA: MIT Press and MIT List Visual Arts Center, 2006). In media theory see M. Cote, 'Technics and the Human Sensorium', *Theory and Event*, 13:4 (2010). In architecture see J. Pallasmaa, 'Toward an Architecture of Humility: On the Value of Experience', *Harvard Design Magazine*, 7 (Winter/Spring 1999); reprinted in J. J. Gieseking and W. Mangold with C. Katz, S. Low and S. Saegert (eds), *The People, Place and Space Reader* (New York and London: Routledge, 2014), pp. 331–2.
4 P. Vannini, 'Senses' in D. Southerton (ed.), *Encyclopedia of Consumer Culture* (Thousand Oaks, CA: SAGE Reference, 2011), pp. 1269–70.
5 T. Puri, 'Fabricating Intimacy: Reading the Dressing Room in Victorian Literature', *Victorian Literature and Culture*, 41 (2013), p. 503. www.moma.org/learn/moma_learning/themes/investigating-identity/the-body-in-art/.
6 T. Chico, *Designing Women: The Dressing Room in Eighteenth-Century Literature and Culture* (Lewisburg, PA: Bucknell University Press, 2005).
7 I. Guzmán, A. and A. B. Marr, 'Issue 18 Introduction', *Invisible Culture: An Electronic Journal for Visual Studies*, 18 (Spring 2013), n.p. Visual & Cultural Studies Program, University of Rochester.
8 D.D. Cali, 'The Interior Sensorium in Media Ecology: Justification for Study', *Dianoetikon*, 1 (2020), pp. 170, 180.
9 'Dressing room, n.1.' *OED Online*, 3 edn, (2020) (accessed 29 May 2020).
10 Tita Chico notes that dressing rooms were introduced into English domestic architecture during the seventeenth century, 'providing elite women with unprecedented private space at home and in so doing promised them an equally unprecedented autonomy by providing a space for self-fashioning, eroticism and contemplation'. Chico, *Designing Women*, p. 26.
11 Michael McKeon observes that in Norfolk House 'the ceremonial function of the quasi-public assembly outweighed all considerations of privacy, and the dressing room, bedchamber, and closet were probably seldom used by an individual'. M. McKeon, *The Secret History of Domesticity: Public, Private, and the Division of Knowledge* (Baltimore, MD: Johns Hopkins University Press, 2006), pp. 249–50.

12  Longleat House in Wiltshire was built in 1570 and remodelled in the early nine-teenth century. The remodelling in 1809 included the addition of a rectangular system of continuous corridors that enables private entry to specialized spaces that include a dressing room next to the main bedroom. See Figures 5.21 and 5.22 in M. Girouard, *Life in the English Country House: A Social and Architectural History* (New Haven, CT: Yale University Press, 1978).

13  'The primary idea here is that of a comparatively small private room attached to a Bedroom for the purposes of the toilet … Gentleman requiring less space unless he use his room as a writing room or study – and the lady requiring always a good deal more – and still more if she makes hers a private Sitting room or Boudoir.' Robert Kerr, *The Gentleman's House Or, how to Plan English Residences, From the Parsonage to the Palace, with Tables of Accommodation and Cost and a Series of Selected Plans* (London: John Murray, 1846), pp. 149–50.

14  K. Leuner, '"The end of all the privacy and propriety": Fanny's Dressing Room in Mansfield Park' in K. Boehm (ed.), *Bodies and Things in Nineteenth-Century Literature and Culture* (New York: Palgrave, 2012), p. 45.

15  J. J. Yorizzo, 'Introduction' in *Madam in Her Boudoir 1870–1940* (Long Island, NY: C.W. Post Art Gallery, 1981), n.p. According to Tita Chico, a private chamber of this type was more prevalent in eighteenth-century English literature than in actual domestic space. Chico, *Designing Women*, p. 9.

16  J. Van Horn, *The Power of Objects in Eighteenth-Century British America* (Chapel Hill, NC: University of North Carolina Press, 2017), p. 302.

17  The appointments for a boudoir are described as 'a writing-desk, with pigeon holes, drawers and cupboards and a comfortable lounge, or lit de repos for resting and reading'. E. Wharton and O. Codman, *The Decoration of Houses* (New York: C. Scribner's Sons, 1898), pp. 22, 130–2.

18  *Ibid.*, p. 22.

19  *Ibid.*, p. 172.

20  L. H. French, *Homes and Their Decoration* (New York: Dodd, Mead and Company, 1903), p. 105. For more specifications on dressing table designs see A. C. Nye, *Furniture Designing and Draughting: Notes on the Elemental Forms, Methods of Construction and Dimensions of Common Articles of Furniture* (New York: W. T. Comstock, 1900), p. 23 and J. H. Elder-Duncan, *The House Beautiful and Useful: Being Practical Suggestions on Furnishing and Decoration* (London and New York: John Lane Co., 1907), p. 176.

21  French, *Homes and Their Decoration*, pp. 105–6.

22  Van Horn makes this point about the relationship between dressing furniture and the activity of dressing – the material objects, she argues, 'scripted the performance of the toilet ritual [giving] material structure to the refinement of [the] body and provided utilitarian aid and ideological cues'. *The Power of Objects*, p. 300.

23  *Ibid.*, pp. 303–9.

24  E. Burbank, *Woman as Decoration* (New York: Dodd, Mead and Company, 1920) (first published 1917), pp. 111–12. Other contemporary observers concur that while the men's dressing room was more utilitarian in nature, the women's boudoir was 'an indulgence in personal taste. The atmosphere of the Boudoir should be such that it stimulates the imagination; it is a room the effect of which is startling or unu-sual it will have the effect of inspiring its user to the accomplishment of unusual and original effects in personal experience.' L. R. and M. E. Pescheret, *The Principles and Practice of Interior Decorating* (Chicago: Pescheret, [1925]), pp. 184–5.

25  G. Wood and E. Burbank, *The Art of Interior Decoration* (New York: Dodd, Mead and Company, 1919), p. 269.

26  Van Horn, *The Power of Objects*, p. 304.

27  See for example 'Dame a sa Toilette' by Henri Bonnart of 1687 as well as François Boucher, 'La Toilette' of 1742 and William Hogarth, 'Marriage a-la Mode: The

Toilet', 1745. Print versions became extremely popular in the eighteenth century especially in England, like W. Humphrey, 'Lady Fritz at Her Toilet', 1780; George Morland, 'Coquette at Her Toilet' of 1787; and James Gillray, 'The Progress of the Toilet' of 1810. Scenes featuring women were most popular but male dressing rooms were also depicted, often used in political satire.

28  According to Vic, the mirror was draped to prevent fine powder from obscuring the individual's image. Vic, 'An 18th Century Lady's Toilette: Hours of Leisurely Dressing and Private Affairs', *Jane Austen's World*, 30 September 2011, https://janeaustensworld.wordpress.com/2011/09/30/an-18th-century-ladys-toilette-hours-of-leisurely-dressing-and-private-affairs/.

29  E. Goodman-Soellner, 'Poetic Interpretations of the "Lady at Her Toilette" Theme in Sixteenth Century Painting', *The Sixteenth Century Journal*, 14:4 (1983), pp. 426–42.

30  The editors of the *Spectator*, a daily paper published in London, in 1711 mocked those women who acted as though 'the Toilet is their great Scene of Business and the adjusting of their hair the principal Employment of their lives'. The authors were seeking to increase their female readership by noting that their paper alone was aimed at women of a more 'exalted sphere of knowledge and virtue' by joining 'all the Beauties of the Mind to the Ornaments of Dress'. J. Addison and R. Steele, *The Spectator*, No. 10 (Mon. March 12, 1711), n.p.

31  M. Davis, *Women's Views: The Narrative Stereograph in Nineteenth Century America* (Lebanon, NH: University of New Hampshire Press, 2015), pp. 1–2.

32  John Plunkett argues that the 'tactile embodied appeal' of the stereograph lay in its 'coupling of the realism of photography with the phenomenological 3-D realism of binocular vision'. J. Plunkett '"Feeling Seeing": Touch, Vision and the Stereoscope', *History of Photography*, 37:4 (2013), pp. 389–96 (390), DOI: 10.1080/03087298.2013.785718.

33  O. Wendell Holmes, 'The Stereoscope and the Stereography', *The Atlantic* (June 1859), p. 1.

34  Holmes observes that through the stereoscope 'we clasp an object with our eyes, as with our arms, or with our hand, or with thumb and forefinger and then we know it to be something more than surface'. *Ibid*, p. 4.

35  The anonymous author of the essay 'Eye and Vision' states: 'The organs of the senses are like mediums placed between thought and the world – mediums yet dim, obscure, deceitful often, and like unfaithful mirrors'. 'The Eye and Vision', *Every Saturday* (28 November 1868), p. 692.

36  Davis observes: 'Mental processing is how we know, but it cannot be easily sorted out between the senses other than to assert … that the eye is really just a receptor for light, color, and motion; all the rest is processing of the visible eye/perception guided by foreknowledge of touch.' Davis, *Women's Views*, p. 31. See also J. Potter, 'The Stereoscope and Popular Fiction: Imagination and Narrative in the Victorian Home', *Journal of Victorian Culture*, 21:3 (2016), pp. 346–62.

37  Earlier versions of this scene often included additional characters who assisted the main subject with her preparations. See for example the French painting, 'Before the Ball' by Jean-François de Troy of 1735 and the unnamed stereoview of the same subject, '[Before the ball]' by Joseph John Elliot published by the London Stereoscopic Company, about 1860.

38  A. Underwood, *The Stereograph and the Stereoscope with Special Maps and Books forming a Travel System. What They Mean for Individual Development. What They Promise for the Spread of Civilization* (New York: Underwood and Underwood, 1909), p. 25.

39  K. Chrisman-Campbell, 'Dressing to Impress: The Morning Toilette and the Fabrication of Femininity' in C. Bremer-David (ed.), *Paris: Life and Luxury in 18th Century* (Los Angeles: The J. Paul Getty Museum, 2011), p. 67.

40  Davis observes that in contrast to today, the mere glimpse of an ankle, décolleté or even petticoat 'managed to be suggestive, erotic even'. M. Davis, 'Doubling the Vision: Women and Narrative Stereography: The United States, 1870–1910' (PhD diss., City University of New York, 2004), pp. 145, 302–3.

41  Melody Davis observes: 'Even when eroticized, the female body is accompanied in American and British views with an amplitude of garments that block the gaze and deflect the codings onto women's culture and realm.' *Ibid.*, p. 145.

42  This corset-dressing scene was based on earlier British print views like 'The Progress of the Toilet – The Stays' from a series by James Gillray of 1810 and the earlier 'Tight Lacing or Fashion before Ease', after John Collett of 1777. The title 'Reducing the Surplus' is more obvious but 'Taking/Pulling in a Reef' referred to the process of reducing the area of a sail, usually by folding or rolling one side in on itself.

43  Valerie Steele observes that this supposedly popular practice of tight lacing to achieve a fashionable hourglass figure was criticized by contemporary observers who used it as an excuse to deride the vanity of the female sex. V. Steele, *The Corset: A Cultural History* (New Haven, CT: Yale University Press, 2003), pp. 87–8.

44  Davis, *Doubling the Vision*, p. 167.

45  Plunkett, 'Feeling Seeing', pp. 389–96.

46  C. A. Jones, 'The Mediated Sensorium' in *Sensorium: Embodied Experience, Technology and Contemporary Art* (Cambridge, MA: MIT Press, 2006), p. 5.

47  Cali observes the full human experience includes both an exterior component in the way the body interacts with the corporeal world and an interior one or the 'senses of the soul'. Cali, 'The Interior Sensorium in Media Ecology', pp. 170, 180.

48  A. Corbin, 'Backstage: The Secret of the Individual' in M. Perrot (ed.), *A History of Private Life: From the Fires of the Revolution to the Great War* (Cambridge, MA: Belknap Press of Harvard University, 1990), p. 482. L. Cameron, 'Interiors and Interiorities: Architectural Understandings of the Mind in Hard Times', *Nineteenth-Century Contexts*, 35:1 (February 2013), pp. 65–79.

# 7

# Site-reading: placing the piano in middle-class homes, 1890–1930

*Michael Windover and James Deaville*

> Now Carrie was affected by music. Her nervous composition responded to certain strains, much as certain strings of a harp vibrate when a corresponding key of a piano is struck. She was delicately moulded in sentiment and answered with vague ruminations to certain wistful chords. They awoke longings for those things which she did not have. They caused her to cling closer to things she possessed. One short song the young woman played in a most soulful and tender mood. Carrie heard it through the open door from the parlor below. ... Now she sat looking out across the park, as wistful and depressed as the nature which craves variety and life can be under such circumstances. As she contemplated her new state, the strain from the parlor below stole upward. With it her thoughts became colored and enmeshed. She reverted to the things which were best and saddest within the small limit of her experience. She became for the moment a repentant.[1]

In this passage from *Sister Carrie* (1900), Theodore Dreiser (1871–1945) evokes the way music can affect an individual and her experience of domestic space. The sounds of the piano in her neighbour's parlour penetrate her apartment and resonate with her emotional state. Carrie – an eighteen-year-old who has travelled from Columbia City, Wisconsin to Chicago and moved in with a man she met on the train there – does not know the young pianist next door but has seen her at the piano and decided that she 'was particularly dressy for her station, and wore a jewelled ring or two on her fingers which flashed upon her white fingers as she played'.[2] Dreiser weaves together immaterial and material aspects of performing on the piano, its senses of sound overcoming the physical barriers that separate city dwellers in their domestic solitudes. On the one hand, the music played is deeply affective and able to modulate the character of domestic atmosphere, even though the performer is not physically present in Carrie's room. In this way, the piano is highlighted as a contributor to the urban soundscape of modernity. On the other, its music represents ideas of social class and materiality, conjuring for Carrie desires for things she does not have and fears that she might lose what she has. Later in the novel, when Carrie had moved to New York City and is installed in an apartment with a new lover, her parlour includes a piano, 'because Carrie said she would like to learn to play'.[3]

In this manner, novelist Dreiser presents to the reader an experience of music as a multisensory, visceral experience that engages more than just the ear; it also involves visual and haptic senses on the part of both performer and audience. Thus, an instrumentalist would require dexterity of hand and sensitivity of touch (or breath for wind and brass players), while vocalists must control lungs, vocal cords, and lips in exercising their art. Such performances in turn evoke both aural and vibrational sensations among their audiences,[4] whereby we could argue that music connects people in material as well as personal relations, as embodied by Carrie. This recognition helps us to understand the words of Methodist pastor A. G. Stacy when he wrote that music was well suited to 'make the atmosphere about us tremulous with soothing sounds'.[5]

The intimacy of the domestic parlour enabled these sensory interactions to take place in the late nineteenth and early twentieth centuries, as documented in numerous sources that include Dreiser's book.[6] That the piano served as the parlour-performance vehicle of choice stands to reason by virtue of its commanding dimensions (and immobility) and versatility as a solo and accompanying instrument. Depending on interior acoustics, its sounds had the capability of disseminating throughout a residence, whether for the pleasure or displeasure of fellow occupants, with proximity to the source being a major factor in the degree of sensory stimulation.[7] However, the parlour piano best fulfilled its potential as the 'primary musical medium of the bourgeois' within its immediate surroundings,[8] a space dedicated to 'genteel' social purposes.[9] The musical activities that transpired in the parlour achieved functional, aesthetic and social ends for both performers and their audiences, be they family members or invited guests.

No doubt for Carrie (and for Dreiser's readers at the turn of the twentieth century), the piano served as a symbol of 'proper' middle-class domesticity. The piano was closely associated with femininity and 'a system of family discipline', with personal cultivation and the demonstration of a strong work ethic.[10] As historian Katherine Grier notes, in 1850 pianos were included among the set of furnishings deemed 'modern' for middle- and upper-class households, and the list of furniture 'would remain essentially unchanged for the rest of the century – at least at the level of popular, rather than fashionable, taste'.[11] Despite critiques of the parlour as artificial, pretentious, and wasteful, and the shrinking of space in middle-class housing in the twentieth century, the practice of parlour-making continued (even as 'living room', as a term designating the main family and public room, began to replace 'parlour' in middle-class houses and apartments).[12] Part of this was due to the lower prices of manufactured furniture, including pianos. Indeed, the high point of piano sales was 1909 in the United States.[13] The piano thus remained an essential element of middle-class living rooms well into the twentieth century.

The concept of a keyboard in the home was helped in part by technological innovations that allowed for mechanized play. With a 'piano-player' (a mechanism pushed up to the instrument), 'player-piano' (an internal system using a perforated roll and pumped by an operator), or 'reproducing piano' (a more dynamic and faithful recording driven by an internal electric motor), auditors could enjoy music without the presence of a skilful player. In addition to its role in private or semi-public entertainment, where the piano would be threatened by the arrival of the gramophone, phonograph, and later radio, it retained an association with (elevated) class and cultural refinement, which may partially explain its longevity. Also, the instrument's tactile and sonorous qualities and its nostalgic associations could not be replicated by the new mechanical surrogates.

In this chapter we examine how the piano played spatially structural and sensually significant roles in the evolving middle-class living room. The piano was a key site of social and personal performance and affected the meaning and sensorial experience of the living room/parlour and broader domestic space. Despite this significance, the home parlour as a locus for musical performance has not received much scholarly attention,[14] nor has the piano's place in the ordering and arrangement of interior space matched the scrutiny paid to other media for musical reproduction.[15] We begin by considering how pianos affected the design of middle-class homes. Architectural plans and depictions in mail-order catalogues of the first decades of the twentieth century provide evidence of the instrument's place in North American living rooms, or at least the imagined ideal. Next, we turn to interior decoration advice literature to illuminate changing attitudes around the placement and meaning of the piano. Here we see how the piano was considered in terms of its visual aesthetic, its spatial implications, and its place in everyday activities. Finally, we explore the design of parlour piano music: the sheet music gives us a sense of not only popular tastes for audiences but also how composers considered the capability of amateur pianists. This provides an idea of the sensescape of the home, as affected by music played either by an individual at the keyboard or via recording on perforated player-piano roll. Ultimately, we contend that the piano literally played a sensually significant part in middle-class homes, visually, haptically, and acoustically.

## Designing homes with pianos

As the influential interior decorator Elsie de Wolfe (1865–1950) suggested in 1913, when a home is designed with music performance in mind, the decorative and utilitarian results can be more effective.[16] While individuals with more means could create elaborate spaces like that which she describes, and the artistically inclined could work with architects to design purpose-built music rooms,[17] more modest homes sometimes evidence music through architectural features. By carefully scrutinizing architectural plans and looking for key elements, we can observe the cultural imprint of the piano and its role in society.

The size and placement of windows can reveal planning for pianos. Natural lighting was an important consideration for the placement of the piano in interior decoration literature: pianos are often placed near windows, though the instruments are best positioned along interior walls to prevent damage from changes in temperature. They also frequently feature near windows in advertisements. More concretely, the performer's need for light occasioned the unique window type identified as the 'piano window'. Historian Wayne Kelly describes the 'piano window' in the parlour, hall, or living room as 'a small rectangle, oval, or octagon of stained and/or bevelled glass ... [positioned] five to six feet from floor level', under which an upright piano would stand.[18] Windows of this type populate many homes in middle-class neighbourhoods built in the first decades of the twentieth century in North American cities, providing visual and lasting evidence for the piano's significance in the design of contemporary homes.

Although not necessarily identified as such, 'piano windows' appear in house catalogues as well. Large mail-order companies sold plans and sometimes fully prefabricated houses to settlers moving into the western provinces, territories, or states of North America.[19] In Canada, for instance, the T. Eaton Company's Winnipeg store offered its customers a catalogue of ideal houses from 1910 to 1932 free of charge.[20] Homeowners (typically farmers) could choose a plan, order the blueprints, then assemble the components, which included lumber from British Columbia and millwork from Winnipeg. An example from the 1919 *Plan Book of Ideal Homes* is the one-and-a-half-storey 'Eadwin', which includes a high, rectangular window in the living room where one could imagine a piano – also ordered by mail from Eaton's – sitting below.

The slightly later *Honor-Bilt Modern Homes* (1925), a catalogue of house plans distributed by Chicago-based Sears, Roebuck and Co., depicts ideal houses fully furnished or with floorplans indicating a layout of furniture. Here we see pianos in most schemes, including grand pianos for more upscale homes like the 'Rembrandt' ($2,553), or when furniture is not depicted on the floor plans, we find references to adequate space for a piano in even very modest houses, like the four-room bungalow called the 'Kimball' ($636).[21] In this sense, the piano became something akin to a unit of measurement, which suggests a cultural standard. In some cases, images of furnished rooms are included in the catalogue to provide evidence of the design's success. For instance, the presentation of the 'Kismet' ($999), a rather humble bungalow, includes an interior photograph of the 'living and dining room' furnished by its owners [Figure 7.1]. This example demonstrates the use of a piano window. Some models, like the 'Fullerton' ($2,294) [Figure 7.2], include images of up-to-date conveniences like the player-piano and radio situated in large living rooms, warmed by a traditional, wood-burning fireplace, and thus they present a picture of modern domesticity on offer from the mail-order company. For many, the pristine images in the catalogue would have been aspirational; however, the inclusion of pianos in nearly all schemes indicates that in the mid-1920s the instrument was still considered an important part of planning one's ideal home.

In a 1929 collection of 254 building plans compiled by the Architects' Small House Service Bureau, the piano features in interior photographs, as well as in the living rooms of floor plans, when furniture arrangements are included.[22] In the discussion of 'Design 6-A-17', a modest, two-storey Colonial house, the architect points out a built-in alcove on an interior wall opposite the fireplace, noting that it would provide 'a splendid location for [a] piano or lounge'.[23] In this instance, rather than being placed in a corner (as is most often the case in the plans), the piano would be situated at the very heart of the home. When in use, its sound would have effortlessly filled the entire house.

The presence of pianos in home catalogues and other builder plans demonstrates its persistent cultural value. Not only were pianos fitted into homes but designers (and large retailers of all manner of home furnishings and homes themselves) made allowances for their presence in modern residences. As the *Honor-Bilt Modern Homes* catalogue makes clear, the piano was a key feature in rooms, sometimes acting as the principal focal point, and thus we could argue it was considered a priority in the design of many, if not most, typical middle-class homes. The instrument was a signifier of middle-class domesticity and a crucial contributor to the emotional warmth and atmosphere of the living room.[24]

## Piano and interior decoration

The piano (and player-piano) presented a spatial problem: how was the homemaker to optimally position the large instrument and symbol of culture in a tasteful parlour or living room? Interior decoration advice literature provided some answers.[25] *The Decoration of Houses* (1897), by Edith Wharton (1862–1937) and Ogden Codman (1863–1951), in some

**FOUR ROOMS AND BATH**

**Honor Bilt**

*The Kismet*

No. 17002X "Already Cut" and Fitted

**$999.00**

IN THE KISMET bungalow we offer a good home at a low price with an absolute guarantee as to the "Honor Bilt" quality of the materials we furnish. This four-room bungalow is suitable for almost any location. In many sections a four or five-room cottage and lot will sell for $4,000.00 to $5,000.00. Notwithstanding the low price which we ask for all of the material required in the construction of this bungalow, there is no sacrifice of quality and there will be no shortage of material. As this house can be built on a lot 25 feet wide, it is suitable for town or country. For a farm house, for a small family, it represents a splendid investment. It is gracefully proportioned and when nicely painted will look well anywhere.

INTERIOR VIEW, HOME OF A CUSTOMER.

**The Living and Dining Room.** From the shady porch, 15 feet by 6 feet, a glazed door opens into the modern combination living and dining room. Size of this room, 10 feet 8 inches by 11 feet 8 inches. The front part is used for living quarters and the part near the kitchen door is used for dining.

**The Kitchen** is 8 feet 8 inches by 7 feet 2 inches. It has space for sink, range, table and chairs; also a closet with shelves. A double window provides light and ventilation. Immediately outside the kitchen door, in the rear entry, is space for the ice box. Here stairs lead to grade door and basement.

**The Bedrooms.** The front bedroom opens from the living and dining room. The rear bedroom and the bathroom are entered from an open hall, right off the dining end of room. Each bedroom has a clothes closet, and is lighted and aired by a window.

**The Basement.** Room for furnace, laundry and storage.

**Height of Ceilings.** Main floor, 9 feet from floor to ceiling. Basement, 7 feet from floor to joists.

*What Our Price Includes*

At the price quoted we will furnish all the material to build this four-room bungalow, consisting of:

Lumber; Lath;
Roofing, Clear Red Cedar Shingles;
Siding, Clear Cypress Bevel;
Framing Lumber, No. 1 Quality Yellow Pine;
Flooring, Clear Yellow Pine;
Porch Flooring, Clear Edge Grain Fir;
Porch Ceiling, Clear Yellow Pine;
Finishing Lumber;
High Grade Millwork (see pages 86 and 87);
Interior Doors, White Pine with Five-Cross Panel of Fir;
Trim, Beautiful Grain Yellow Pine;
Windows of California Clear White Pine;
Medicine Case;
Eaves Trough and Down Spout;
40-Lb. Building Paper; Sash Weights;
Stratford Design Hardware (see page 107);
Paint for Three Coats Outside Trim and Siding;
Varnish and Wood Filler for Interior Doors and Trim;
Complete Plans and Specifications.
See Description of "Honor Bilt" Houses on Pages 12 and 13.

Can be built on a lot 25 feet wide

FLOOR PLAN

KITCHEN 8'-8"x7'-2" — BED ROOM 8'2"x9'2" — DINING ROOM — HALL — BATH 4'x6'4" — LIVING ROOM 10'-8"x17'-8" — BED ROOM 8'2"x9'2" — PORCH 15'-0"x6'0" — 20'-0"

OPTIONS

*Sheet Plaster and Plaster Finish, $97.00 extra. See page 90.*

*Maple Flooring furnished for kitchen and bathroom, instead of yellow pine, no extra charge.*

*Oriental Asphalt Shingles, guaranteed 17 years, instead of wood shingles, $21.00 extra.*

*Storm Doors and Windows, $34.00 extra.*

*Screen Doors and Windows, galvanized wire, $23.00 extra.*

For prices of Plumbing, Heating, Wiring, Electric Fixtures and Shades see page 106.

Page 66     597     SEARS, ROEBUCK AND CO

**Figure 7.1**    'The Kismet', in *Honor-Bilt Modern Homes* (Sears, Roebuck and Co., 1925), p. 66.

ways set the tone for early twentieth-century interior decoration advice, with its Edwardian emphasis on simplicity (in contrast with the seeming decorative excesses of the Victorian era) and consideration of architectural elements derived from analyses of plan and room elevations.[26]

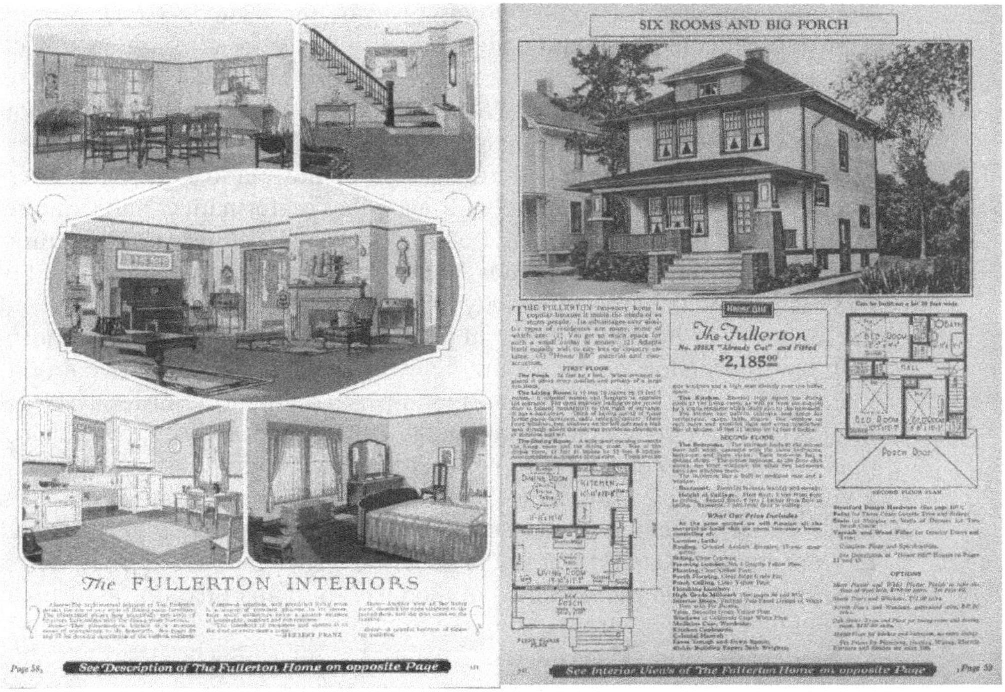

**Figure 7.2**   'The Fullerton', in *Honor-Bilt Modern Homes* (Sears, Roebuck and Co., 1925), pp. 58–9.

They make reference to the piano only twice: first, in passing, they note that a writing table ought to be in a well-lit space near a window, one 'usually sacred to the piano'. The other reference occurs in their discussion of remodelling a music room. A music room, they explain, should be decorated in light, serene tones and 'should always appear as though there were space overhead for notes to escape'.[27] With regard to the piano itself, they describe it as a decorative challenge: 'It is difficult to understand why modern music-rooms have so long been disfigured by the clumsy lines of grand and upright pianos, since the cases of both might be modified without affecting the construction of the instrument.'[28] Perhaps in their desire to see simpler forms, they suggest that an upright would be improved by 'straightening its legs and substituting right angles for the weak curves of the lid'; it 'might also be made of plainly panelled mahogany, with a few good ormolu ornaments; or of inlaid wood, with a design of musical instruments and similar "attributes"'.[29] They similarly call for a redesign of the music stand and music stool to match the simplified piano case.[30] While the advice offered by Wharton and Codman is aimed at an upper-middle-class audience – those who might be able to afford a designated music room – their calls for 'mellow' colour schemes and simplification of form could be employed by more modest (if upwardly aspiring) homemakers, and indeed were echoed in subsequent advice literature.

In some ways, *Homes and Their Decoration* (1903), by Lillie Hamilton French (1854–1939), is more helpful in its descriptions and prescriptions. She is less concerned with the aesthetic of the piano and more interested in situating it appropriately for everyday performance. She cautions against using the piano as a kind of prop to visually signify one's culturation.[31] Instead, she advises readers to create rooms designed around utility and comfort, with zones of activity marked by the placement of sofas and the piano.[32] For French, an upright piano is ideally situated at right angles with a corner, allowing for natural light from a window and the concealment of the keys. The piano and piano-playing should effortlessly blend into the visual and social environment. To this end, she suggests that a piano ought to be 'draped with a piece of rich brocade' to harmonize with a nearby table's covering as well as with the sofa that sits at right angles to the piano, softening its presence, and meanwhile protecting the 'timid or embarrassed player' from visual scrutiny.[33] The emphasis here is on the distinctly domestic performance of modesty (perhaps private) rather than the public display of virtuosity.

A decade later, Elsie de Wolfe offered similar advice about keeping a piano from dominating a room in *The House in Good Taste* (1913). Writing for an ideal audience of greater means than French's book did, she argues that the piano 'belongs in the living-room, if it is in constant use'; however, she concedes that being placed in larger rooms could be useful for small dances.[34] This reminds us of the piano's established role in activating domestic space for a variety of different purposes and performances. De Wolfe's comment about 'constant use' no doubt alludes to practising, and we can imagine the sometimes tedious sounds of scales, repetition of particular songs, and other exercises resonating in the living room; meanwhile, her reference to 'small dances' signals ways that amateur performers entertained guests for listening pleasure or instrumental accompaniment for vocal performances (or sing-a-longs) and dancing. The piano becomes a central part of the domestic soundscape, marking moments in time (with periods of practice and performance) and activating other sounds of human voices, tapping feet, swishing clothes, and so on.

Like French before, de Wolfe emphasizes utility and notes that if pianos are to be included in a decorative scheme, they ought to be considered in the planning as early as possible, as noted above. Her comments on the decorative potential of pianos resonate with Wharton and Cogman's earlier work as she describes typical piano cases as 'hideous' but points to possibilities for artistic embellishment (she cites successful designs by Arts and Crafts artists, including Sir Edward Burne-Jones (1833–98), Sir Lawrence

Alma-Tadema (1836–1912), Sir Robert Lorimer (1864–1929), and Phoebe Anna Traquair (1852–1936)).[35]

Importantly, de Wolfe's text reveals changes in the meaning and use of pianos in the face of modern inventions:

> I am going to admit that in my opinion there is nothing more abused than the piano, I have no piano in my own house in New York. I love music – but I am not a musician, and so I do not expose myself to the merciless banging of chance callers. Besides, my house is quite small and a good piano would dwarf the other furnishings of my rooms. I think pianos are for musicians, not strummers, who spoil all chance for any real conversation. [...] Musicians are not born every day, but lovers of music are everywhere, and I for one am heartily in favor of doing away with the old custom of teaching every child to bang a little, and instead, teaching him to *listen* to music. Oh, the crimes that are committed against music in American parlors! I prefer the good mechanical cabinet that offers us 'canned' music to the manual exercise of people who insist on playing wherever they see an open piano. Of course the mechanical instrument is new, and therefore, subject to much criticism from a decorative standpoint, but the music is much better than the amateur's. We are still turning our noses a little at the mechanical piano players, but if we will use our common sense we must admit that a new order of things has come to pass, and the new 'canned' music is not to be despised.[36]

De Wolfe's commentary indicates changing perceptions about the piano. When faced with 'canned music' – whether from phonographs, gramophones, or player-pianos – a kind of professionalism in music is being lauded while amateurism (which was accommodated in French's scheme) is now to be replaced with new, more attentive forms of listening if not performing.

The incursion of the phonograph or gramophone neither dislodged the piano from its important place in middle-class homes nor in consumer culture. As historian Craig Roell asserts, the technological shortcomings of phonograph recordings (e.g., limits of disc time to only four minutes and relatively poor quality of recording) meant that the player-piano became a key component of what he dubs a 'musical democracy' through the first three decades of the twentieth century.[37] Reporting in *Style & Home Furnishing* in 1916, Alwyn T. Covell noted that contemporary American homes increasingly included *both* pianos (or player-pianos) and phonographs,[38] in other words allowing for both creative and recreative technologies of music. After discussing some strategies for decorating a music room (with comments about colour schemes and utilitarian concerns reminiscent of early interior decorating advice literature), he notes that the 'music alcove, or piano and phonograph occupying a place in the living room itself are certainly most characteristic of the American home of today, and the informality of such an arrangement is conducive to more frequent performance of such music as the household enjoys'.[39]

He proceeds to argue that 'the introduction of the piano, phonograph and music and record cabinets in the living room calls [... simply] for an appreciation of good taste, conformity and the importance of place-ment'. Comfort, especially for musicians, should trump 'what looks best' in design considerations.

Pianos and player-pianos remain interests for interior decorators into the 1920s. Representative of the post-war literature is *Be Your Own Decorator* (1923) by Emily Burbank. Echoing sentiments from earlier in the century, she prescribes groupings of seats around the piano 'to indi-cate that if some one is good enough to play, some one else is courteous enough to listen!'[40] For Burbank, the decoration of domestic space should express the interests, tastes, and personality of the occupants first and foremost. Indeed, as the foregoing survey of interior decorating literature indicates, over the first few decades of the twentieth century, the piano gradually shifted from an essential component of the home based on moral grounds (the ostensible morality of music and the discipline of a work ethic) to an expressive component of one's personality, interests, and tastes.[41]

We should note that while most interior decoration manuals reference the piano in one form or another, the instrument could sometimes be oddly overlooked. For example, in a section from *The Modern Priscilla Home Furnishing Book* (1925), the author explains how the home decorator could compensate for the lack of a fireplace in the living room by directing atten-tion to windows and lamps.[42] A diagram employing an eighteenth-century drawing technique, which allows a view of floor plan and elevations at once, is used to demonstrate the harmonious arrangement of furniture [Figure 7.3]. We observe a grand piano in the corner, and yet the accompa-nying text makes no reference to its presence (not to mention the nearby phonograph); instead it focuses on the tables and sofas. The absence of any notice of the piano is curious. As an advice manual for all homemak-ers, perhaps avoiding reference in the text made the lessons more broadly applicable to those who may not own a piano; the instrument's inclusion in the diagram, however, underlines the continued significance of the piano in designing an ideal living room or, indeed, home. In its advice on furnish-ing 'A Living Room for Six Hundred Dollars', the contemporary *Ross Crane Book of Home Furnishing and Decoration* makes the point explicit: 'In case of a budget even more limited, the desk and one table might be omitted; but a musical instrument of some sort is always an indispensable in a real home.'[43] While a piano might be difficult to accommodate spatially, its social and cultural value made it imperative for homeowners who desired the art and entertainment of the instrument to try. Without it, a crucial multisensorial element of the home would be missing.

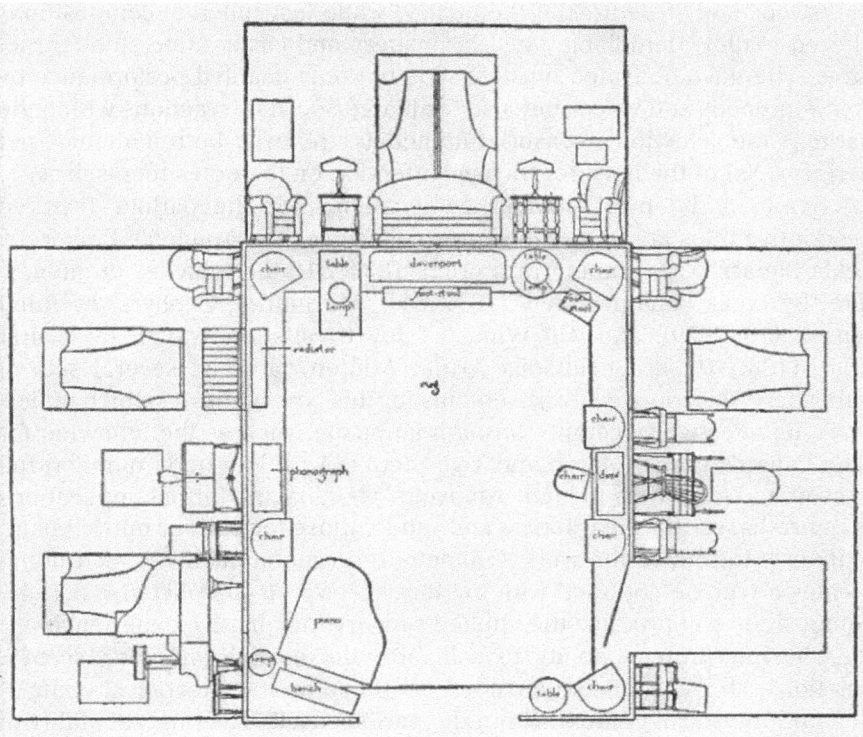

**Figure 7.3**   Living room floor plan with elevations. *Modern Priscilla Home Furnishing Book: A Practical Book for the Woman Who Loves Her Home* (Boston: The Priscilla Publishing Company, 1925), p. 161.

## Designing music for the parlour piano

Home parlour performers had a wide array of sheet music at their disposal, ranging from technical exercises and pedagogical studies for personal advancement to sentimental parlour ephemera for the enjoyment of family and friends and the 'classical' repertoire for grander affairs. In the never-ending battle between popular and elite tastes, the designation 'parlour music' came to acquire a pejorative meaning when describing works that were 'sentimentally vapid' and 'structurally mechanical'.[44] Nevertheless, as an unnamed critic observed, 'even in its shallower illustrations, parlor music is a large social force, bringing myriads of persons into touch with tonal art'.[45] In doing so, of course, it also brought those same people in touch with others, whatever the level or quality of the music itself.

Stylistic features of parlour music aimed at a direct expression of sentimentality through emotion-laden texts, tuneful and memorable melodies, moderate tempos, and basic formal designs. Songs unambiguously reflect the moods and structures of the poetry, while instrumental compositions offered readily identifiable musical imagery and easily understood structures. The uncomplicated musical style not only enabled performance by amateur hands and voices but also facilitated social interactions within the parlour: the selection's sensorial immediacy relieved both audience and performer(s) of the need for focused attention on the notes themselves.

Some of the most popular compositions for the parlour featured descriptive titles and musical elements, such as 'The Maiden's Prayer' by Tekla Bądarzewska-Baranowska (1829/1834–61), 'Les cloches du monastère' by Louis Lefébure-Wély (1817–69), 'Murmuring Zephyrs' by Adolf Jensen (1837–79), and 'On Wings of Joy (Hesitation Waltz)' by Walter Rolfe (1880–1944). Sociologist Arthur Minton gathered several sets of publishers' descriptive advertisements for this type of music, which underscore its affective viscerality through language, such as the following for 'The Panama Canal (March and Two Step)': 'A rattling good number, full of snap and go. – Sets the feet a-moving.'[46] Unlike the formal implications of genre-based titles like sonata and rondo, those for parlour music unambiguously introduce the work's mimetic representationality – such titling creates a type of 'contract' with the purchaser/performer/listener that the composition will produce the implied sensory-imaginative experience.

The interpreter's ability to call forth the music's intended scenes, emotions, and sensations depended of course on their technical completion and the social context within the parlour itself. The musical ability of most bourgeois parlour pianists could accommodate a simple sentimental ballad for voice with piano self-accompaniment like 'I Love You Truly' by Carrie Jacobs-Bond (1862–1946) or 'After the Ball' by Charles K. Harris (1867–1930) or a descriptive piano piece of limited technical demands such as 'On Wings of Song' by Felix Mendelssohn (1809–47) or the 'Souvenir de bal' by Henri Rosellen (1811–76). Although home musicians could perform these works in the parlour alone, for their own enjoyment, communicating the music's affective properties to family and friends would contribute to the space's intimacy and sociable domestic atmosphere. If the Jacobs-Bond song might invoke romantic sentiments within the room, the Mendelssohn and Rosellen could transport both performer and audience to another place or another time. Eliciting these diverse moods would rely on music's capacity to function as a multisensory experience within the social frame of the home parlour, as activated by the piano.

The moods evoked by music in performance might be visually represented by advertisements for instruments, like that for the reproducing pianos manufactured in Toronto by Mason & Risch [Figure 7.4]. In the advertisement, lyricist George Cooper (1840–1927) is photographed sitting next to the technologically advanced instrument, apparently listening to the ballad 'Sweet Genevieve'. Meanwhile, nearby floats the spectral presence of Genevieve, who had been a 'real character' according to the accompanying

**Figure 7.4**   Advertisement for Mason & Risch Duo-Art reproducing piano, *Canadian Homes and Gardens* (February 1926), p. 8.

text. Outside the frame, we see a drawn rendering of a couple, arm-in-arm, standing inside a picket-fenced property and looking at a two-storey sub-urban house, with steeply pitched roof and garden. Altogether, the images and copy paint a nostalgic picture of music at home. Perhaps akin to Carrie's experience with her pianist-neighbour's performance, viewers of this advertisement are drawn to the power of music to carry them wistfully away 'on wings of song'. Interestingly, this escape to the past is premised on modern design: the novel piano allows for a multisensory experience of music from earlier times. And while the piano has the capability of repro-ducing great concert pianists, the choice for this advertisement is a melan-cholic ballad, designed for performance at home.

After the turn of the century, the sentimental style of parlour music would increasingly yield to the musical trends of the day, which intro-duced to domestic spaces the lively syncopated rhythms of instrumental ragtime and the jazz- and blues-inflected tunes and harmonies of Tin Pan Alley songs. Even as the parlour piano made room for the Victrola and the piano itself underwent transformation into various mechanical instruments, the home space dedicated to music shifted from a place for warm and intimate domestic sociality to one for the expression of personal tastes and abilities. The new repertoire of up-tempo jazz as well as songs based on the blues facilitated this transformation of the parlour into a site for the entertainment of others on the one hand and the introspection of the individual on the other. And as the text on the 1936 Ampico piano roll recording of 'It's De-Lovely' by Cole Porter (1891–1964) makes clear, the piano (here a 'reproducing piano') was still at the centre of a multisensory experience in the living room [Figure 7.5]. The roll not only reproduces the Sherry Brothers' performance of the song, with all the dynamism and excitement one might expect of a foxtrot, but notes that it is a 'Recording with words for singing and dancing.' Domestic audiences could simply enjoy listening to the professional performance or could more actively sing or dance along with the hit song from *Red, Hot and Blue*.

## Conclusion

In the late nineteenth and early twentieth centuries, the piano, as both material and conceptual instrument of culture, was ubiquitous to the point of being overlooked, yet it made a deep impression on the domestic sense-scape. Our chapter reveals its presence in interior design through readings of plans, architecture, and decorating literature, and by returning to par-lour music, advertisements, and contemporary fiction we indicate ways of remembering its sonic place and imaginative potency in a period that wit-nessed substantial changes to home entertainment. By 'site-reading' – that is, emphasizing the embodied place of music in the domestic environment – our chapter encourages interdisciplinary perspectives on both the study of

**Figure 7.5**   Piano roll for an Ampico reproducing piano of 'It's De-Lovely' (Cole Porter) performed by the Sherry Brothers, 1936. Collection of Bruce and Dale Scott. Photo: Michael Windover.

interiors and parlour music. Narrowing in on the piano as an object rich with multisensorial effects, this chapter offers a way of locating sound and other sensory experiences in interior design history. For instance, we sense the piano's physicality and spatial impact on often quite confined rooms, as well as the way it affected lighting (placement of windows, piano lamps, or other fixtures) and of course the sonic dimensions of domestic interiors.

Importantly, this chapter highlights some of the ways the piano acted as a node in a series of design narratives. It affected the spatial and visual layout of the living room and the performance of everyday activities in the home, while itself invoking a particular set of compositions (design propositions in their own way). These imbricated activities amplify for us the multisensorial place of the piano in the early twentieth century, a time when the instrument entered more North American homes than ever before and carried with it associations with culture, class, and social prestige. It was a site of work and entertainment and an agent in the creation of social relations. It could mark the rhythm of everyday life or larger calendrical cycles of special events or holidays. As a result, it could operate as a kind of hub around which social and family life circulated and be entwined with sensorially potent memories and perhaps for some a kind of nostalgia. By drawing attention to sound, studies like this one emphasize the significance of the temporal if not ephemeral and evanescent. Even if only imagined from a historical distance, interiors come to life with movement and performance through careful consideration of a conversely fixed piece of furniture.

'Site-reading' for the piano allows us to see how professionals were grappling with the instrument's enduring presence as new technologies and attendant activities began to change the social and sensory character of middle-class homes. The second third of the twentieth century witnessed some fundamental changes to the soundscape of domestic life. Better quality recordings and speakers for gramophones and radio threatened the primacy of the piano as an acoustic point of interest in the living room. Radio and later television brought in different spatial and sensory experiences. The 'live' quality of the piano (even if played on a player-piano) and the haptic element of engaging with the instrument was replaced with electro-acoustic production and a different set of visual, audio, tactile, and spatial experiences. Over the course of time, the piano lost its spatio-structural status in living rooms as it no longer served as a primary source of entertainment at home, yet for those individuals with the motivation to possess it, the piano has remained a site for multisensory satisfaction.

## Notes

1 T. Dreiser, *Sister Carrie* (New York: Double Day, Page & Co., 1900), pp. 114–15.
2 *Ibid.*, p. 114.
3 *Ibid.*, p. 331.
4 N. S. Eidsheim, *Sensing Sound: Singing and Listening as Vibrational Practice* (Durham, NC: Duke University Press, 2015).
5 A. G. Stacy, *The Service of Song: A Treatise on Singing* … (New York: A. S. Brown, 1874), p. 74.
6 H. R. Haweis, *Music and Morals* (London: Strahan & Co., 1871). See also G. Carson, 'The Piano in the Parlor', *American Heritage*, 17:1 (1965), pp. 54–9, 99; S. Levine, 'Parlor Pianos, Homespun, and Ahab's Leyden Jar: The Arts and American Life', *Canadian Review of American Studies*, 14:4 (1983), pp. 361–82; and R. A. Solie, '"Girling" at the Parlor Piano' in *Music in Other Words: Victorian Conversations* (Berkeley, CA: University of California Press, 2004), pp. 85–117.
7 A. J. Kolarik, B. C. J. Moore, P. Zahorik, S. Cirstea and S. Pardhan, 'Auditory Distance Perception in Humans: A Review of Cues, Development, Neuronal Bases, and Effects of Sensory Loss', *Attention, Perception, & Psychophysics*, 78 (2016), pp. 373–95.
8 T. Christensen, 'Four-Hand Piano Transcription and Geographies of Nineteenth-Century Musical Reception', *Journal of the American Musicological Society*, 52:2 (1999), pp. 255–98.
9 T. C. Hubka and J. T. Kenny, 'Examining the American Dream: Housing Standards and the Emergence of a National Housing Culture, 1900–1930', *Perspectives in Vernacular Architecture*, 13:1 (2006), pp. 49–69.
10 Solie, '"Girling" at the Parlor Piano', p. 95; C. Roell, *The Piano in America, 1890–1940* (Chapel Hill, NC: University of North Carolina Press, 1989), pp. 3–12.

11 K. C. Grier, *Culture & Comfort: Parlor Making and Middle-Class Identity, 1850–1930* (Washington, DC and London: Smithsonian Institutional Press, 1988), p. 73.
12 *Ibid.*, p. 212.
13 Roell, *The Piano in America*, p. 32. According to the *Biennial Census of Manufactures: 1921* (Washington, DC: Government Printing Office, 1924), p. 1153, over 350,000 pianos were manufactured. In Canada, the number of pianos rose from 10,000 in 1900 to 32,000 in 1913 then slid back down to 24,762 in 1917. See J. A. Ross, '"Ye Olde Firme" Heintzman & Company, Ltd., 1885–1930: A Case Study in Canadian Piano Manufacturing' (M.A. thesis, University of Western Ontario, 1994), p. 73.
14 However, see K. Guiguet, *The Ideal World of Mrs. Widder's Soirée Musicale: Social Identity and Musical Life in Nineteenth-Century Ontario* (Gatineau, QC: Canadian Museum of Civilization, 2004).
15 For example, see K. Barnett, 'Furniture Music: The Phonograph as Furniture, 1900–1930', *Journal of Popular Music Studies*, 18:3 (2006), pp. 301–24; D. Harris, 'A Tiny Orchestra in the Living Room: High-Fidelity Sound, Stereo Systems, and the Postwar House' in J. Archer, P. J. P. Sandul and K. Solomonson (eds), *Making Suburbia: New Histories of Everyday America* (Minneapolis, MN: University of Minnesota Press, 2015), pp. 305–28; K. Keightley, '"Turn it down!" She Shrieked: Gender, Domestic Space, and High Fidelity, 1948–59', *Popular Music*, 15:2 (1996), pp. 149–77; L. Spigel, *Make Room for TV: Television and the Family Ideal in Postwar America* (Chicago: University of Chicago Press, 1992); T. D. Taylor, 'The Commodification of Music at the Dawn of the Era of "Mechanical Music"', *Ethnomusicology*, 51:2 (Spring/Summer 2007), pp. 281–305; J. Vest, 'Vox Machinae: Phonographs and the Birth of Sonic Modernity, 1877–1930' (PhD diss, University of Michigan, 2018); M. Windover and A. MacLennan, *Seeing, Selling, and Situating Radio in Canada, 1922–1956* (Halifax: Dalhousie Architectural Press, 2017).
16 E. de Wolfe, *The House in Good Taste* (New York: The Century Co., 1913), pp. 185–6 (available online through The Project Gutenberg eBook, #14715, 17 January 2005). De Wolfe describes a house that included a music alcove that was built into a mezzanine overhanging a large living room (separating the player from the audience below).
17 Recently, music rooms and acoustic dimensions of architect-designed domestic architecture have seen scholarly attention. For example, see D. de Muzio, 'Wharton Esherick's Music Room from the Curtis Bok House, Gulph Mills, Pennsylvania, 1935–1938', *Winterthur Portfolio*, 46:2–3 (2012), pp. 58–74; and J. Quinan, 'Frank Lloyd Wright's Intuitive Sound Modernity', *Journal of Architecture*, 23:6 (2018), pp. 961–85.
18 W. Kelly, *Downright Upright: A History of the Canadian Piano Industry* (Toronto: Natural Heritage/Natural History Inc., 1991), p. 10.
19 For a history of prefabricated houses focusing on Sears, see A. Cooke and A. Friedman, 'Ahead of Their Time: The Sears Catalogue Prefabricated Houses', *Journal of Design History*, 14:1 (2001), pp. 53–70.
20 For more on mail-order houses in Canada, see L. Henry, 'Mail-Order Houses', *Before E-Commerce: A History of Canadian Mail-order Catalogues*, Virtual Museum of Canada, www.historymuseum.ca/cmc/exhibitions/cpm/catalog/cat2104e.html (accessed 25 May 2020).
21 https://archive.org/details/SearsRoebuckandCoHonorbiltmodernhomes0001/mode/2up (accessed 25 May 2020).
22 R. T. Jones (ed.), *Authentic Small Houses of the Twenties: Illustrations and Floor Plans of 254 Characteristic Homes* (New York: Dover Publications, 1989). It is a reprint of *Small Homes of Architectural Distinction: A Book of Suggested Plans Designed by The Architects' Small House Service Bureau, Inc.* (New York and London: Harper & Brothers Publishers, 1929).
23 *Ibid.*, p. 126.

24 For more about the atmospheres created by and surrounding the parlour piano, see M. Windover and J. Deaville, 'Setting the Tone in Early 20th-Century North American Living Rooms: The Parlor Piano' in A. Sioli and E. Kiourtsoglou (eds), *The Sound of Architecture: Acoustic Atmospheres in Place* (Leuven: Leuven University Press, 2022), pp. 45–58.

25 Design historians have made good use of interior decoration advice literature to inform studies of interiors. For instance, see G. Lees-Maffei, 'From Service to Self-Service: Advice Literature as Design Discourse, 1920–1970', *Journal of Design History*, 14:3 (2001), pp. 187–206 (and her subsequent *Design at Home: Domestic Advice Books in Britain and the USA since 1945* (London: Routledge, 2013)); E. Ferry, '"Decorators May be Compared to Doctors": An Analysis of Rhoda and Agnes Garrett's *Suggestions for House Decoration in Painting, Woodwork and Furniture* (1876)', *Journal of Design History*, 16:1 (2003), pp. 15–33; and the special issue of the *Journal of Design History*, 18:1 (2005), edited by J. Aynsley and F. Berry.

26 E. Wharton and O. Codman Jr, *The Decoration of Houses* (New York: Charles Scribner's Sons, 1897 [1901]).

27 *Ibid.*, p. 142.

28 *Ibid.*, p. 143.

29 *Ibid.*

30 *Ibid.*, p. 144.

31 L. H. French, *Homes and Their Decoration* (New York: Dodd, Mead and Company, 1903), p. 19.

32 *Ibid.*, p. 197.

33 *Ibid.*, pp. 373–4.

34 De Wolfe, *The House in Good Taste*, p. 183.

35 *Ibid.*, p. 187. For other examples of Arts and Crafts contexts with reference to decorated pianos, see G. Zelleke, 'Harmonizing Form and Function: Mackay Hugh Baillie Scott and the Transformation of the Upright Piano', *Art Institute of Chicago Museum Studies*, 19:2 (1993), pp. 160–73, 203–5; and L. Lacroix, 'The Pursuit of Art and the Flourishing of Aestheticism amidst the Everyday Affairs of Mankind' in C. C. Hill (ed.), *Artists, Architects & Artisans, Canadian Art 1890–1918* (Ottawa: National Gallery of Canada, 2013), pp. 20–55.

36 De Wolfe, pp. 184–5.

37 Roell, *The Piano in America*, Chapter 2.

38 A. T. Covell, 'Music in the Home: What Modern Furniture Offers to the Music Lover', *Style & Home Furnishing* (February 1916), pp. 2–4.

39 *Ibid.*, p. 4.

40 E. Burbank, *Be Your Own Decorator* (New York: Dodd, Mead and Company, 1923), p. 8.

41 For more on this historical change, see K. Halttunen, 'From Parlor to Living Room: Domestic Space, Interior Decoration, and the Culture of Personality' in S. J. Bronner (ed.), *Consuming Visions: Accumulation and Display of Goods in America 1880–1920* (New York: Norton, 1989), pp. 157–89 (158).

42 C. A. Byers et al., *Modern Priscilla Home Furnishing Book: A Practical Book for the Woman Who Loves her Home* (Boston, MA: The Priscilla Publishing Company, 1925), pp. 160–1. Our thanks to musicologist Dr Michael Saffle for providing this and other references. His book *Selling Pianos with Pictures: Commercial Art and Keyboard Instruments from the Eighteenth Century to the 1920s* (Turnhout, Belgium: Brepols, 2021) provides an insightful history of piano marketing that draws visual evidence from such diverse sources as magazine ads, sheet music covers, and trade cards.

43 C. E. R. Crane, *Ross Crane Book of Home Furnishing and Decoration; A Practical, Authoritative and Sympathetic Guide for the Amateur Home Decorator* (Chicago: Frederick J. Drake & Company, 1925), p. 29. In this room the musical instrument is

a phonograph; however, elsewhere in the book, the piano is discussed in terms of providing a secondary if not primary centre of interest (p. 100).

44  W. S. Pratt, *The History of Music* (New York: G. Schirmer, 1907), p. 533.
45  *Ibid.*
46  A. Minton, 'Parlor Music', *American Speech*, 13:4 (1938), p. 261.

# 8

## The *Herrenzimmer*: masculinity, the senses and interior design in turn-of-twentieth-century Germany

### *Änne Söll*

The description of an 1899 design for a *Herrenzimmer*[1] by Henry van de Velde (1863–1957) at the exhibition of *Angewandte Kunst der Münchner Sezession* (Applied Arts at the Munich Secession) as 'ein Raum konzentrirter Geistes-Tätigkeit' (literally, 'a room of concentrated thinking')[2] indicates that interior design for men around 1900 focuses on the mind rather than the senses. Thus – one suspects – actual bodily and *sensory* experience within men's interiors is tangential, serving only as a means to the end of disembodied (male) thinking. My aim is to investigate as well as question this assumption by examining the discourse on the *Herrenzimmer* at the turn of the century as it manifests itself in German magazines and advice books. I also trace the role of the senses in the conception of rooms dedicated to male/masculine living and design by asking: How is the bourgeois male sphere created, and what role do the senses play within this realm of domestic masculinity? Drawing from a selection of interior design magazines and advice literature, I focus on a set of examples aimed at a male consumer imagined to be the head of an affluent household, a husband with wife and, possibly, children. This focus excludes an examination of apartments designed for bachelors, as has been performed in recent publications by John Potvin, Paul B. Preciado and Bill Ogersby.[3] As will become apparent, the men living in the *Herrenzimmer* were not imagined to be (queer) bachelor 'Deco Dandies', as Potvin has shown so convincingly for 1920s French magazines such as *Monsieur*[4] who were 'suggestively offered hybrid "furnishing orientation"'.[5] The men addressed within the pages of the German literature examined here were implicitly white, middle to upper class and heterosexual.[6] In fact, one could argue that these visions of male domesticity 'suggest that home played an important role in the articulation of bourgeois men's gendered and class identity'.[7] As Pamela Warner astutely argues in her discussion on men's domestic portraiture in nineteenth-century France, '[M]an's domestic life did not emasculate him';[8] it is rather an important part in the make-up of a heteronormative vision of bourgeois masculinity at the turn of the last century. Consequently, what concerns me here is how this normative 'vision' of white, heterosexual masculinity is housed through and within the *Herrenzimmer*. How is (heterosexual) masculinity created through this sensual environment, and how are the senses involved in creating a specific environment that is thought of as masculine? How does the design of the *Herrenzimmer* partake in the ordering of the senses along social and gendered lines?

## Separate spheres? Feminine salons v. masculine *Herrenzimmer*

The nineteenth-century division of life into separate, gendered spheres, both in the home and in society at large, is well documented and discussed in a wealth of research, only a selection of which I can refer to here for reasons of space.[9] The general consensus is that, as the nineteenth century wore on, the public sphere, mainly work and politics, became increasingly the domain of middle- and upper-class men, while women of the same classes were relegated increasingly to the private sphere, chiefly the domestic realm of the home. As historian Adleheid von Saldern points out, however, these 'separate spheres' were not strictly distinct from one another but deeply connected and intertwined.[10] Women were indeed never completely absent from the public sphere[11] and men were naturally present in the home. Nevertheless, as a rule, middle- and upper-class women were closely tied to the home, and the home was seen primarily as a private 'female sphere'.[12] In fact, femininity was conceived as intimate and private by its very nature, whereas masculinity was associated with public engagement and work outside the home. Yet, married, middle- and upper-class men lived within their family homes and inevitably made their mark on this domestic space. As such, in the words of Temma Balducci, Heather Belnap Jensen and Pamela Warner, the idea of nineteenth-century interiors as 'Spaces of Femininity'[13] 'needs to be expanded to include men's presence there'.[14] Taking up Penny Sparke's argument, the *Herrenzimmer* must be seen within the dynamics of the modern interior as 'the result of the two-way movement between the private and the public spheres'.[15] If, as Sparke points out, the 'domestic interior moved outside the home, rendering ambiguous the spaces of feminine modernity as it did so'[16] the *Herrenzimmer* as a space of bourgeois male domesticity, as I will show, blurs the lines of 'feminine' domesticity and, as part of the 'two-way movement' of private and public spheres, offers a specific space of male modernity *within* the home.

Irene Nierhaus argues that the nineteenth-century bourgeois home was to serve as a sanctuary for the family, protecting its members from the outside world and providing them with intimate spaces.[17] Women, whether as wife or maid, bore responsibility for creating and maintaining this family home, whereas men were to function as head of the household. This 'intimate' gendered space called 'home' is, as Nierhaus has shown, also charged with feelings and moral codes that make it 'a real and imagined space for the development of the bourgeois subject and his/her emotional ties and virtues'.[18] As the concept of intimacy and privacy took greater hold in the second half of the nineteenth century, the differentiation of spaces within the home became more pronounced. If possible, parents and children slept in their own rooms and 'private' living quarters, such as bedrooms, were separated from the 'public' salon reserved for entertaining visitors.[19]

The design of upper-class homes, in particular, shows this differentiation of gendered public and private zones within the house or apartment, providing its inhabitants with individualized living quarters that were based on aristocratic architectural concepts of separate apartments for husband and wife. Consequently, *Herrenzimmer* were found largely in the homes of affluent bourgeois families that were able to afford large houses or apartments.[20] The *Herrenzimmer* could be the site for a variety of different activities, such as working, reading, writing, smoking and leisure pursuits like billiards. When used for entertaining, the *Herrenzimmer* became the counterpart to the salon, leaving this space to the company of middle- and upper-class women.[21] Depending on income and social standing, quarters might incorporate just one *Herrenzimmer* that would serve several of these functions at once, or it might have an entire array of *Herrenzimmer*, each with a separate function. This is nicely illustrated by Alexander Koch's multivolume *Handbuch neuzeitlicher Wohnkultur* from 1912, the first of which is dedicated to the *Herrenzimmer*.[22] Koch splits his collection of photographs of interiors into nine sections: 'Arbeits-Zimmer' (study), 'Bibliothek-Zimmer' (library), 'Rauch-Zimmer' (smoking room), 'Jagd-Zimmer' (hunting room), 'Kneip-Zimmer' (socializing room/bar), 'Billiard-Zimmer' und 'Spiel-Zimmer' (billiard room and gaming room), 'Privat-Bureaux' (study for official use within the home), or even 'Sitzungs-Zimmer' (meeting room).[23] Describing the main functions of these rooms, Koch writes:

> The master's room, the real domain of the master of the house, *plays* a significant role in the organism of the modern home. Considering the increased professional and social demands, the master of the house needs a space for concentrated work and undisturbed recreation, away from the unrest of family life. In these two terms [work and recreation] are given the two main functions of the master's room.[24]

The *Herrenzimmer* is thus a retreat, a space of concentrated work and quiet rest, that is a private 'male' space *within* the privacy of the family home. Pamela Warner even called it a 'sanctuary' offering a withdrawal 'from the pressures of the outside world',[25] providing solitude, if not isolation. The interior design of the *Herrenzimmer* should, as Koch continues, facilitate work and rest, foremost by providing a practical desk, shelves and bookcases (or a separate library), a comfortable sofa or armchairs and 'atmospheric wall covering using wallpapers or fabrics, resulting in a good, cohesive unit of space'.[26] Koch's descriptions make clear that the *Herrenzimmer* and its furnishings are part of what Nierhaus has called a 'visualized choreography of gender'[27] within the home that can also be expressed through different decorative styles associated with femininity or masculinity.[28] As in all other rooms within the German middle- and upper-class home at the end of the nineteenth century, the *Herrenzimmer* creates a *Stimmung* (mood or atmosphere) giving the room and its furnishings 'an essential, psychic-subjective character [...], which is supposed to express ideally and poetically what goes on' within it.[29] The use of large, straight and austere forms to create a predominantly dark and business-like ambience was intended to evoke the masculine space defining the *Herrenzimmer*:

> Following its counterpart, the characteristics of an adequate male interior can be summarized in the terms big, strong, firm and straightforward. At the same time, these qualities characterize the ideal male body constitution, as well as male character, if one translates straightforwardness with determination or firmness with will and steadfastness, for example.[30]

So, what do these masculine spaces actually look like? What characterizes these male spaces? How are they furnished and decorated?

## Looking into the *Herrenzimmer*

Leafing through three of the most prominent German interior design journals *Deutsche Kunst und Dekoration* (*DKD*), *Innendekoration* (*ID*) and *Moderne Bauformen* (*MB*), from the end of the nineteenth century up until the 1930s, it is striking how often we are shown images of *Herrenzimmer*.[31] The 'master's room' seems to be an undisputed element of every affluent household or architectural plan in all magazines and advice literature. Its significance is made clear when, in an article in *Innendekoration* from 1903 summing up the potential costs of furnishing for an affluent household, the *Herrenzimmer* is the most expensive.[32] If financially possible, investing in a representative *Herrenzimmer* seems to have been a standard procedure and the large sum signals the importance of the head of the bourgeois household and his right to representative rooms of his own. Only at the end of the 1920s, with women's emancipation exerting a stronger influence and the rise of Bauhaus design, do we detect occasional signs that a clear-cut division between male and female 'spheres' within middle- and

upper-class households is losing its foothold.[33] For example, Armand
Weise writing in *Deutsche Kunst and Dekoration* in 1927 argues for col-
lapsing the *Herrenzimmer* and the women's salon into a single living room:

> The independence of women and their entry into the struggle of the economic
> life brought about the equalization of the sexes. In this consequence the ladies'
> room and the boudoir will have to fall at the same time as the *Herrenzimmer*.
> Or rather, the rooms intended for sociability will lose their hitherto rigidly held
> character of a strong separation between masculine – powerful and austere
> and, on the other hand, feminine – delicate, soft and playful. A new type of
> socializing room will gradually develop, combining both extremes.[34]

It is also argued that the use of tubular steel furniture prompted pre-war
separate spheres within the home to give way to a more 'neutral mood,
giving all rooms and their furnishings something homogenous or even
monotonous'.[35] Nevertheless, the term *Herrenzimmer* continued to be
used for interiors furnished with tubular steel furniture[36] and with the rise
of National Socialism, especially after the Nazi seizure of power in 1933,
the *Herrenzimmer* reasserted its significance, reviving the rhetoric of separate spheres for husband and wife.[37]

While the necessity of the *Herrenzimmer* is questioned only for a brief
interlude between the late 1920s and early 1930s, remaining a staple of
the decoration trade until after the Second World War, the design of this
decidedly masculine space as shown in the magazines and advice books of
the period reveals notable differences – for example, looking at images of
*Herrenzimmer*, especially in the journal *Moderne Bauformen*, the disparity
between the design of *Herrenzimmer* featured at exhibition or showrooms
and those of privately owned *Herrenzimmer*. The latter display a greater
range of styles, mixing furniture and decoration from different epochs to a
much higher degree.[38] The ideal of the sober, straight, firm and predominantly dark *Herrenzimmer* conjured up within the texts of these journals
and advice books, in fact, contrasts with changing styles not always adher-
ing to this masculine ideal. Instead, they bear witness to men's individual
circumstances, adapting this ideal to their taste and financial means. What
all these rooms do have in common, though, is that they are thought of as
a man's exclusive domain within a family home offering a calm space for
work and/or repose.

As noted above, the character of the *Herrenzimmer* – 'big, strong, firm
and straightforward' – generally coincides with the nineteenth-century
ideal of the masculine body,[39] giving rise to the presumption that we are
dealing with a constant, unchanging design. In fact, the images and descriptions of the *Herrenzimmer* in all three journals and advice books examined
here tell a different story. Over the course of the years, beginning in
about 1880, there are *Herrenzimmer* in virtually every imaginable style and
decoration, ranging from opulent historicist styles deemed 'masculine',

Herrenzimmer
Entwurf: Prof. Bruno Paul, Berlin. Ausführung: Vereinigte Werkstätten für Kunst
im Handwerk H.-G., Hemelingen bei Bremen

Die Möbel find praktifch und nur auf den Bewohner hin entworfen und gearbeitet, der Künftler alfo tritt ganz in
den Hintergrund, fein Werk wirkt anonym. Und das ift wohl die Hauptaufgabe des Mobiliars, nämlich: D i e n e r zu
fein, nie Herr.

**Figure 8.1**    B. Paul, 'Herrenzimmer', in P. Klopfer, *Wie baue ich mein Haus und wie beschaffe
ich mir eine gediegene Wohnungseinrichtung?* (How do I build my house and how do I obtain an
appropriate interior design?)

such as neo-Gothic, through to neo-Renaissance interiors.[40] Equally varying are the suggestions for *Herrenzimmer* design from 1900 onwards:
we find a mixture of club sofa, striped wallpaper and neo-Biedermeier
furniture designed by Bruno Paul [Figure 8.1] or the soft curved style of
*Jugendstil* interiors by Henry van de Velde,[41] as well as the more geometric design of the Wiener Werkstätten by Josef Hofmann[42] or Hans Ofner's
*Herrenzimmer* sporting white, geometric furniture, light-coloured walls
and carpets [Figure 8.2]. All these designs offer a wide range of differing
designs for the 'master's room'. As mentioned, *Innendekoration* even features *Herrenzimmer* furnished with Bauhaus tubular steel chairs and desk
[Figure 8.3]. It would seem, then, that the prerogative was to find straight-
ness, strength, firmness and sobriety *within* these vastly different, competing styles and redefine the *Herrenzimmer* for each of these decorative
options.[43] Moreover, there are even designs for *Herrenzimmer* that vary
only very slightly from that of the lady's room. Looking at Valentin Mink's
designs[44] for a *Spielecke eines Herrenzimmers* (master's room corner for

**Figure 8.2**   H. Ofner, 'Herrenzimmer von Architekt Hans Ofner, Wien. Ausgeführt von
F. Mittringer' (*Herrenzimmer* by architect Hans Ofner, Vienna. Realized by F. Mittringer), in
*ID*, Band 17, Heft 2 (1906), pp. 46–7.

games) and a *Fenstersitz eines Damenzimmers* (window seat for a lady's
room) in an issue of *Innendekoration* from 1903, the *Jugendstil* design is
applied equally to both rooms without a discernible difference in style
or atmosphere [Figure 8.4]. Aside from the upholstered benches in the
*Herrenzimmer* grouped around a small table to accommodate card games
and the bench in the lady's room positioned to face an open space with
walls showing a higher density of decoration, there is no essential decorative difference between the two rooms. Consequently, there seems to
be no singular, essential style for the *Herrenzimmer* equally applicable
throughout the last half of the nineteenth century nor at the beginning of
the twentieth century. It is the *Herrenzimmer*'s purpose and, indeed, its
appeal to the senses, I argue, that makes it primarily a 'man's space' over
the course of the years.

## Male senses in the *Herrenzimmer*

As Constance Classen has convincingly demonstrated, the sensory world
has not only been subject to classification by social standing but is equally

**Figure 8.3**    'A. Lorenz, "Herrenzimmer", schwarz Kunstharz und Chromstahl'; 'Arch. Luckhardt und Anker, "Herrenzimmer", Deutsche Stahlmöbek, G.M.B.H.', in *ID*, Band 42, Heft 1 (1931), p. 31.

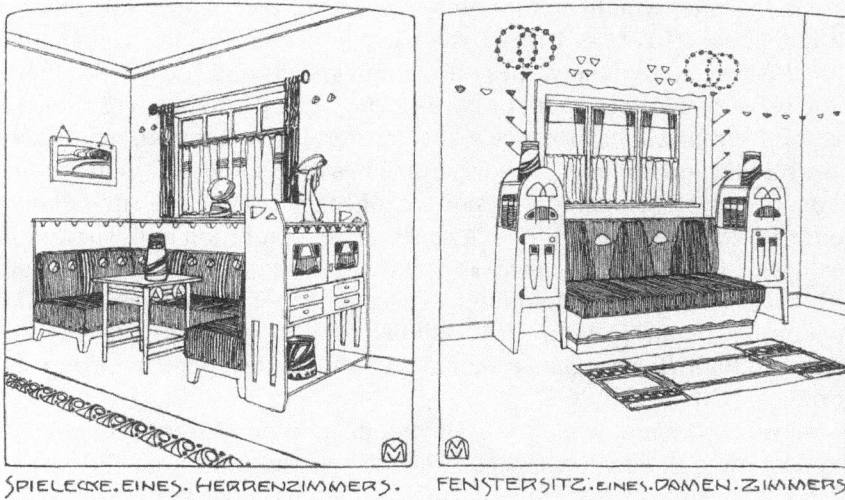

SPIELECKE.EINES. HERRENZIMMERS.    FENSTERSITZ.EINES.DAMEN.ZIMMERS

**Figure 8.4**    V. Mink, 'Entwürfe für Interieurs in Feder-Zeichnung von Architekt Valentin Mink, Darmstadt' (Designs for interiors in pen by architect Valentin Mink), in *ID*, Band 13, Heft 1 (1902), p. 40.

gendered: 'As the "lower" sex, women of all classes were associated with the "lower" senses of touch, taste and smell. [...] Men, by contrast, were conceptualized as masters of sight and hearing, while women stayed at home, they went out to see and oversee the world and take part in public discourse'.[45] Classen also argues that as a result of industrialization and the mechanization of work-processes, as well as the introduction of wide-spread schooling and compulsory army service during the nineteenth and early twentieth centuries, the senses became socially regulated: 'the sense of touch was disciplined, the sense of smell suppressed, the sense of taste controlled, the sense of hearing attuned to directives, and the sense of sight habituated to perceiving the world as assemblage of units'.[46] Under the additional influences of 'transnational commerce, conquest and colonization and industrial systems, this led to a certain homogenization of perception across cultures'.[47] Modern societies were not only confronted with homogenization but also required a degree of specialization, which also had an effect on the sensing systems and resulted in spaces dedicated to specific sensory activities (restaurants, museums, concert halls).[48] These divisions, Classen claims, were also mirrored in the modern house 'with its separate rooms for dining, sleeping, bathing and its parlour serving for visual display, music and conversation'.[49] Additionally, Freudian psychology and Darwinism championed the idea of a sensory evolutional model in which the 'lower' senses, such as smell and touch, were part of an earlier stage 'whether in the development of the species or in that of the individual'.[50] Yet, as I make clear in my analysis of the conceptions of the *Herrenzimmer* below, these hierarchies, divisions and developments of the sensory world are not always as clearly cut. It will become apparent that the *Herrenzimmer* provides a space where (heterosexual, white) men of the middle and upper classes were able to satisfy almost all their sensory needs, from taste, smell, touch, sight and hearing. While, at a first glance, the *Herrenzimmer* appears to be a space of concentration and work, in its ideal 'cosy' (*wohnlich/behaglich*) incarnation, it is equally as much a space for the 'lower', so-called 'feminine' senses such as smell, touch and taste. Smoking, drinking, playing cards and listening to music are all practised by men in their *Herrenzimmer*, stimulating all senses deemed appropriate for men.

As we have seen, while the style and decoration of *Herrenzimmer* can vary according to time, style, taste, financial means and status, the desired effect it is to have on its inhabitant is what remains constant over the years. According to magazines and advice books, *Herrenzimmer* are generally supposed to provide a calm, almost sedate atmosphere for relaxation after work. Or, if working from home, men should be able to sit at a practical desk and concentrate on the tasks at hand. This contradictory mixture of concentration and relaxation is achieved through different 'zones' within the *Herrenzimmer*, creating a space for thinking and working at a desk and another for relaxation – that is, drinking, smoking, reading, collecting and entertaining while sitting in a comfortable armchair, lying on a daybed or relaxing in a sofa, preferably close to a fireplace.[51] A vivid example of this particular calming atmosphere is provided by a description in *Innendekoration* dating from 1927. In the *Herrenzimmer*, the author writes, a man 'wants to spend some hours immersed in a thick book only now and then startled by the crack of a log in the fireplace'.[52] Devoid of any other sounds but the fire, the *Herrenzimmer* is imagined to be a quiet, peaceful, comfortable and warm space.[53] *Ruhig* (quiet, still, peaceful) is the German term most frequently used by the authors writing in magazines or advice books when describing the mood of the *Herrenzimmer*.[54] The adjective *ernst* (serious, solemn, grave) is also routinely used to define the atmosphere of the *Herrenzimmer* by contrast to the lady's salon that is described as playful, delicate and graceful.[55]

Most designs in Koch's volume on the *Herrenzimmer*[56] feature some kind of carpet, either on the floor or recommended as a wall-hanging.[57] Going by the illustrations in the books by Koch and Klopfer and the magazines *Innendekoration*, *Moderne Bauformen* and *Deutsche Kunst und Dekoration*, all *Herrenzimmer* were furnished with upholstered armchairs or even sofas that, in addition to the carpets, would have contributed to a reduction of sounds within and from without the room. The upholstery and carpets would also have provided a certain 'soft' touch contrasting with the different sorts of stained wood most commonly used in *Herrenzimmer* design. Various types of leather were used quite often, especially for club sofas and chairs.[58] Many of the rooms were fitted out with predominantly dark wooden panelling of varying descriptions and built-in cupboards or bookcases, further reducing sound and contributing to a unified look.[59] The illustrations show that light coming through the windows was dimmed by thin curtains or even leaded stained glass. Additionally, a set of darker curtains was used to further dim natural light or provide privacy at night.[60] Most rooms had a ceiling lamp and one for the desk, illuminating the room at night with several artificial light sources. Colours are described as dark, rich and saturated; most frequently mentioned are grey, brown and green, although there were exceptions, such as the interiors from designers associated with the Wiener Werkstätten, as noted above.[61] Taken together, the effects of mainly dark, saturated colours, dimmed light, dark woods, curtains and upholstery are what most authors describe in German as *wohnlich*, *behaglich* or *gemütlich*, which translates as 'comfortable', 'cosy' or 'snug'. With the introduction of Bauhaus design (and tubular steel furniture) this concept of cosiness (*Behaglichkeit*) is exchanged for a much cleaner, lighter and 'cooler' look, but the requirements for the *Herrenzimmer* remain the same: a quiet room for repose and/or work.

As we have seen, colour, carpets and upholstery all go to satisfying the senses of sight, sound and touch in the *Herrenzimmer*, but that is not all. The appeal to a man's taste and smell amplifies the sensory experience of this masculine space, turning the *Herrenzimmer* into a room for *all the senses*. The introduction to Koch's *Herrenzimmer* volume suggests smoking was a standard pleasure reserved for the *Herrenzimmer*[62] and in an earlier article the *Herrenzimmer* is presented as the location within the home 'where one drinks black coffee, tastes liqueur and smokes'.[63] Some years later, the *Herrenzimmer* of a rich Hamburg merchant is portrayed as 'a small world of books and other pleasures (bar with specially constructed dishwasher)'.[64] Tellingly, Koch's volume on the *Herrenzimmer* ends with an image of a round, small wooden *Likörschrank* (liqueur-cabinet) designed by Julius Gipkens,[65] giving the sense of taste the last word, as it were. In this three-dimensional, multisensorial space, the senses were obviously not addressed separately. Take for example this vivid, striking description of a kinaesthetic recreational soundscape which is created while contemplating a photograph written by Paul Klopfer in 1917:

> I once sat in a Herrenzimmer which included a piano that was positioned next to a wall. While I was resting in the club chair, my kind host played a nocturne by Chopin and I was able to immerse my eyes in the beauty of an image titled 'Wind strength 11'. This was a rather large photograph of about 80cm by 50cm showing the sea: the rolling of the waves, the swaying of the crests and the unfathomable vastness of the water; and all this combined with the sound waves that hit my ear in one blissfully uplifting feeling. And even without the music this image opens up great depths, expands and clears the horizon of the viewer, that might have been clouded during the day.[66]

Clearly, then, the *Herrenzimmer* could offer multisensual, pleasurable and recreational experiences through the stimulation of sight, sound, smell, touch and taste, calling into question a strictly distinguished gendered world of the senses. Ideally, as Klopfer described it, this sensory experience is so intense that it can virtually transport men to a place far away from their everyday activities, potentially improving men's moods as well as calming stressed male nerves by 'clearing away the clouds from the horizon'. It is not the design and the furnishing as such that create the sedate atmosphere of the *Herrenzimmer*, but rather their overall effect on the senses – mostly calming, sometimes stimulating – that makes it a room suitable for men. Stimulating the brain through reading is as much part of the *Herrenzimmer* as triggering the tastebuds by drinking liqueur or inhaling and/or smelling smoke from a cigar or a pipe. What is implied, especially through the written descriptions of these spaces, is that only by harmoniously combining mental and sensual stimulation can genuine *Wohnlichkeit*, *Behaglichkeit* and *Gemütlichkeit* (cosiness) be created for men who need to relax their 'nerves'.

## Calming the nerves in the *Herrenzimmer*

Why, one might ask, are men especially in need of relaxation and calm? Why are men imagined to be *nervös* (nervous) and therefore in need of a room with calming effects on the senses? As Robert Jütte has argued, with the development of modern medical and physiological research over the course of the nineteenth century, the senses and the physiological concept of the functioning of 'nerves' were very closely tied to an ever more differentiated world of the senses and subject to in-depth experiments and competing ideas.[67] Joachim Radkau has persuasively described how nervousness from about 1880 until roughly the beginning of the First World War turned into 'a cultural phenomenon of the first order, generating strong momentum on a broad emotional basis and creating a new experience of the world and its time frame'.[68] Concentrating on a very broad set of different German sources such as literature, private diaries, scientific discourse and psychoanalysis, Radkau shows that nervousness functioned as a 'synonym for irritable aggressiveness',[69] creating an 'aura of sensitive intimacy (sensible Intimität) and hidden insinuations'.[70] In fact, discourses on nervousness worked as a cipher for various stress-induced illnesses or psychological problems. Nervousness was a condition to which both sexes were susceptible, Radkau argues, but men could suffer especially, since they were more and more subjected to a form of living usually associated with women:

> The total filling of time, [...] and the fragmentation of attention – this constant having-to-do-something, this back-and-forth and having to think of several things at once – this had earlier characterized the world of women, now a growing number of men had to deal with this type of stress as well. [...] This might explain why the most eminent examples for neurasthenia were men, most men were not used to this type of strain.[71]

Even though neurasthenia and nervousness were a phenomenon not reserved to the middle and upper classes, '[i]t was the privilege of the middle classes to stylize and act out the stress of the industrial age, but the nervousness registered by the public was only the visible part of an otherwise often unarticulated unease'.[72] Not surprisingly, the home, and especially the *Herrenzimmer*, is imagined as a space in which the strains inflicted on men's nerves through the impact of modern life, industrialization, ever faster travel and communication (and a strenuous family life) are alleviated. Koch's assertion in his 1912 volume on the *Herrenzimmer* that 'the master's room, the real domain of the master of the house, plays a significant role in the organism of the modern home'[73] can be turned around: the master's room plays a significant role for men's own organism, their bodies as a whole, nerves and *all* senses included. As a multisensory space, the *Herrenzimmer* was supposed to provide a calming experience for the stressed man, head of the household, husband and father. Away from family demands, the *Herrenzimmer* offered a world that relied on the senses as much as it did on purely 'mental/cerebral' stimulation. As Walter Benjamin describes in his discussion of the interiors of the *fin de siècle*:

> The private individual, who in the office has to deal with realities, needs the domestic interior to sustain him in his illusions [...]. From this derives the phantasmagorias of the interior ... in the interior, he brings together remote locales and memories of the past. His living room is a box in the theatre of the world.[74]

This interior box 'in the theatre of the world' makes room not only for *konzentrierte Geistes-Tätigkeit* (working of the mind), as Henry van de Velde's *Herrenzimmer* was described; in fact, it equally makes room for *Sinnes-Tätigkeit* (working of the senses) that encompasses all the bodily senses.

## Notes

My heartfelt thanks go to Stefan Krämer and Eva da Silva Antunes Alves for their help and ideas when researching the interior decorating magazines for this article. I also thank Staci von Boeckmann for improving my written English.
  If not otherwise mentioned, all translations are my own.

1 I will use the German term *Herrenzimmer* throughout this chapter. It means 'master's room' or 'men's room', which is not to be confused with a bathroom or lavatory for men, but is a designated place for men to gather, more like a living room or study for men.
2 Anon., 'Angewandte Kunst in der Secession zu München', *Deutsche Kunst und Dekoration*, 5 (1899), p. 6.
3 J. Potvin, *Deco Dandy* (Manchester: Manchester University Press, 2020); J. Potvin, *Bachelors of a Different Sort* (Manchester: Manchester University Press, 2014); P. B. Preciado, *Pornotopia: An Essay on Playboy's Architecture and Biopolitics* (New York: Zone Books, 2014); B. Osgerby, 'The Bachelor Pad as Cultural Icon: Masculinity, Consumption and Interior Design in American Men's Magazines, 1930–55', *Journal of Design History*, 18:1 (Spring 2005), pp. 99–113.
4 Potvin, *Deco Dandy*, pp. 148–93.
5 *Ibid.*, p. 155.
6 This is not to say that all rooms shown in these magazines and books were exclusively and actually inhabited by this idealized vision of white, heterosexual male of the middle classes.
7 P. Warner, 'The Competing Dialectics of the Cabinet de Travail: Masculinity at the Threshold' in T. Balducci, H. Belnap Jensen and P. Warner (eds), *Interior Portraiture and Masculine Identity in France 1789–1914* (Farnham: Ashgate, 2011), p. 171.
8 Warner, 'The Competing Dialectics of the Cabinet de Travail', p. 160.
9 J. Landes (ed.), *Feminism: The Public and the Private* (Oxford: Oxford University Press, 1998); M. Hurd, 'Class, Masculinity, Manner and Mores: Public Space and Public Sphere in Nineteenth Century Europe', *Social History*, 24 (Spring 2000), pp. 75–110; T. Balducci and H. Belnap Jensen, 'Introduction' in T. Balducci and H. Belnap Jensen (eds), *Women, Femininity and Public Space in European Visual Culture 1789–1914* (Farnham: Ashgate, 2014), pp. 1–16.

10  A. von Saldern, 'Im Hause, zu Hause: Wohnen im Spannungsfeld von Gegebenheiten und Aneignungen' in J. Reulecke (ed.), *Geschichte des Wohnens Bd. 3: 1800–1918 Das bürgerliche Zeitalter* (Stuttgart: Deutsche Verlags-Anstalt, 1997), p. 147.

11  Balducci and Belnap Jensen, 'Introduction'.

12  I. Nierhaus, *Arch 6, Raum, Geschlecht, Architektur* (Vienna: Verlag Sonderzahl, 1999), pp. 104–5; von Saldern, 'Im Hause, zu Hause', pp. 175–8; B. Colomina, *Privacy and Publicity* (Cambridge, MA: MIT Press 1994).

13  G. Pollock, 'Modernity and Spaces of Femininity' in G. Pollock, *Vision and Difference: Feminism, Femininity and the Histories of Art* (London: Routledge, 1988), ch. 3.

14  T. Balducci, H. Belnap Jensen and P. Warner, 'Introduction' in Balducci, Belnap Jensen and Warner (eds), *Interior Portraiture*, pp. 1–14, p. 5.

15  Penny Sparke, *The Modern Interior* (London: Reaktion Books, 2010), p. 16.

16  *Ibid.*, p. 33.

17  Nierhaus, *Arch 6*, p. 94.

18  *Ibid.*

19  *Ibid.*, p. 95.

20  Von Saldern, 'Im Hause, zu Hause', pp. 175–8, pp. 314–17; J. Releuke, 'Die Mobilisierung der "Kräfte und Kapitale": der Wandel der Lebensverhältnisse im Gefolge von Industrialisierung und Verstädterung' in Reulecke (ed.), *Geschichte des Wohnens*, pp. 22–5.

21  E. Siebel, *Der Großbürgerliche Salon 1850–1918* (Berlin: Reimer Verlag, 1999), pp. 97–8.

22  A. Koch, *Handbuch neuzeitlicher Wohnungskultur, Vol. 1 Herrenzimmer* (Darmstadt: Verlag Alexander Koch, 1912).

23  This spelling is used by Koch in his table of contents (*ibid.*). In the text he uses *Herrenzimmer*. I will use the modern spelling without the hyphen.

24  *Ibid.*, n.p.

25  Warner, 'The Competing Dialectics of the Cabinet de Travail', p. 163.

26  Koch, *Handbuch neuzeitlicher Wohnungskultur*, n.p.

27  Nierhaus, *Arch 6*, p. 102.

28  For example, Rococo-style interiors are thought of as 'feminine' whereas Renaissance-style interiors are considered 'masculine' (see also A. Rossberg, 'Wie Frauen Zimmer wurden – Zur Wohnkultur im 18. Und 19. Jahrhundert' in S. Hackenschmidt and K. Engelhorn (eds), *Möbel als Medien* (Bielefeld: Transcript, 2011), pp. 143–53).

29  Nierhaus, *Arch 6*, p. 100.

30  Rossberg, 'Wie Frauen Zimmer wurden', p. 14.

31  For example, a digital search of the years 1898 to 1932 of *Deutsche Kunst und Dekoration* yields at least two to five entries for almost every issue. Only very few issues have no mention of the *Herrenzimmer*. *Deutsche Kunst und Dekoration* was digitized by Universitäts Bibliothek Heidelberg and can permanently be accessed at https://digi.ub.uni-heidelberg.de/diglit/dkd. In addition, *Moderne Bauformen* and *Innendekoration* have also been digitized and can be accessed at https://digi.ub.uni-heidelberg.de/diglit/moderne_bauformen and https://digi.ub.uni-heidelberg.de/diglit/innendekoration.

32  Anon., 'Aufführung der preisgekönten Entwürfe und deren Kosten', *Innendekoration*, 14:3 (1903), p. 84.

33  A. C. Rüdenauer, 'Das Kleinmöbel', *Innendekoration*, 45:4 (1934), p. 139.

34  A. Weiser, 'Fritz Groß – Wien: Eine Landhaus-Einrichtung', *Deutsche Kunst und Dekoration*, 60 (1927), p. 179.

35  A. Wenzel, 'Die neutral Stimmung', *Innendekoration*, 42:10 (1931), pp. 388–9.

36  H. Ritter, 'Eine modern Wohnung', *Innendekoration*, 44:8 (1933), p. 274.

37  W. Michel, 'Umbau einer Wohnung', *Innendekoration*, 47:2 (1936), pp. 55–60; Anon. 'Falsche Begriffe', *Innendekoration*, 50:6 (1939), p. 192; H. Henniger, 'Räume der Gräfin Margot Besozzi, Mailand', *Innendekoration*, 52:10 (1941), p. 282.

38  M. Lutz, 'Das Herrenzimmer des Herrn Rochau-Jent zu Bern', *Moderne Bauformen*, 15 (1916), p. 24; K. Pullich, 'Entwurf für ein Herrenzimmer, Stuttgart', *Moderne Bauformen*, 15 (1916), plate 13; G. A. Nietsch, 'Aus einem Herrenzimmer', *Moderne Bauformen*, 15 (1916), plate 20; W. Schönhofer, 'Aus einem Herrenzimmer, Berlin', *Moderne Bauformen*, 15 (1916), plate 30; M. H. Baillie Scott, 'Das Herrenhaus "The Cloisters" zu London, Regent's Par – Aus dem Herrenzimmer', *Moderne Bauformen*, 19 (1920), p. 140.

39  Rossberg, 'Wie Frauen Zimmer wurden', p. 14.

40  W. Friedrich and O. Mothes, *Unser Heim im Schmuck der Kunst. Ein Bildercyklus* (Leipzig: Verlag Edwin Schloemp, 1879), pp. 6, 28.

41  H. van de Velde, 'Herren-Zimmer im Haus des Verlegers I. I., in Charlottenburg, ausgeführt 1899', *Innendekoration*, 13:1 (1902), p. 25; V. Mink, 'Entwürfe für Interieurs in Feder-Zeichnung von Architekt Valetin Mink, Darmstadt', *Innendekoration*, 13:1 (1902), p. 40.

42  J. Hoffmann, 'Haus des Herrn Pollak, Wien', *Innendekoration*, 13:5 (1902), p. 133.

43  This range of styles becomes especially apparent in Alexander Koch's compendium of photographs: Koch, *Handbuch neuzeitlicher Wohnkultur*.

44  V. Mink, 'Entwürfe für Interieurs in Feder-Zeichnung von Architekt Valetin Mink, Darmstadt', *Innendekoration*, 13:1 (1902), p. 40.

45  C. Classen, 'Introduction: The Transformation of Perception' in C. Classen (ed.), *A Cultural History of the Senses, Vol. 5: The Age of Empire* (London: Bloomsbury, 2014), pp. 1–24; see also C. Classen, 'Engendering Perception: Gender Ideologies and Sensory Hierachies in Western Society', *Body and Society*, 3:2 (June 1997) pp. 1–19.

46  Classen, 'Introduction: The Transformation of Perception', p. 16.

47  *Ibid.*, p. 17.

48  *Ibid.*, pp. 17–18.

49  *Ibid.*, p. 18.

50  *Ibid.*

51  P. Klopfer, *Wie baue ich mein Haus und wie beschaffe ich mir eine gediegene Wohnungseinrichtung?* (Stuttgart: Verlag Wilhelm Meyer-Ilschen, 1917), p. 66–70; Koch, *Handbuch neuzeitlicher Wohnkultur*, n.p.

52  H. Eulenberg, 'Austellung Gebrüder Schürmann: betrachtet von Herbert Eulenberg', *Innendekoration*, 38:3 (1927), pp. 105–6.

53  ML. H., 'Raum des Geistes', *Innendekoration*, 54:4 (1943), pp. 88–9.

54  Klopfer, *Wie baue ich mein Haus*, p. 66; Koch, *Handbuch neuzeitlicher Wohnkultur*, n.p.; O. Gardmann, 'Die I. wüttembergische Ausstellung für Wohnungs-Ausstellungen', *Innendekoration*, 16:10 (1905), p. 260; R. Breuer, 'Das neue Kunst-Ausstellungshaus Keller & Reiner, Berlin', *Innendekoration*, 21:3 (1910), p. 123.

55  Klopfer, *Wie baue ich mein Haus*, p. 66; G. J. Wolf, 'Schloss Wolfsbrunn im Erzgebirge: die Innenräume des Schlosses', *Innendekoration*, 32:4 (1921), p. 106; H. Post, 'Bruno Paul als Architekt', *Deutsche Kunst und Dekoration*, 25 (1909/10), p. 175.

56  Koch, *Handbuch neuzeitlicher Wohnkultur*.

57  Klopfer, *Wie baue ich mein Haus*, p. 69.

58  Gardmann, 'Die I. wüttembergische Ausstellung', p. 260; Koch, *Handbuch neuzeitlicher Wohnkultur*, pp. 10, 17, 18, 24, 40, 58, 61, 68, 80, 106.

59  Koch, *Handbuch neuzeitlicher Wohnkultur*, pp. 20, 21, 22, 23, 24, 25, 26, 28, 32, etc.

60  *Ibid.*, pp. 2, 12, 13, 43, 55, 69, 70, 83, 84.

61  H. van de Velde, 'Einige Künstler Holland's und die Ausstellung Hugo Kochs in Düsseldorf', *Innendekoration*, 13:8 (1902), p. 206; Red., 'Bruno Pauls Räume auf der "Grossen berliner Kunst-Ausstellung"', *Innendekoration*, 18:7 (1907), p. 232; I., 'Räume von Ludwig Preetorius in Hamburg', *Innendekoration*, 23:4 (1912),

p. 166; O. A. Schneider, 'Prof. Edmund Körner, Darmstadt-Essen', *Innendekoration*, 27:2 (1916), p. 59.

62  Koch, *Handbuch neuzeitlicher Wohnkultur*, n.p.

63  A. Jaumann, 'Unser Wettbewerb: Spiel- und Billard-Zimmer', *Innendekoration*, 17:1 (1906), p. 28.

64  W. Michel, 'Umbau einer Wohnung', *Innendekoration*, 47:2 (1936), pp. 55–60.

65  Koch, *Handbuch neuzeitlicher Wohnkultur*, p. 158.

66  Klopfer, *Wie baue ich mein Haus*, p. 70.

67  R. Jütte, *Geschichte der Sinne: Von der Antike bis zum Cyberspace* (München: C. H. Beck, 2000), pp. 236–54; P. Sarasin, *Reizbare Maschinen: Eine Geschichte des Körpers 1765–1914* (Frankfurt: Suhrkamp Verlag, 2001), pp. 344–53.

68  J. Radkau, *Das Zeitalter der Nervosität. Deutschland zwischen Bismarck und Hitler* (München: Ullstein Verlag, 2000 [1998]), p. 28.

69  *Ibid.*, p. 33.

70  *Ibid.*

71  Radkau, *Das Zeitalter der Nervosität*, p. 147; on the same issue see also Sarasin, *Reizbare Maschinen*, pp. 423–33.

72  Radkau, *Das Zeitalter der Nervosität*, pp. 249–50.

73  Koch, *Handbuch neuzeitlicher Wohnungskultur*, n.p.

74  W. Benjamin, 'Paris: Capital of the Nineteenth Century' (1935) in R. Tiedemann (ed.), *Arcades Project*, trans. H. Eiland and K. McLaughlin (Cambridge, MA: Harvard University Press, 1999), pp. 8–9.

# 9

# Hands at home? Textures, tactility and touch in interior design

## Grace Lees-Maffei

### Introduction: touching home

The interior spaces that we occupy are not all the work of professional interior designers but they are all designed, whether with forethought (design in the sense of planning) or with less intentionality and more organic accrual. It follows that the sensory experiences we have in those spaces are also designed, and that they contribute to our understanding of interior design.

Touch looms large in our experience of the world; after all the skin is our largest organ. But touch, feeling, is also critically important for wellbeing, how we feel.[1] Interior designer Catherine Bailly Dunne notes: 'Interior design has traditionally focussed its energies on pleasing the eye. But a room that looks right doesn't necessarily feel right'. She explains that 'Humans can survive without hearing, sight, smell – even without the pleasures of taste. But without touch, we cannot survive psychologically […] Always include touch in your decorating equation'.[2] Rather than seeking to prioritize any one of the senses, though, Bailly Dunne advocates designing for all of them, as does architect Juhani Pallasmaa.[3] Our senses – the proverbial five senses, plus proprioception, and even the sixth sense, intuition – work in concert to deliver our experiences of the world, including interiors. Some of our senses have obvious affinities: every meal we eat demonstrates that taste and smell are connected, and any task requiring hand-eye coordination shows that sight and touch are sister senses. The experiences of people with disabilities, who develop enhanced senses, both challenge and confirm normative sensory experiences, however those are understood.

Given that the senses work collectively, why isolate the sense of touch in understanding interior design? One answer is practical:

because we cannot hope to articulate a total sensory experience, isolating a sense (touch in this case) makes the task more manageable. Also, because the information we receive from our senses is highly personal, we cannot generalize about sensory experiences. Isolating touch allows greater focus and promises potentially more useful commentary and analysis. Another reason to focus on touch is that it is not a singular entity; there are many different touch receptors on our hands and bodies and by foregrounding touch we can better appreciate its variety. We engage with the world – and with interiors therefore – by stroking, patting, squeezing, grasping and lifting. These touches – plural – facilitate the sensing of surface texture, volume and weight. Touch is not only a manual activity; it is a whole-body sense. We sense how a room feels using touch alongside other senses and social and cognitive functions such as intuition. We are touching interior design when we stand and walk on the floor, sit and lie on furniture, open and close doors, cupboards, drawers, curtains and blinds. We feel carpet or other flooring under our feet, whether or not we are wearing shoes. We sense air on our skin. Regardless of 'do not touch' signs in museums and certain shops, we touch every interior that we enter. Therefore, if we wish to understand interiors, their design and design history, it is essential to consider touch.

Interior design involves a range of different touch experiences, again working collectively to form a concerted sensory experience. Different materials perform diverse functions and offer varied sensory experiences. Is the floor under your feet floorboards, parquet or tile? Is it carpeted or covered with rugs, linoleum or vinyl, rubber or plant fibre matting? Is the chair you are sitting on upholstered? Is it made of plastic (see below), metal, wood or a combination of those? Is your table glass, wood, metal or plastic? Are your walls covered in fabric, tapestry or velvet-flocked wallpaper? Or are your walls stained plaster, fresco, *trompe l'œil* or decorated with a mural? Are they papered and, if so, is the paper embossed? If you have printed wallpaper, is it machine-printed or hand-blocked? The texture will tell you. If you are your own interior designer, these variables were chosen by you, and touch will have played a part. If not, interior designers have undertaken a combinatory process which determines your sensory experience.

While some interiors are designed with all of the senses in mind, others prioritize one sense over the rest; for example, in appealing to the eye but not the hand. Things that look good do not always feel good, and vice versa, as the users of poured concrete staircases and polyester bedsheets might attest. Some plastic chairs, paints or textiles admired for their visual appeal may carry odour that mars the sensory enjoyment they promise. A focus on touch needs to recognize its interaction with other senses such as smell and sight. Indeed, focusing on touch enables an analysis which counterbalances the ocularcentrism of the design print media, as I will discuss later in this chapter.

Interior design history has largely focused on domestic interiors rather than public, commercial, transport and other kinds of interior.[4] Most of the examples in this chapter are domestic, partly for the practical reason that it is a more manageable subcategory but also, and more importantly, due to the association of touch and comfort. The phrase 'home comforts' indicates that the home is not merely a place; it is a group of sensory experiences which collectively produce a distinctive comfort. This chapter, then, explores the mutually constitutive relationships between touch and interior design for the home, in an analysis attentive to modernisms and mediation.

Interior design has developed as a professional practice during the modern period, broadly defined, in ways increasingly distinct from both architecture, on the one hand, and decoration, on the other.[5] The central importance of comfort in the nineteenth-century bourgeois interior, communicated in contemporary domestic advice books, was challenged by modernist designers who reimagined the home and its comfort.[6] The Modern Movement in design provided a context for the professionalization of interior design in the twentieth century.[7] Modernism is best understood as a collection of tendencies, or even modernisms in the plural, rather than as a style or as a singular, wholly coherent cultural movement. Here, I examine three key tendencies of modernism, showing how a focus on touch yields new understanding about the interplay of people and their object worlds in domestic interiors.

## Hand and machine: producing and consuming modernist interior design

Interior design is a process of planning. A meaning of 'design' is the verb 'to plan'; another is the noun 'plan'. Interior designers focus on spatial planning – how people move through and use spaces and places – as well as how best to deploy furniture and furnishings, including 'soft furnishings' such as curtains and cushions. This planning precedes, or occurs alongside, the practical activities of realizing a planned interior such as construction, fabrication, installation and decoration. Planning is not simply intellectual: it involves ideation but also sourcing materials using manufacturers' samples. Decisions about materials are made with budget, utility and application in mind, but also in response to aesthetics and how things feel. Interior components fabricated by the designer or studio commissioned to design an interior usually sit alongside a combination of pre-existing manufactured elements, such as floor finishes, furniture, wall treatments and lighting. Touch is key in their selection.

That touch is a crucial aspect of interior design is demonstrated by the persistence in the age of computer-aided design (CAD) of physical mood boards, a tactile mix of inspiration and information. The interior that is produced in the mind's eye of the designer is visible in design sketches, and imagining how the space will feel is assisted by sample swatches on mood boards and in manufacturers' catalogues. The mood board is a place where interior designers collect their ideas and plan their designs, but it is also a tool of communication with studio colleagues, clients, contractors, fabricators and stakeholders. Mood boards ensure that touch is part of interior design process as well as its end result. The planning that interior designers undertake includes anticipating and designing users' sensory experiences, including touch. Sensory responses to design are not purely a factor of consumption; they are designed into products and places. An analytical approach to interiors focused on the senses – here, touch, specifically – brings together the production and consumption of design in three examples focused on aspects of modernism.

## Elimination: enhancing the sense of touch

A key modernist design tendency is elimination, from Mies van der Rohe's (following Peter Behrens) 'personal motto, "less is more"' to Dieter Rams' 1984 injunction that we must 'omit the unimportant', because 'Good design is as little design as possible'.[8] Adolf Loos (1870–1933) infamously associated ornament with degeneracy and crime.[9] A striking example of elimination in design is the 1903 bedroom Loos designed for his wife, Lina Loos (1882–1950) [Figure 9.1].[10] This remarkable room provides only what is essential for a bedroom, albeit in luxurious, sensual style. It is dominated by an enormous white Angora rabbit fur rug which climbs up the sides of a divan bed covered in a simple white silk bedspread. The walls and window(s) alike are shielded by a white wraparound curtain, made from cambric, with a flounce at the hem that exactly matches the flounced skirts for two bedside tables and a dressing table. The effect is both dramatic and calming. Through elimination, Loos has reduced the visual load of the space and intensified the impact of its tactile, textural appeal. He has set the stage for sleep, or passion, or splendid isolation. A person contemplating the room may wish to lie on the rug more than the bed, and true relaxation in the space may require first pulling back the curtain to see what it conceals. Loos here presents a version of luxury updated for modernism: he employs longstanding status symbols in the form of luxury materials made from animal products – fur and silk – in conjunction with qualities which might retrospectively be termed 'stealth wealth': luxuries of space, and the ability to resource the labour required to maintain a white or cream interior. Through elimination, Loos intensifies the experience of comfort

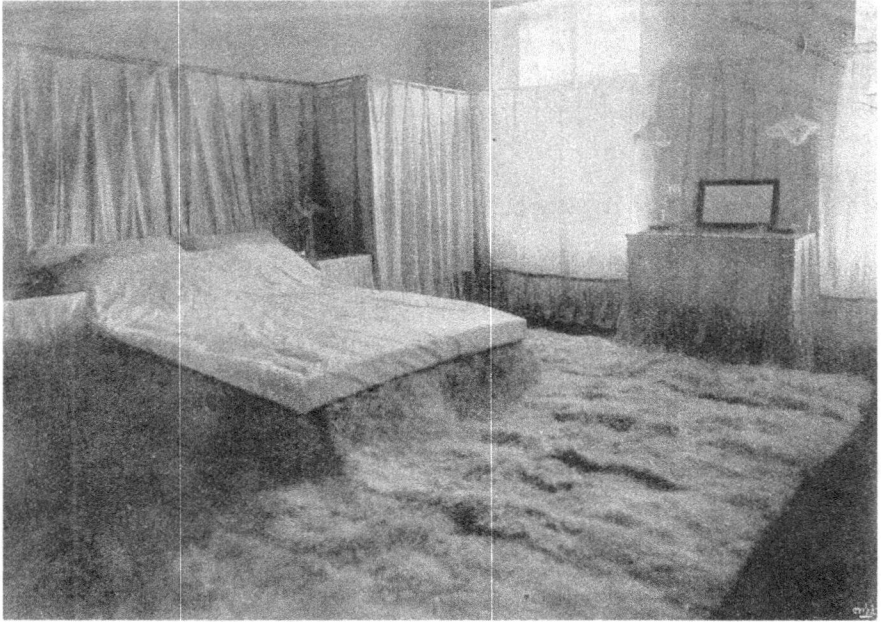

**Figure 9.1**    Adolf Loos, 'Das Schlafzimmer meiner Frau' (My wife's bedroom) in *Kunst: Halbmonatschrift für Kunst und alles andere*, no. 1 (1903).

through textures which appeal to the sense(s) of touch – deep-pile fur, smooth silk, crisp drapery.

This 1903 interior could not be a clearer rejection of the overstuffed nineteenth-century domestic interior; it can also be seen, in retrospect, as anticipating both the white moderne[11] interior designs of Syrie Maugham and minimalism in interior design exemplified by the work of architect John Pawson (1949–). See, for instance, Pawson's Home Farm (2013–19), 'where architect and client are one':

> Over the course of more than thirty years, a body of work has accumulated based on the objective of making simple spaces, with just what is required and nothing more, where the eye feels as comfortable as the body. At the heart of everything has been the idea of refining by removing, meticulously paring away until what is left cannot be improved by further reduction: sensual space, where the primary experience is of the quality of light, materials and proportions.[12]

Feminist design historians have contributed much to the understanding of modernism, interior design, the relationship of architecture, design, and decoration and domesticity, often critiquing minimalism and its variants as masculinist practices.[13] An interior design history attentive to touch enables deeper recognition of what elimination offers, as much as what it takes away.

In interior design, elimination and minimalism are strategies which reduce sensory stimuli and thereby enable an enhanced sensory experience.

## Functionalism at home: a cog in the machine for living in

Another modernist design tenet is that of appropriateness of form, derived from the design reformers of the nineteenth century. Architect Louis Sullivan's proposal that 'form follows function' underpins the machine aesthetic, the idea that machines are beautiful.[14] Le Corbusier (1887–1965) regarded the house as a machine for living in.[15] His interiors form some of the clearest demonstrations of the machine aesthetic, characterized by shiny metal, painted metal, tiles on the floor and walls, and minimal furniture and furnishings. Although they may seem devoid of home comforts when compared with many other homes, Le Corbusier's domestic interiors engage the sense of touch just as resoundingly as Loos' furry bedroom. As Ilse Crawford notes: 'Early Modern Movement houses, although clinical in appearance, were meant to be temples of the senses'.[16] Visitors to Le Corbusier's interiors are guided by the interior elements that he designed into them. Tim Benton's 1975 filmed visit to Villa Savoye (1928–31), designed by Le Corbusier and Pierre Jeanneret (1896–1967), makes clear that the house was designed to be experienced as a continuous route up and around, from the galleried pathway created by the pilotis on which the house sits, up through the rooms, to the roof terrace.[17] While not necessarily forming part of the visitors' promenade tour, the pantry shown here [Figure 9.2] has good sightlines throughout the first floor of the home, and shows Le Corbusier's attention to detail in terms of hardware.

When visitors grasp and turn the metal door handles at Villa Savoye (which match the ones at Maison La Roche, another one of Le Corbusier's houses in Paris),[18] and open the window locks, ascend staircases and sloping walkways, in these houses, they become cogs in Le Corbusier's living machine. The role of the designed world in scripting human behaviour through the affordances it offers to users follows the Actor Network Theory of, among others, Bruno Latour.[19] Kjetil Fallan has written, 'Latour's construction metaphor seems to be more about homes than about houses, to use a familiar distinction from the sphere of architecture. […] It is not just about erecting a building, but about co-producing architecture'.[20] Le Corbusier and Jeanneret have designed our sensory experiences and left a script for us in the forms and affordances of these interiors. In elaborating instructions for the house-machine, 'the manual of the dwelling', Le Corbusier concludes: 'Every modern man has the mechanical sense. The feeling for mechanics exists and is justified by our daily activities.'[21] He says of the 'House-Tool' that 'it is essential to create the right state of mind for living in mass-production houses'.[22] We might see the same didacticism in Charlotte Perriand (1903–99), Pierre Jeanneret and Le Corbusier's

**Figure 9.2**  Le Corbusier and Pierre Jeanneret, pantry, Villa Savoye, Paris, 1931.

metal and leather chaise longue LC4 (1929), a common addition to Le Corbusier's domestic interiors. Although it is comfortable, and adjustable, it anticipates and scripts the positions the user may adopt.[23] Not every inhabitant of Le Corbusier's house-machines behaves in the way that the architects intended.[24] A difference between the experiences of the original inhabitants of Le Corbusier's homes and today's visitors is that the smooth, shiny metals and other construction materials have accrued markers of time: patina, dust, rust and efflorescence.

## Hard bodies: plastics and liquid modernity

A third defining characteristic of modernism that has been important in transforming nineteenth-century bourgeois notions of home comforts is the technological developments which extended the possibilities of design. Let us consider just one example: the materials we collectively term 'plastic'.[25] Plastic is derived from oil and, like oil, it is liquid during the production process. Once solid, a plastic object can take almost any form and texture, including ones which recall its liquid phase. This makes it quite different to existing furniture construction processes and materials, even those which best approximate fluidity in appearance, such as the steamed bentwood bistro chairs manufactured by Thonet (1859), of which Le Corbusier approved,[26] the serpentine, whiplash forms of art nouveau fine cabinetmaking and the tubular metal of modernism in design, such as the aforementioned LC4 chaise longue of 1929 (which was also made by Gebrüder Thonet).

Just as entering an interior is a kind of touch – touching the floor, touching the air, touching the handles and surfaces – so is sitting.[27] Early applications of plastic to products for the interior include Charles and Ray Eames' DAR armchair (Herman Miller Furniture Company, 1948–50) [Figure 9.3] where their goal was to produce an armchair from a single

**Figure 9.3**   Charles Eames and Ray Eames, DAR armchair with rod base, 1950. Fibreglass shell seat, metal legs, plastic feet.

piece. This chair was recognized by the Museum of Modern Art in 1950.[28] The next year, Phillips Petroleum established the polymerization of propylene, and from 1954, Giulio Natta and Karl Rehn, at the Politecnico di Milano, developed polypropylene further. First commercially exploited by Montecatini from 1957,[29] subsequently manufacturers including Kartell took advantage of the properties of plastic to create new furniture forms. In 1960, Verner Panton (1926–98) designed the first single-form injection-moulded plastic chair, the organic 'S chair'.[30] Panton's aesthetic legacy persists, for instance, in the smooth plastic curves favoured by Egyptian Canadian designer Karim Rashid (1960–), such as his roto-moulded polyethylene 'Woopy' chair of 2011.[31]

Plastic introduced new tactile experiences into the domestic interior. In some cases, the shiny new forms that plastic enabled became the entire interior as shown in many of the room and dwelling proposals showcased in the exhibition *Italy: The New Domestic Landscape* at the Museum of Modern Art in 1972 and some of these ideas were put into production. Sitting on an Eames plastic chair, the sitter experiences not the responsive bounce of upholstery but rather the small flex plastic affords. Production of the Eames chairs switched from fibreglass to polypropylene, and there is a discernible difference between the feel of the two materials,[32] but in neither case does the sitter sink into an Eames chair as they would into an upholstered one; rather they are enclosed by it, and it moves with and next to them.[33]

Inflatable plastic chairs such as the Blow chair (Zanotta, 1967), designed by Paolo Lomazzi (1936–), Donato D'Urbino (1935–) and Jonathan De Pas (1932–91), offer a sitting experience more akin to upholstery than the Eames shell chairs do, but they share with all plastic chairs the fact that skin sticks to them in a way that it doesn't with furnishing fabric [Figure 9.4]. Sitting in an Eames chair, or a Blow chair, feels different depending on whether the sitter is wearing trousers or a skirt, shorts or a bikini. Ingrid Halland has theorized that the Blow chair is immaterial because it is inflated with air. Closely following Felicity Scott's analysis of Manfredo Tafuri's critique, Halland suggests that 'plastic-moulded mass-produced objects alienated the designer from work and increased the distance between the designer and the object'.[34] If we accept this theory, we must also recognize that plastic chairs decrease the distance between the user and the object to nothing. Here my analysis of the plastic chair, focused on touch, has shown that it is wholly material, whether moving with and alongside the sitter, or sticking to them.

## Seeing and touching: mediating and consuming interior design

So far, this chapter has examined how interiors – and interior elements in the form of plastic chairs – engage the sense of touch. While I have

**Figure 9.4**  Model in a swimsuit lying on the Blow inflatable chair, designed by Paolo Lomazzi, Donato D'Urbino and Jonathan De Pas, produced by Zanotta, 1967.

deliberately selected examples of which I have primary, direct experience (architecture and interior design by Le Corbusier and John Pawson, chairs designed by Charles and Ray Eames) I did not visit Lina Loos' bedroom and have responded to that space using the available evidence. Loos himself recognized the problem: 'a true building makes no impression as a picture reduced to two dimensions. It is my greatest pride that the interiors I have created are completely lacking in effect when photographed.'[35] Yet, as Ellen Lupton puts it, 'Touch is visual. The eye is a surrogate for the skin. We can look at things and see if they are sticky or slick, nubby or smooth, sharp or blunt, before we ever touch them.'[36] As noted, the senses work together. Seeing is usually a prelude to touching and when we cannot see what we are touching, the sense of touch is heightened to make up for the lost information we would gather from sight.[37] Imaginatively occupying an interior is a skill we develop as consumers in a variety of contexts from browsing home decorating and domestic advice books, shelter magazines and catalogues, visiting retail environments, handling products and entering shops' room sets, and visiting historic interiors and period rooms. Yet, as I noted at the outset of this chapter, appearances can be deceptive; things can look better than they feel, or look as if they feel better than they do. It is necessary to distinguish between interiors we can touch, and those we cannot, and to consider how in the latter case, touch, as a constitutive element of interior design, is mediated to consumers.

## Press

Ironically named after a kind of touch, the press offers merely an oblique touch experience. We flip through the glossy pages of aspirational magazines such as *World of Interiors*, and turn the slubby, recycled paper pages of publications such as *Kinfolk*, feeling them, smelling the ink and perusing the interiors shown. The shelter magazine, home decorating book or online equivalent accessed via a device such as a touchscreen or keyboard are tangible artefacts providing touch experiences, but they do not allow direct contact with interiors depicted. So how have design commentators promoted attention to the sense of touch? Two women who have each combined the roles of interior design consultant, design journalist and editor-in-chief of *ELLE Decoration*, Ilse Crawford (1962–) and Michelle Ogundehin (1967–), have called attention to the sensory, textual affordances of objects, materials, furniture and furnishings, and how interiors can make inhabitants feel. Crawford designed a hotel, Ett Hem, with the intention that guests should feel at home.[38] Ogundehin has written a lifestyle guide called *Happy Inside*, a title communicating the connection she promotes between interior design and wellbeing.[39] Their insistence on the importance of texture may be understood as an antidote to the visuality of the interior design press.

## Retail

We cannot usually step into windows displays; the appeal of seeing window dressers at work comes from them being real people in an environment of fabrications, samples and models, caught in the act of constructing an alluring illusion, moving in a context which is usually uninhabited and static (unless uncanny animatronic and other dynamic display techniques are used). But we can imagine, from the other side of the glass, that we inhabit those spaces, just as we can imaginatively enter interiors shown in the press. Interior design retail incorporates physical touch in a variety of ways, from the swatches given to customers in stores, for planning and colour matching, to the retail environments themselves, where we can pick up lamps and open drawers, sit on sofas and wheeled office chairs, pat cushions, stroke fabrics and rummage through remnant bins. The 'big box' US homewares retailer Bed, Bath and Beyond provides something of the retail tour experience epitomized by IKEA. Antonia Mantonakis, Professor of Marketing at Brock University, explains that

> [c]ustomers want to touch, feel, and get all of the senses when they shop [...] In Bed Bath, you can feel the towels and linens. Even if you do the research online, there are certain categories of items consumers will always want to check out in stores. It's a different, more engaging, more emotional, involved experience consumers enjoy.[40]

Interiors retailers often go further, providing small mock-up scenes, such as dummy beds (sometimes full length, sometimes – to save retail space – strangely abbreviated like early modern beds in stately homes) made up with bedlinen. Bed retailers encourage customers, individually or as couples, to lie down to test the texture of mattresses. In IKEA we are guided through apparently endless 'room' sets, entering a trance state in which we become more easily impressed by mesh storage solutions and rugs. While these mock-up interiors enable touching and feeling as a prelude to purchase, they still require imaginative labour from consumers who envisage the store's products in their homes, just as potential home buyers do in show homes.[41]

## Museums

The room sets we encounter in interiors stores are sisters of the period rooms we see in museums, albeit with some key differences: museum period rooms exist not to sell but rather to educate; the objects they contain are usually prized or remarkable in some way; unless they form part of a house tour, we are not always allowed to enter period rooms.[42] Handling collections are provided by museums not only because manual handling enhances learning but also to preserve the main collection from the damages wrought by touch. When I toured Elvis Presley's house Graceland in Memphis, Tennessee, the only thing I touched was my camera.[43] The Museum of the Home in London has repurposed a group of almshouses as an enfilade of period rooms to communicate a chronological history of the middle-class interior, where visitors are kept out of the successive period rooms by a low rope. On a visit there, I saw a man simply step over the rope into one of the rooms. This transgression earned the censure of the security staff (and myself). Visitors to England's National Trust properties are used to seeing teasels or holly sprigs placed on seats as instructions not to sit, as well as disincentives (both are spiky). Those same visitors are now being coaxed into the touch practices, such as playing the pianos, that are increasingly integrated into the National Trust visitor experience.

## Conclusion: touch as/and consumption and interiority

This chapter has reflected on the importance of touch, as a whole-body sense, as the defining experience of interiority and as a primary medium for interior design. We touch every interior we enter (not always with our hands but always with our bodies). When we enter interiors, they envelop us. Just as we consume them, they consume us. It is not easy to replicate in words the feeling of touching interior design – however hard the design press might try – but when we read about interiors in home and shelter magazines, and browse the images they show, we imagine what it would feel like to inhabit those homes.

While touch as a way of knowing interiors is a whole-body experience, it is constrained. We learn rules about what we can and cannot touch, how and when.[44] This is demonstrated by children who identify affordances more creatively.[45] The interiors we can touch unguardedly do not extend much beyond our own homes and – potentially – any interior in which we are left unattended and unobserved. Even in the homes of friends and family we cannot touch what we want, when we want. Fragile items must be handled carefully and infrequently, perhaps only by certain people. Firearms, ceramics, paintings are out of bounds, whether for safety or propriety. By refraining from running our fingers over everything in sight, we show deference to other inhabitant(s). In workspaces where space, equipment and facilities are shared, we are not at liberty to riffle through items on other people's desks or to enter certain spaces without permission. When we travel, we may feel temporary (illusory) ownership over our reserved seat, while a visit to the cockpit of a plane is an invitation-only treat. Sometimes not being allowed to touch is an expression of care. The interior can be a retreat and place of safety. In a hospital ward, hygiene and safety are paramount, as they are in a prison cell, albeit for different reasons. Constraints and denial can be self-imposed, too.

As well as the social rules and expectations which variously constrain and allow touch, tactile engagement with interiors develops over months, years and decades. We reach out and grasp a door knob, stair rail, drawer pull or light switch. When the light, or our eyesight, is insufficient, we feel our way around our homes, using familiarity and sense-memory. Touch over time is evidenced in patterns of wear, such as worn sections of floor in a heavily trafficked hall, next to a kitchen counter, by a bed, and threadbare soft furnishings such as chair arms. The decisions made by interior designers, and the choices we make for ourselves about the design of our homes directly condition this tactile experience without always anticipating its effects.

## Notes

1 For a remarkable study of how home feels, albeit not focused on touch, see P. J. J. Pennartz, 'Home: The Experience of Atmosphere' in I. Cieraad (ed.), *At Home: An Anthropology of Domestic Space* (Syracuse, NY: Syracuse University Press, 1999).

2 C. B. Dunne, *Interior Designing for all Five Senses* (London: St Martin's Press, 1998), pp. 3, 85.

3 J. Pallasmaa, *The Eyes of the Skin: Architecture and the Senses* (Chichester: Wiley, 2005).

4 P. Sparke, 'The Modern Interior: A Space, a Place or a Matter of Taste?', *Interiors*, 1:1 (2010), pp. 7–17.

5 For a precursor to nineteenth-century bourgeois notions of comfort, see J. E. Crowley, *The Invention of Comfort: Sensibilities and Design in Early Modern America* (Baltimore, MD: Johns Hopkins University Press, 2003). On nineteenth-century bourgeois notions of comfort, see K. C. Grier, *Culture and Comfort: Parlour Making and Middle-Class Identity, 1850–1930* (Washington, DC: Smithsonian Institution Press, 1988); D. Cohen, *Household Gods: The British and Their Possessions* (New Haven, CT and London: Yale University Press, 2006) and L. Young, *Middle-Class Culture in the Nineteenth Century: America, Australia and Britain* (Basingstoke: Palgrave Macmillan, 1992).

6 P. Sparke, A. Massey, T. Keeble and B. Martin (eds), *Designing the Modern Interior: From the Victorians to Today* (Oxford: Berg, 2009).

7 G. Lees-Maffei, 'Introduction: Professionalization as a Focus in Interior Design History', *Journal of Design History*, 21:1 (2008), pp. 1–18.

8 P. C. Johnson, *Mies van der Rohe* (New York: Museum of Modern Art, 1947), p. 49. Dieter Rams, 'Omit the Unimportant', *Design Issues*, 1:1 (Spring 1984), pp. 24–6. 'Less is more' was later replaced by postmodern architect Robert Venturi with 'Less is a bore': R. Venturi, *Complexity and Contradiction in Architecture* (New York: Museum of Modern Art, 2002 [1966]), p. 17.

9 A. Loos, 'Ornament and Crime', *Neue Freie Presse*, Vienna (January 1908). Reprinted in Le Corbusier's *Esprit Nouveau*, 1920. Just as the racial politics of this essay have been critiqued, so has its bibliographic history: see C. Long, 'The Origins and Context of Adolf Loos's "Ornament and Crime"', *Journal of the Society of Architectural Historians*, 68 (2009), pp. 200–23.

10 A. Loos, 'Das Schlafzimmer meiner Frau' ('My Wife's Bedroom') in *Kunst: Halbmonatschrift für Kunst und alles andere*, 1 (1903). See T. Gronberg, 'Haptic Homes: Fashioning the Modern Interior' in T. Gronberg, *Vienna: City of Modernity 1890–1914* (Bern: Peter Lang, 2007).

11 'Moderne' refers to an interwar style in interior design and decorative arts, between high modernism and consumerist variations on modernism as a style. See T. Washington, 'Moderne' in C. Edwards (ed.), *Bloomsbury Encyclopedia of Design*, vol. 2 (London: Bloomsbury 2016), p. 386; T. Benton, C. Benton and G. Wood (eds), *Art Deco 1910–1939* (London: Victoria & Albert Museum, 2003).

12 J. Pawson, 'Home Farm', www.johnpawson.com/works/home-farm website (accessed 31 March 2021). See also J. Pawson, *Minimum* (London: Phaidon, 2006); J. Pawson, *Anatomy of Minimum* (London: Phaidon, 2019). Pawson has also addressed the sense of touch with his textile collections and the sense of taste with his two cookbooks: J. Pawson and A. Bell, *Living and Eating* (New York: Clarkson Potter, 2001) and C. Pawson and J. Pawson, *Home Farm Cooking* (London: Phaidon, 2021).

13 B. Colomina, *Privacy and Publicity: Modern Architecture as Mass Media* (Cambridge, MA: MIT Press, 1994); B. Colomina, 'The Split Wall: Domestic Voyeurism' in B. Colomina (ed.), *Sexuality and Space* (New York: Princeton Architectural Press, 1992). B. Colomina (ed.), *The Century of the Bed* (Vienna: Verlag für modern

Kunst, 2014), pp. 18–23 mentions and illustrates Lina Loos's bedroom but does not discuss it. P. Sparke, *As Long as it's Pink: The Sexual Politics of Taste* (London: Pandora, 1995) refers to a telling scene in the documentary series *Signs of the Times* in which an architect's wife laments the loss of curtains in their shared house. The episode referred to is probably 'Marie Louise Collects Bric-a-Brac', *Signs of the Times*, directed by Nicholas Barker. 5 January 1992, 49 minutes, BBC. Available online at www.bbc.co.uk/iplayer/episode/p03rff4k/signs-of-the-times-marie-louise-collects-bricabrac (accessed 31 March 2021). For a discussion of women, windows, curtains and vulva, see M. M. Petty, 'Scopophobia/Scopophilia: Electric Light and the Anxiety of the Gaze in American Postwar Domestic Architecture' in R. Schuldenfrei (ed.), *Atomic Dwelling: Anxiety, Domesticity, and Postwar Architecture* (Abingdon: Routledge, 2012).

14  L. Sullivan, 'The Tall Office Building Artistically Considered' (1896) in R. Twombley (ed.), *Louis Sullivan: The Public Papers* (Chicago: University of Chicago Press, 1988). The Alessi company's postmodern retort to this was 'family follows fiction'; see Centro Studi Alessi, *F.F.F. Family Follows Fiction Workshop 1991/1993* (Crusinallo: F.A.O. S.p.A., 1993).

15  Le Corbusier, *Towards a New Architecture* (*Vers une Architecture*, 1924, Paris), trans. F. Etchells (London: The Architectural Press, 1927, 1952), p. 89, p. 100.

16  I. Crawford, *The Sensual Home: Liberate Your Senses and Change Your Life* (London: Quadrille, 2000), p. 15.

17  A305/13: 'Le Corbusier: Villa Savoye', written by T. Benton, directed by N. Levinson, produced by the BBC/Open University, aired 14 June 1975 on BBC2 as part of The Open University course A305, History of Architecture and Design 1890–1939, https://youtu.be/40I7y-3Wvcg (accessed 31 March 2021). This promenade experience might be seen, in retrospect, to anticipate Frank Lloyd Wright's continuously sloping art promenade for the Guggenheim Museum (1943–59) in New York City.

18  Le Corbusier and Pierre Jeanneret, Maison La Roche (1923–5) is one of two homes, known collectively as Les Villas La Roche-Jeanneret, and now housing Fondation Le Corbusier. I visited Villa Savoye and Maison La Roche in Paris, and the Wesisenhof Museum in houses designed by Le Corbusier as part of the 1927 Deutscher Werkbund exhibition 'Die Wohnung' (The Home) on the Weissenhof Estate in Stuttgart, Germany, as part of my embodied research for a broader project on hands and touch in design history and the history of design.

19  B. Latour, *Reassembling the Social: An Introduction to Actor Network Theory* (Oxford: Oxford University Press, 2005); A. Yaneva, 'Making the Social Hold: Towards an Actor-Network Theory of Design', *Design and Culture*, 1:3 (2009), pp. 273–88.

20  K. Fallan, 'Architecture in Action: Traveling with Actor-Network Theory in the Land of Architectural Research', *Architectural Theory Review*, 13:1 (2008), pp. 80–96, p. 87.

21  Le Corbusier, *Towards*, p. 115, p. 119.

22  *Ibid.*, p. 115, p. 245.

23  I experienced firsthand the comfort of Perriand, Le Corbusier and Jeanneret's Chaise Longue at the exhibition 'Charlotte Perriand: Inventing a New World', Fondation Louis Vuitton, Paris, 2 October 2019 to 24 February 2020, where examples of Perriand's furniture were available for visitors to sit and lie on, to enjoy a full-body experience of their ergonomic excellence.

24  P. Boudon, *Lived-In Architecture*, trans. Gerald Onn (Cambridge, MA: MIT Press, 1969), p. 2 cited in J. M. Malnar and F. Vodvarka, *Sensory Design* (Minneapolis: University of Minnesota Press, 2004), p. 68.

25  On the etymology of the word 'plastic', see J. L. Meikle, *American Plastic: A Cultural History* (New Brunswick, NJ: Rutgers University Press, 1995), p. 4.

26  Le Corbusier, *The Decorative Arts of Today* (*L'art décorative d'aujourd'hui*, 1925), trans. J. Dunnett (Cambridge, MA: MIT Press, 1987).

27  On sitting as touch see E. Lupton, 'Notes on Touch' in E. Lupton and A. Lipps, *The Senses: Design Beyond Vision* (New York: Princeton Architectural Press and Cooper Hewitt National Design Museum, 2018).

28  E. Kaufmann, Jr, *What is Modern Design?* (New York: Museum of Modern Art, 1950), p. 11; Meikle, *American Plastic*, p. 202.

29  P. J. T. Morris, *Polymer Pioneers: A Popular History of the Science and Technology of Large Molecules* (Philadelphia, PA: Chemical Heritage Foundation, 2005), p. 76; P. Sparke (ed.), *The Plastics Age: From Modernity to Post-Modernity* (London: Victoria & Albert Museum, 1990).

30  Later known as the 'Panton chair', it was produced by Vitra from 1967. www.vitra. com/en-gb/product/panton-chair (accessed 31 March 2021).

31  www.b-line.it/prodotti/woopy/ website (accessed 5 April 2021).

32  Based on direct personal experience of living with a variety of Eames chairs, in both plastic and fibreglass, DAR, RAR and DSR.

33  On Eero Saarinen's design of plastic chairs with upholstery for comfort see C. McAtee, 'Taking Comfort in The Age of Anxiety' in Schuldenfrei (ed.), *Atomic Dwelling*.

34  I. Halland, 'The Unstable Object: Glifo, Blow and Sacco at MoMA, 1972', *Journal of Design History*, 33:4 (December 2020), pp. 329–45, cites F. D. Scott, *Architecture or Techno-Utopia: Politics after Modernism* (Cambridge, MA: MIT Press, 2010), discussing M. Tafuri, 'Design and Technological Utopia' in E. Ambasz (ed.), *Italy: The New Domestic Landscape: Achievements and Problems of Italian Design* (New York: Museum of Modern Art, 1972), and M. Tafuri, *Architecture and Utopia: Design and Capitalist Development* (Cambridge, MA: MIT Press, 1976).

35  A. Loos, 'Architecture' (1910) in A. Loos, *On Architecture*, p. 78, cited in Gronberg, 'Haptic Homes', p. 101. On Adolf Loos, Le Corbusier, architecture and photography, see Colomina, *Privacy and Publicity*. On Loos and Corbusier, see Colomina, *Sexuality and Space*.

36  Lupton, 'Notes on Touch', p. 42.

37  Crawford, *The Sensual Home*, p. 66.

38  Kinfolk (N. Williams) and Norm Architects (J. Bjerre-Poulsen) (eds), *The Touch: Spaces Designed for the Senses* (Berlin: Die Gestalten Verlag, 2019), pp. 248–57.

39  M. Ogundehin, *Happy Inside* (London: Ebury Press, 2020).

40  C. Lieber, 'Calculated Chaos: Examining the Brilliant Strategy Behind Bed Bath & Beyond', *Racked.com* website, 26 February 2015. www.racked.com/ 2015/2/26/8110031/bed-bath-beyond-home-goods-market (accessed 1 April 2021).

41  See T. Chapman, 'Stage Sets for Ideal Lives: Images of Home in Contemporary Show Homes' in T. Chapman and J. Hockey (eds), *Ideal Homes: Social Change and Domestic Life* (London: Routledge, 1999). Chapman also refers to an episode of the BBC television series *Signs of the Times*, featuring the purchasers of a furnished show home.

42  See P. Sparke, B. Martin and T. Keeble (eds), *The Modern Period Room: The Construction of the Exhibited Interior, 1870 to 1950* (Abingdon: Routledge, 2006).

43  On Graceland as a mediated experience see J. Hari, *Stolen Focus: Why You Can't Pay Attention* (London: Bloomsbury 2022), pp. 1–5.

44  See D. Wood and R. J. Beck with I. Wood, R. Wood and C. Wood, *Home Rules* (Baltimore, MD and London: Johns Hopkins University Press, 1994).

45  On children's creativity with regard to interior affordances and design for children, see M. Gutman and N. De Coninck-Smith, *Designing Modern Childhoods: History, Space and the Material Culture of Children* (New Jersey: Rutgers University Press, 2008). For a recent examination of James J. Gibson's concept of affordances, as applied by Donald A. Norman to design, see J. L. Davis, *How Artifacts Afford: The Power and Politics of Everyday Things* (New Haven, CT: MIT Press, 2020).

# PART III

## Sensual economies

# 10

# Forging foam at the 1925 Paris Exhibition

*Claire I R O'Mahony*

In his famous analysis of the 1896 Berlin Trade Exhibition, Georg Simmel (1858–1918) identified a contrast between the desensitization of the producer and the sensorial overstimulation of the consumer amidst the spectacle of the world's fair.[1] The nomenclature of the 1925 Exposition Internationale des Arts Décoratifs et Industriels Modernes held in Paris signposted a purposeful attempt to reconcile these tensions between the seductive pleasures of interior decoration and the dehumanizing toil of standardized manufacture required by reconstruction after world conflict.[2] Sensorial experiences of the 1925 Exposition from the pyrotechnics of night illuminations to the haptic allure of luxury goods also activated overexcitement in the consumer engaging sight, touch, atmosphere, motion. Amidst this solipsistic feast, guidebooks and publicity materials directed visitors, and indeed subsequent scholars, to focus on a repertoire of iconic interiors that have come to typify stylistic and ideological polarities ascribed to interwar design. A symphony of caressing tactility amidst warm, plush, lavish hand-crafted organic leathers, patterned silks and hard woods immersed the individual visitor to the Salon in the Pavilion du Collectionneur orchestrated by Jacques-Émile Ruhlmann (1879–1933) and Pierre Patout (1879–1965) into a synaesthetic fantasy of sensual delight. Collective interiority could congregate amongst the unupholstered plain wood chairs around a table of instructive pamphlets in a worker's club designed by Alexander Rodchenko (1891–1956) amidst a bold colour scheme of red, black and white illuminated by transparent walls of glass and steel grids in the Soviet Pavilion designed by Konstantin Mel'nikov (1890–1974).[3]

Visitors strolling along on the Esplanade des Invalides who instead happened upon the Pavilion of Nancy and Eastern France situated between the Pavilions of the Sèvres National Manufactures, also designed by Patout with André Ventre (1874–1951), and of Lyon and Sainte Etienne, designed by Tony Garnier (1869–1948), encountered a sensorial environment where such ideological and design polarities cohabited. The Pavilion of Nancy and Eastern France, a large longitudinal iron and concrete tripartite environment, was 'surprising in its combination of energy and grace'.[4] One entered the structure through a permeable open-air octagonal central hall covered by an iron cupola supported by sixteen polished polygonal iron columns fluctuating between light and dark. Two metal and glass thresholds on either side afforded glimpses of two enclosed interiors, to the right, a commercial museum and, to the left, a conference hall.[5] In this 'iron' pavilion, pathways and thresholds signposted in stone, metal, paint and glass decoration connected these three symbolic interior spaces through strategies of 'flow', 'symbiosis' and 'foam'.[6] Methodological synergies between psychological theorizations of cognitive and spatial 'flow'; meditations on the 'symbiosis' of organic and industrial architectural modernist practices and the philosophical construct of 'foam' in which interpenetrating collective and isolated being facilitate the exploration of 'world forming' rival sensorial experiences and identities that coalesce, whilst remaining distinct, within the pavilion.

These intermediate spaces, thresholds and frameworks also express contiguities across rival identities forged by the creative industries and geopolitics of these borderlands, where microspheres (artisan, factory worker, educator, entrepreneur, politician, devasted regions) preserved their discreteness whilst cohabiting macrospheres (France, the Republic, Society). The sensorial experience of the pavilion embodied a material and ideological hybridity one might term as 'co-isolation' conceptualized by Peter Sloterdijk as 'foam':

> 'Society' is understood here as an aggregate of microspheres (couples, households, businesses, associations) of different formats that like the individual bubbles in a mountain of foam, border on one another, yet without being truly accessible or effectively separable from one another ... 'many chambers in the world' – but they have no doors ... The bubbles in foam ... are self-referentially constituted microcontinents ... Each of the symbiotic units is world forming in itself and for itself – alongside neighbouring groups of world formers who do the same in their own way and with whom they are drawn into an interactive network based on the principle of co-isolation.[7]

Valuable mineralogical deposits and ensuing concentrations of metallurgy industries had made Alsace and Lorraine the most prized war trophies in the Treaties of Frankfurt of 1871 and of Versailles in 1919.[8] Ensuing multiple mass migrations of materials, objects, populations, skills and businesses associated with both industrial arts and metallurgy displaced static identity politics into fluid microcontinents of 'co-isolation'.[9] This pavilion operated as a sensorial manifestation of this 'foam', enacting a fragile creative and geopolitical symbiosis. The medium of metal was deployed and mythologized both through the sculptural iconography of metalworking and makers and by sensorial experiences enacted when traversing the pavilion's membranous metallic thresholds (iron and glass doors, leaded stained glass). An overlooked protean interwar borderland culture existed where creative and economic localism aspired to international dialogue, far from the chauvinist parochialism traditionally ascribed to regionalism. The pavilion and the place it represented embodied a 'foam' forged by the interpenetration of micro-macrospheres.

## Sensorial memories: mediation as micro/macrosphere

Attempting a sensorial history of the Pavilion of Nancy and Eastern France might at first appear to be a fool's errand. Dismantled and then dispersed when the 1925 Exposition closed, the surviving material trace of this pavilion is a frieze painted by Victor Prouvé (1858–1943).[10] Postcards and Parisian press coverage mostly illustrated distant longitudinal perspectives in which even the complex proscenium decoration of the façade and domed roofline were hardly discernible, let alone the interiors. Interwar eastern French periodicals and reports on the Exposition yielded a richer harvest, including the architects' floorplan, sanguine sketches of Prouvé's panels and photographs of both the pavilion's construction and completed three interior zones. Rival economic and cultural formations of producers and consumers of industry and craft flowed through the iconographies and materials deployed in the pavilion's three interiors.

Inspired by the psychological frameworks of Mihaly Csikszentmihalyi, 'flow' has been persuasively positioned by Penny Sparke as a design strategy whereby the physical, professional and metaphorical permeability of architecture, interiority and landscape interpenetrate each other.[11] In the Pavilion of Nancy and Eastern France, this 'liquid modernity' was a sensorial experience communicated through fluid spatial dynamics and gradients in atmospheric luminosity. Decorative friezes in the three internal zones of the pavilion linked across an upper spatial register facilitating ambulatory and spectatorial flow echoed in metallic and glass thresholds at ground level. Haptic traces of the blacksmith's hammer and the painter's brush engaged the visitor in the living memory of the process of making. A sensorial history of a specific interior provides a strategy through which to address Sloterdijk's 'mischievous question' of Heideggerian 'being': 'When you say *Dasein* is thrown into the world, where is it thrown? What's the temperature there, the colour of the walls, the material that has been chosen, the technology for disposing of refuse, the cost of the air-conditioning and so on?'.[12] Archival and discursive research can divulge detailed traces of embodied experience of the 'where and what' of a historically located instance of 'being'. The embodied figuration and tactile traces of making in these friezes and thresholds of the Pavilion of Nancy and Eastern France expressed collaborative synergies between rival microspheres of professional identity (art/science; industry/craft). The co-isolation of multiple forms of creative labour required to reconstruct the devasted regions was represented figuratively as workers in metal, textile and construction long championed as equal, if different, collaborators by the École de Nancy. The immersive sensations of illumination and gloom, tactility and transparency, flow and rootedness across the pavilion's interiors enacted a volatile experience resonant with permeable borderlands, always both micro- and macrosphere, the quintessence of 'foam'.[13]

Since the 1880s, the École de Nancy had deployed hybrid pedagogies, practices and politics which informed the new economic models and creative questions in play in 1925. In defining the rubric of the Exposition, François Carnot (1872–1960) aligned the 'modern' with innovative metallic construction and the industrial arts in glass of Émile Gallé (1846–1904) within the Expositions of 1889 and 1900, both products of Lorraine.[14] In 1923, Carnot wrote directly to Prefects in each of the newly formed seventeen economic regions devised by Minister of Commerce Étienne Clémentel (1864–1936) and implemented by law in 1919. He invited them to form local committees to disseminate details of the aims of the Exposition, to identify 'artists, artisans, industrialists and editors who might contribute to its success' and to 'facilitate individual and collective participation from the region'.[15] The economic geographer Louis Lafitte (1873–1914) had originally proposed this zoning model and translated it into physical form in the transnational installations and events of the 1909 Exposition of Eastern France held in Nancy [Figure 10.1].[16] Low relief ornament of the façade of the Pavilion of Nancy and Eastern France echoed the 1909 Exposition, which had secured this contested economic zone one of the largest and more prominent footprints in the 1925 Exposition. On either side of the entrance, the arms of Nancy and Lorraine were emblazoned above a panel of kinetic cascades of metallic components.[17] For an eastern French observer, these dynamic cogs and wheels not only expressed the renewal of region's industrial prowess and interwar machine age aesthetics but also resonated with memories of the Nancy 1909 Eastern France Exposition. Actual standard wheels and girders produced by Lorrain industrial firms had been welded together to create a vast, yet delicate, iron lacework monumental entrance circular arch demonstrating how the collaboration of industry, craft and education could reimagine bloodied borderlands as a symbiotic microcontinent.

The Hachette guide to the 1925 Exposition offered glimpses of how the physical elements and visitor experience of the Pavilion of Nancy and Eastern France were understood through the complex interwar identity politics of this borderland microcontinent. The 'iron architecture' of Pierre Le Bourgeois (1879–1971) and Jean Bourgon (1895–1959) embodied the 'robust and energetic character of the inhabitants of the region'.[18] The vast open-air hall accessed through a colonnade of iron and steel

**Figure 10.1**    Commercial postcard of the façade of the Pavilion of Nancy and Eastern France at the 1925 Exposition des Arts Décoratifs et Industriels.

columns supported a sculpted frieze representing metalworkers by Émile J. Bachelet (1891–1982) which continued around the base of an iron cupola, 'giving an impression of power'.[19] Beneath this rotunda, an illuminated metal and glass fountain symbolized molten blast furnaces at work in Lorraine.[20] Two permeable thresholds to either wing extending from the rotunda were created by iron and glass doors forged by Jean Prouvé

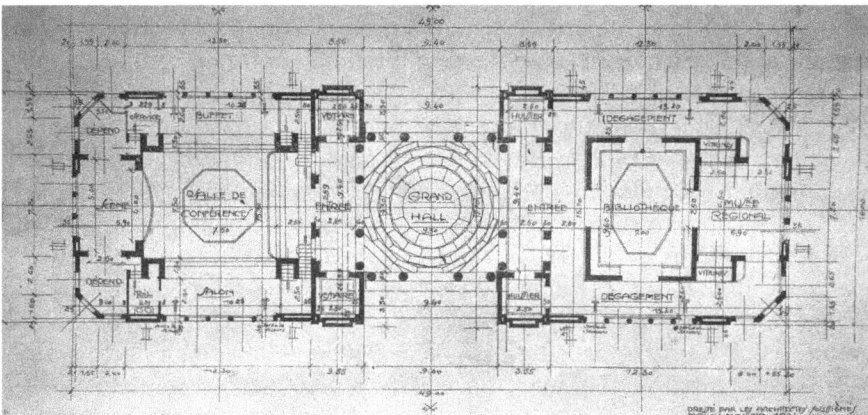

**Figure 10.2**    Floor plan of the Nancy and Eastern France Pavilion reproduced in *L'Est Illustré*, March 1925.

(1901–84) [Figure 10.2]. To the right, a commercial museum showcased regional products in vitrines below the frieze of ten painted panels by Victor Prouvé, celebrating collective spaces of production: mines, furnaces, ceramic, glass, printing and textile factories. To the left, in a hall with cinema-style flip-up seating designed by Auguste Vallin (1881–1967), visitors enjoyed conferences and concerts. A vast stained-glass wall by Jacques Gruber (1870–1936), visualizing a village being rebuilt, extended along the full length of the hall. In both wings, the visitor could leaf through educative periodicals seated in Majorelle cosy armchairs 'with a touch of coquetterie'.[21] The economic vitality of the eastern region was both represented decoratively and performed socially in this pavilion where producer and consumer experiences coalesced.

In his review of the 1925 Exposition, the art critic Waldemar George (1893–1970) objected to the typologies of the pavilions designed by the Société des Artistes Décorateurs, Pavilion de l'Ambassade Française and Le Pavilion du Collectionneur. He chastised this professional body and its members for being 'reactionary not only in their devotion to the "powers of money" but also in their failure to understand the needs that modern life imposes'.[22] He asked why had they not used the opportunity to create a 'Maison du Peuple'? The collaborative construction process, multiple functionalities and decorative registers of the Pavilion of Nancy and Eastern France took up his challenge. Its spatial flow, intimated by pathways of sculpted, forged, painted and vitreous figuration of Lorrainers rebuilding their devastated regions, articulated a microhistory of mixed economies of making and progressive, transnational cultural exchange distinctive to borderlands. Its fluid shifts between illumination and gloom reimagined labour and consumption as intersecting.

Gallan and Gibson have not only questioned the unchallenged 'binaristic conceptions' of dark and light but also alert us to how the sensorial experience of these polarities within interiors connote 'productivity' or 'recuperation'.[23] Their reassessment of the fluidity of the 'frontiers' of day and night positions light/dark intersectionality as multivalent; light is no longer the normative temporality of public work nor darkness a zone of 'deviance' or risk. This flow subverts conservative configurations of dark as a 'dangerous void' to be repressed.[24] The volatile sensorial experience across and around the Pavilion of Eastern France ebbed and flowed between multiple registers of luminosity, transparent and obstructed spatiality, immersion in auditory performance and internalized reading amidst representations of industrial and artisanal labour, museology and commerce, natural landscape and constructed shelter. Such permeability afforded potential encounters and collaborations across spatial, societal and temporal binaries, a fluidity central to the progressive pedagogic, professional and entrepreneurial practices of the École de Nancy and its interwar successors.

Eastern French press coverage celebrated the cooperation between multiple actors in the creation of the building. The construction was declared an 'intelligent initiative of two important Nancy firms to collaborate': the Pantz factory realizing the complex metal armature needed to materialize the architects' designs for multiple glass and metal domed ceiling structures and the firm of Gustave Simon (1868–1926), leftist Republican Mayor of Nancy (1914–19) and Vice-President of the Eastern France Committee, executing the brickwork and external harling.[25] Funded by the metallurgy and creative industries, the project was overseen by an alliance drawn from multiple localities and professions from across the region.[26] This committee combined surviving members of the École de Nancy's Provincial Alliance of Art Industries founded in 1901 with a second generation of the Daum, Majorelle, Prouvé and Vallin dynasties recently returned from their military service.[27] This neglected pavilion in the 1925 Exposition suggested that the foam of multiple professions, generations and consumers might collaborate to rebuild distinct microspheres into a borderland microcontinent. Immersion in the iconography and deployment of metal in the rotunda reveals how materiality expressed the progressive agendas of multiple generations of the École de Nancy.

## Flow and intermediary space: temporality in the rotunda

The directionality of Bachelet's metalworkers' posture propelled the visitor from the proscenium façade towards the open-air colonnaded rotunda at the centre of the pavilion embodying metallurgy as the core economic and cultural identity of the region. The continuance of Bachelet's sculpted workers in four further panels poised between the industrial metal of the rotunda's coffered ceiling, exposed rivets, massive columns and a furnace-fountain suspended the visitor in a spatial and temporal vortex of gravitas and dynamism [Figure 10.3]. Bachelet's representational idiom juxtaposed the grandeur of overlapping horsemen in the metopes carved by Phidias (480–430 BCE) for the Parthenon with the claustrophobic space of contemporary industrial work, affording a volatile spectatorial experience in the visitor. The centrifugal pull of the rolling machine anonymized the hunched bodies of Lorrain metallurgical workers, yet periodic individualizations of gaze and pose, a syncopated rhythm of caps and sabots interrupted this dehumanization. Bachelet's metalworkers, at once heroic and dystopian, static and kinetic, also resonated with the tympanum for Nancy's Université Populaire of 1902 where the muscularity of Victor Prouvé's blacksmith contested the confines of the architectural frame. This quotation signposted how the commercial museum in the 1925 pavilion sustained the idealism and pedagogic practices of the Provincial Alliance of Industrial Arts founded in Nancy in 1901.[28]

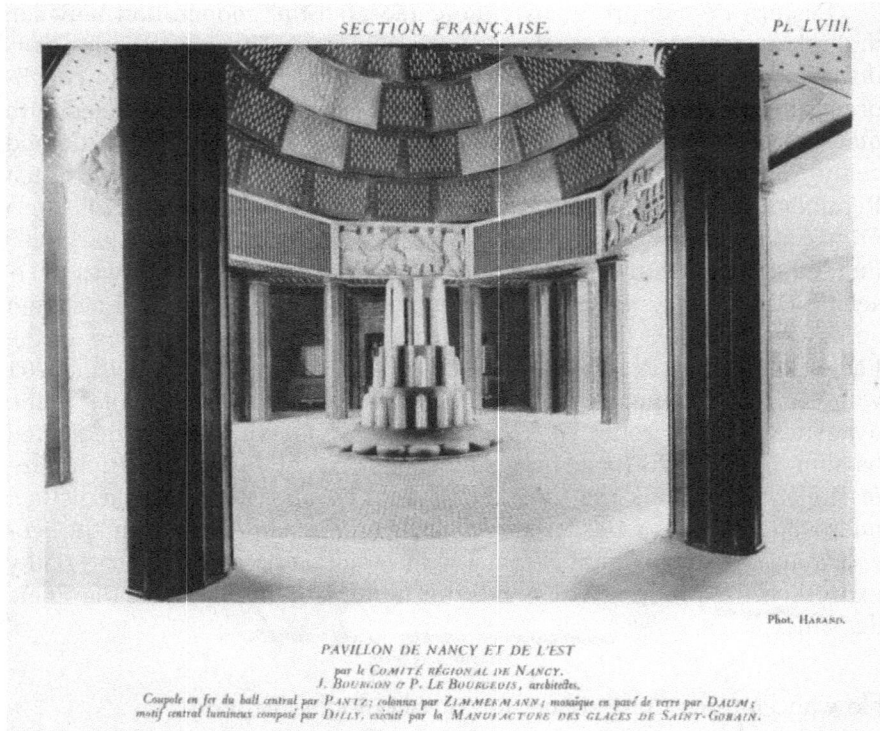

**Figure 10.3** Central rotunda of the Nancy and Eastern France Pavilion illustrated in *L'Encyclopédie des arts décoratifs et industriels modernes au xx siècle*, volume 2 (1927) as Plate LVIII (n.p.).

This collective promoted economic cooperation and workers' education as progressive strategies for creative industry. Founding members were all polymaths who taught evening classes at the Université Populaire incentivizing potential and employed decorative workers to enhance their skills and prospects. They persuaded Lorrain entrepreneurs to fund public competitions, such as the lingerie firm of Albert Heymann (1862–1940) which funded an embroidery competition for women makers for the 1925 Exposition.[29] The sensorial affects of the pavilion's tripartite interior space materialized the ideals of the École de Nancy, enacting a symbiosis where the potentially rival practices and temporalities of the metallurgy industries and industrial arts collaborated in the aspiration to create a better future for eastern France. Entering the collective space of the concert hall, consumer-visitors were immersed in coloured light and the auditory impact of performed music and speech. Illumination through the leaded membranes of stained glass both differentiated microspheres and connected them into a future macrosphere of reconstructed villages embedded in borderland landscape. This material and ideological 'foam' of co-isolation embodied the fragile interwar peace of this borderland microcontinent.

The transitional tripartite internal space materialized the therapeutic affect of 'flow' identified by Sparke with temporal and spatial freedom.[30] The sensorial experience of the pavilion suspended the visitor somatically and psychically. It connected interior and exterior space, light and dark, solid and liquid in metal and glass, the cognitive and gestural flow required by individual handicraft and collective industrial labour. However, the serial rupture of these borderlands also allowed for Sloterdijk's 'interactive network based on the principle of co-isolation'.[31] Durable peace amidst this reinvented economic region would require a pliancy embodied in the progressive identity politics of the pavilion. Such fluidity would soon prove impossible amidst the economic and ideological hardening of the 1930s.

The sensorial experience of metal and glass in the rotunda integrated flow and co-isolation through intersections of kinetic and static power, friction and glide, illumination and gloom. The grounded vertical force of the massive, fluted iron columns mediated between the circular motion of both the interlocking metal plates of the cupola's ceiling coffering and the mosaic floor. The tactility of exposed rivets suggested not only the tensile strength required to hold these axes in balance but also the malleable metal and worker's blows of their making. The vortex of cascading rivulets of the foundry/fountain, a modern Lorrain furnace of Vulcan, was arrested in suspended animation. The fluidity of these chimerical transformations of metal and glass from liquid and solid states expressed temporal and professional alliances between modernity and antiquity, craft and mass production and the confluence of sensorial experiences of makers and visitor-consumers.

The open-air colonnaded rotunda flowed through two translucent metal and glass thresholds designed and executed by Jean Prouvé into the commercial museum and meeting hall respectively. As Kishō Kurokawa (1934–2007), who participated in the post-war reconstruction of Japan through his project of Metabolism (c.1959–80), has persuasively argued, such 'intermediary space' can achieve a 'vibrant symbiosis that incorporates opposition' where opposing narratives of the 'age of the machine' and the 'age of life' coexist.[32] The symbiosis of the rotunda also informed the making and mediation of Prouvé's doors, in which the sensorial affordances of transparency and tactility mediated between craft traditions of the forge and modern metal construction.

## Forging foam: the Prouvés' intergenerational pedagogy and practice

The shadowy geometry of the massive metal and glass doors designed and executed by Jean Prouvé discernible in installation photographs of the rotunda space suit the received wisdom about his career. Most anglophone scholarship on Prouvé avoids considering his early years in Lorraine, his historiographical place being instead within modernist paradigmatic and Paris-centric narratives focused upon his roles in founding of Union des Artistes Modernes in 1929, innovating modular house construction and presiding over the Centre Pompidou competition in 1971.[33] However, a high-resolution illustration of the doors reproduced in a collector's album devoted to ironwork in the 1925 Exposition reveals how a sensorial inter-pretation of these thresholds better recognizes how in 1925 Prouvé's prac-tice itself was a threshold between historical and future trajectories of metalwork in Nancy [Figure 10.4].[34] The striking visual traces of Prouvé's hammer-blows demonstrate the vital importance of attempting to recuper-ate histories of the embodied sensorial experiences of an interior.[35] This illustration complicates our perception of the primacy of proto-modernist abstract pattern as the defining feature of these thresholds. These doors required interaction, where touch, temperature, weight, motion as well as the shifting visuality of transparency and opacity immersed the visitor-consumer in the sensorial experiences of materials and makers. These thresholds remained poised in time and space, connecting and dis-tinguishing between the making and consuming visualized within the dec-oration and in the use of the conference hall and the commercial museum. The illustration shows the irregular tactility of the surfaces of the central panels and frame of the doors – no 'age of the machine' smoothness here. Instead in the impact of the hammer-blow, 'the age of life' is eternalized in the metal.[36] The unsettling orthogonal compositional elements create a further disruption. Although these linear elements appear to be flush to the internal geometry of the frame and central panels, the ambiguity of their diagonal directionality pushes these two rectangles in and out of recession and projection, constantly flowing between two- and three-dimensional spatiality.

This sensorial volatility surely engaged the visitor viscerally in the process of creation by an individual maker. Prouvé's doors proposed a counternarrative to the principally visual delectation of symmetrical pat-terns favoured by proponents of oxyacetylene welding Edgar Brandt (1880–1960) and Raymond Subes (1893–1970). Metalwork attracted the attention of many critics' responses to the 1925 Exposition, which often juxtaposed Prouvé and Brandt, contrasting their ideals and practices. In the popular science journal *Nature*, Jacques Boyer typified the gen-eral acclaim accorded to Brandt and Subes, relishing the mechanics of new tools and working practices. He concluded by pondering what Jean Lamour (1698–1771), the master ironworker of the gilded Rococo metal grilles of Nancy's Place Stanislas, could have done with the opportunities of these technologies, exhorting 'an industrialization of this art in our country. Thanks to the serialization of models, simplified and perfectly adapted to use, sober and graceful ironwork will soon replace the glitzy

**Figure 10.4**  Door designed in glass and iron forged by Jean Prouvé (1901–84) for the central open-air rotunda of the Pavilion of Nancy and Eastern France 1925 illustrated as Plate 10 in Henri Clouzot, *La ferronerie moderne* (Paris: Ch. Moreau, 1925).

fake objects and *décorations-similis* which render *les homes modestes* ugly'.[37] Guillaume Janneau (1887–1981), future director of the National Manufactures of Beauvais, Gobelins and Sèvres and later professor at the Conservatoire des Arts et Métiers, characterized two distinct paths for modern metalwork, aligning Brandt's adoption of the new welding process with Delacroix's 'great art of effect produced by any means … the concretisation of vast ideas' whereas Prouvé's artistry 'was grounded in execution ... and the power to stir emotion, to engage through the direct address of his making'.[38] Janneau captures the sensorial history embodied in the 'rough beauty of the materiality and labour' expressed in 'the great blows frankly imprinted on this hard material' in Prouvé's doors.[39]

The metalwork of both Jean Prouvé and Brandt was rewarded by the 1925 Exposition's Jury with an honourable mention and medal respectively. The methods and environments in which each practised and promoted their metalwork signified how the experience of war in eastern France had transformed each man's relationship to the medium. Brandt's innovations in munitions design secured him both financial and reputational advantages that culminated in private, corporate and national war memorial commissions. His figurative idiom deployed in symbolic revanchist sites reveals the distance between Brandt's stance and the progressive microcontinent suggested by Prouvé's abstracted, yet embodied, thresholds in the Pavilion of Nancy and Eastern France. Prouvé's experience of lightweight metal construction for war production of bicycles, automobiles and aviation would inform his principles of fluid, serial, economical and transportable construction. However, this standardization was never at the cost of the wellbeing of the metalworkers themselves. Both men had created workshops just after the war; their contrasting employment practices underlined the political distance between them. Brandt's impressive commercial premises opened in 1919 with separate hierarchal entrances for clients and workers embodying a business inspired by a Fordist division of labour with migrant workers hired on piecework contracts.[40] Prouvé opened his first workshop in Nancy in 1923, where the rationalization of collaborative work was translated into profits shared collectively by all employees. Brandt's oxyacetylene welding ensured cost-efficient serial production of furnishing, fittings and screens which were ubiquitous across the elite interiors of the exhibition. Prouvé made three sets of doors: two for the Pavilion of Nancy and Eastern France and a third for the stand of the École des Beaux-Arts of Nancy, environments that celebrated the cohabitation of collective industrial and individual craft identities.

Jean Prouvé's own transformation from artistic ironworker and locksmith to 'constructor' was witnessed in the changing nomenclature and graphic design of his letterhead and stamp.[41] His acquisition of machines for electric-arc welding, punching, trimming, grinding, polishing and folding have been positioned as the key actors in his reconfiguration. However, in a 1980 interview Jean also championed the importance of the embodied learning strategies and 'worker-participation' he experienced during his apprenticeships in the workshops of Émile Robert (1860–1924) in Enghien.[42] Victor Prouvé had entrusted his son Jean to Robert, who fostered imagination and egalitarian comradeship in the workshop, core tenets of Victor's own restructuring of the syllabus and practice of Nancy's art school. By contrast, Jean recounted walking out after only one week working for Subes, whose dehumanizing treatment of young staff and the misapplication of new technologies such as the acetylene welding torch felt intolerable. Student recollections of Jean's performative drawing during his lessons at the Conservatoire National des Arts et Métiers in Paris in the 1960s stressed his commitment to embodied thinking and craft processes in his pedagogy and practice.[43]

Prouvé's evolving practice was generated not only by the acquisition and use of machines but also by earlier intergenerational and transnational networks congregating and conversing in Nancy. As Dutch designer-architect Theo van Doesburg (1883–1931) declared: 'We think of Nancy as an artistic city worthy of being a centre for aesthetic propaganda'.[44] Having experienced the slow process of reconstruction ensuing from conflict in the 1870s, Victor Prouvé forged new pedagogic aims as Director of the École des Beaux-Arts (1919–39), instilling interdisciplinary approaches to practical skills, better preparing young Lorrainers to enter craft and industrial professions available amidst limited materials in the devastated regions. These formal institutional networks facilitated a second generation of popular education as well. George Sadoul (1904–67) formed the Comité Nancy-Paris which involved the older generation of the École de Nancy alongside a band of youthful veterans of the trenches, all engaged in the enlightened pedagogic traditions and collective working practices encouraged by formations in this culture of polymaths. The synergies amongst these fathers and sons ensured that the people of Nancy experienced the latest examples and debates about modern creativity at first hand, from the modern architecture of André Lurçat (1894–1970) to projections of *L'Inhumaine* the 1924 film directed by Marcel L'Herbier (1888–1979) and surrealist painting.

In 1923, Victor Guillaume (1880–1942), a key member of the Comité Nancy-Paris, published an arresting article about Prouvé's ironwork in Nancy's main broadsheet newspaper, *L'Est Républicain*. Embodied sensation pulsates throughout the piece, the grip of Prouvé's 'strong, calloused hands' and the movement of his 'outdoor athletic body' imprints itself on the materiality of the metal object, 'malleable and resistant, ductile and tenacious'.[45] The first ingot held by adolescent Jean is an 80-kilo projectile of rail track which crashed into the Prouvé family home and studio during the aerial bombardment of Nancy. Guillaume aligns ironwork with a new collective architecture of reinforced concrete, deriving from the genius of both thousands of anonymous artisans and the spirits of Émile Gallé and his own tutor in wood carving, Eugène Vallin (1856–1922). Amidst the puff of the bellows, the rhythm and clang of the mallet, the heat and energy of the forge, Prouvé's ironwork embodies 'A new order which under the influence of science, hygiene and sports, variations of private or public fortunes, dominates the intense life of today'.[46] The vestigial sensorial experience of Prouvé's hammer-blow reverberated in the effort required to open these massive doors to enter the side wings of the pavilion, engaging the visitor in the physicality of this new way of living.

The 1925 Pavilion of Nancy and Eastern France demonstrated this now largely forgotten politically engaged context through the sensorial experiences enacted by the interior design choices intersecting across its three zones. Multiple seating formats of the conference hall and commercial museum catered to distinct publics. The cinema-style flip-up collective seating designed by Auguste Vallin resonated with the innovative performances orchestrated by the Comité Nancy-Paris, alongside armchairs for improving reading by Louis Majorelle (1859–1926). Antonin Daum (1864–1931) championed the use of his new colour-infused industrial glass manufactured using the latest technologies, not only in tesserae of the circular mosaic flooring of the central rotunda but also in the ceiling light and stained-glass wall created by Jacques Gruber [Figure 10.5].[47] This radiant space of encounter and exchange contrasted boldly with the chiaroscuro juxtapositions of the fountain-furnace of the central rotunda. Gruber's translucent vista of the reconstruction of Lorraine located the participant-consumer in a vista of a brighter future during the events hosted in this meeting hall. Metal was transfigured from the contrasting centrifugal forces of columns and coffered ceiling

**Figure 10.5**   Concert hall with stained-glass wall designed by Jacques Gruber (1870–1936) in the Pavilion of Nancy and Eastern France, 1925.

constraining Bachelet's metalworkers into a lacework of lead membranes connecting and differentiating the materials, makers and landscapes of the devasted regions. This encounter with a mutuality particular to contested borderlands resonated with the interdependent fragility Sloterdijk ascribed to 'foam':

> In this framework of stable-unstable, large polyhedrons, it is potentially impossible for any one cell to burst without tearing the whole construct along with it into nothingness. These tragic geometries contain such a high degree of internal tension, tensegrity, between the remaining co-isolated spaces that their shared existential risk can be expressed in a co-fragility formula.[48]

## Epilogue

Victor Prouvé chose to use a sanguine crayon for his sketches for the ten panels for the pavilion's commercial museum reproduced in *L'Est Illustré*. The haptic sensoriality of this medium suffused his frieze of modern workplaces where metalwork, textiles and glass were made and consumed [Figure 10.6]. Gestural movements and postures of makers flow across the discrete practices represented in each panel. Sloterdijk's 'interactive network based on the principle of co-isolation' is materialized in Prouvé's

**Figure 10.6**    Musée Commercial with frieze painted on linoleum by Victor Prouvé (1858–1943) in the Pavilion of Nancy and Eastern France, 1925.

painted 'chambers' of creative work: interiors where designer, lace-maker, embroiderer, textile-worker and modern consumer were connected and yet remained self-contained in their respective tasks and pleasures. Painted on the backs of mass-produced linoleum flooring sheets, each panel was easily demountable in preparedness for their return and reuse in the devasted regions. The Pavilion of Nancy and Eastern France deployed the sensorial experience of metal and glass to signify materials, makers and participant-consumers as generators of the region's economic industrial might as well as therapeutic self-realization through craft. Contrasting practices of manufacture and interactive use across the exhibition's multiple thresholds attested to sensorial history's revelation of how ideological stances can be experienced through designed environments. Experiences of metal and glass captured synergies flowing between learning, making and consuming expressed through contrasts of illumination and gloom, tactile weight and kinetic translucency. As fixities of geopolitical and disciplinary borders in the wake of tragedy are once more being mobilized, might the sensorial traces of these microspheres suggest counternarratives where tolerant, hybrid fluidity imagines strategies for symbiotic coexistence?

## Notes

1  G. Simmel. 'The Berlin Trade Exhibition' (1896) translated in 'Appendix' in A. Geppert, *Fleeting Cities Imperial Expositions in Fin-de-Siècle Europe* (New York: Palgrave Macmillan, 2010), p. 284.
2  Anonymous, 'Programme de l'Exposition', *Rapport Général*, I (1925), 95, http://cnum.cnam.fr/CGI/fpage.cgi?4XAE94.1/99/100/324/103/303 (accessed 1 March 2019).
3  V. Paperny, 'Chapter 9: Temporary Architecture and Life Building, 1925–40' in A. Aronova and A. Ortenberg (eds), *A History of Russian Exposition and Festival Architecture: 1700–2014* (Abingdon: Routledge, 2018), pp. 188–91.
4  'Le Pavillon de Nancy à l'Exposition de Paris', *L'Immeuble et La Construction dans l'Est* (5 July 1925), n.p.
5  The building's footprint of 50 by 16 metres sat within an 800 square metre site; the façade was 4 metres in height.
6  P. Sparke, P. Brown, P. Lara-Betancourt, G. Lee and M. Taylor (eds), *Flow: Interior, Landscape, and Architecture in the Era of Liquid Modernity* (London: Bloomsbury, 2018); K. Kurokawa, *The Philosophy of Symbiosis* (London: Academy Editions, 1994); and P. Sloterdijk, *Foams: Spheres Volume III: Plural Spherology*, trans. W. Hoban (Los Angeles: Semiotext(e), 2016).
7  Sloterdijk, *Foams*, p. 56.
8  The destruction of almost 70 per cent of metallurgy factories (2,238 out of 3,265) in the annexed zones of eastern France by retreating German forces in 1918 and the accessioning of mining and manufacturing in Germany's Saarland for nine years to France as reparation underlined the centrality of metal manufacturing in the recalibration of economic and diplomatic power structures. G. Eisenmenger, *La Lorraine au Travail* (Paris: Librarie Pierre Roger, 1925), p. 217 ; V. Prott, *The Politics of Self-Determination: Remaking Territories and National Identities in Europe, 1917–1923* (Oxford: Oxford University Press, 2016).

9 When required to opt for French or German nationality by the Treaty of Frankfurt approximately 70 per cent of Lorrains and 10 per cent of Alsatians in the annexed regions migrated to France, 8,614 settled in Nancy composed of business owners, their employees and over 2,000 skilled manual workers (pre-1873 population of Nancy: 6,965) according to H. Sicard-Lenattier, *Les Alsaciens-Lorrains à Nancy 1870–1914: une ardente histoire* (Haroué: Gérard Louis, 2000), pp. 45–78, 92–9.

10 V. Thomas, 'Études', *Révue du Louvre*, 5:4 (December 2008), pp. 82–6.

11 Sparke et al., *Flow*, p. xvii.

12 B. Latour, 'Spheres and Networks: Two Ways to Reinterpret Globalization. Transcription of a Lecture at Harvard University Graduate School of Design, 17 February', *Harvard Design Magazine*, 30 (2009), www.harvarddesignmagazine.org/issues/30/spheres-and-networks-two-ways-to-reinterpret-globalization (accessed 28 April 2021).

13 A. Calvera, 'Local, Regional, National, Global and Feedback: Several Issues to Be Faced with Constructing Regional Narratives', *Journal of Design History*, 18:4 (2005), pp. 371–83; G. Adamson, G. Riello and S. Teasley, *Global Design History* (New York: Bloomsbury, 2011).

14 Carnot was President of the Union Centrale des Arts Décoratifs (1910–59) and of the 1925 Exposition General Committee. Original typescript, D2 96, Musée des Arts Décoratifs Paris, published as F. Carnot, 'L'Exposition des Arts Décoratifs et Industriels Modernes', *La Revue Bleue*, Année 61, vol. 23 (Oct. 1923), p. 687.

15 Archives Departmentales Meurthe et Meuse 8 M 26.

16 L. Lafitte, 'L'Evolution économique de la Lorraine', *Annales de géographie*, 21:120 (1912), pp. 393–417; B. Damamme-Gilbert, 'The 1909 Nancy International Exhibition: Showcase for a Vibrant Region and Swansong of the Ecole de Nancy', *Art on the Line* (special issue: Emile Gallé and la Lorraine Artiste), 1:5 (2007) www.bristol.ac.uk/artontheline/journal_20071/articles/pdf/20071_05.pdf (accessed 18 May 2021).

17 Anonymous, 'Le Pavillon de Nancy à l'Exposition de Paris', *L'Immeuble et La Construction dans l'Est* (5 July 1925).

18 Anonymous, 'L'Exposition en 6 Visites', *Guide Hachette* (Paris: Hachette, 1925), pp. 325–6.

19 'L'Exposition en 6 Visites', p. 326.

20 'Le Pavillon de Nancy à l'Exposition de Paris' (5 July 1925).

21 'L'Exposition en 6 Visites', p. 326.

22 W. George. 'L'Exposition des Arts Décoratifs et Industriels de 1925: Les tendances générales', *L'Amour de l'Art*, 8 (August 1925), pp. 285–6.

23 B. Gallan and C. Gibson, 'Commentary', *Environment and Planning A: Economy and Space*, 43:11 (2011), pp. 2509–15. See also T. Edensor, *From Light to Dark Daylight, Illumination and Gloom* (Minneapolis, MN: University of Minnesota, 2017).

24 Gallan and Gibson, 'Commentary', p. 2514.

25 'Le Pavillon de Nancy à l'Exposition Internationale des Arts Décoratifs de 1925', *L'Est Illustré* (29 March 1925), p. 7. The columns were manufactured by Ateliers Zimmermann of Nancy; the glass and iron cupola was forged by Louis Beyssen. The Glaceries de Cirey-Saint-Gobain created the metal and glass light feature. The mosaic floor utilized a new industrial glass produced by Daum. Four polished granite seating fixtures were carved by Roches frères of Senones. 'Le Pavillon de Nancy à l'Exposition de Paris' (5 July 1925).

26 Archives Departmentales Meurthe et Moselle 8 M 26.

27 C. Coley, 'L'effort moderne à Nancy dans les années vingt: Chronique du comité Nancy-Paris', *Le Pays Lorrain*, 67:1 (January–March 1986), pp. 5–20; C. Coley and D. Pauly (eds), *Quand l'architecture internationale s'exposait 1922–1932* (Lyon: Fage Éditions, 2007).

28  Nancy Galeries Poirel, *L'Ecole de Nancy, 1889–1909: Art nouveau et industries d'art* (Nancy: Réunion des Musées Nationaux, 1999); Musée de l'Ecole de Nancy, *L'Ecole de Nancy Art nouveau et industrie d'art* (Paris: Éditions Somogy, 2018); Musée des Beaux-Arts, *Victor Prouvé 1858–1943* (Paris: Gallimard; Nancy: Ville de Nancy, 2008).
29  'Concours de Broderie', *L'Est Républicain* (3 March 1925), p. 2.
30  Sparke et al., *Flow*, p. xvii.
31  Sloterdijk, *Foams*, p. 56.
32  Kurokawa, *The Philosophy of Symbiosis*, p. 29.
33  C. Wilk, 'Jean Prouvé: The Poetics of the Technical Object', *The Journal of Modern Craft*, 1:3 (2008), pp. 423–6.
34  C. Coley, *Jean Prouvé en Lorraine* (Nancy: Presses universitaires de Nancy; Archives de l'architecture Lorraine, 1991); C. Froment. 'La ferronnerie à Nancy dans l'entre-deux guerres' in *Jean Prouvé* (Nancy: Musée des Beaux-Arts, Paris: Somogy Éditions d'Art, 2012), pp. 169–75; B. Otter and J. Perrin, 'Jean Prouvé ferronnier d'art' in *Jean Prouvé* (Nancy: Musée des Beaux-Arts, Paris: Somogy Éditions d'Art, 2012), pp. 159–68.
35  Plate 10 in H. Clouzot, *La ferronerie moderne* (Paris: Ch. Moreau, 1925).
36  Kurokawa, *The Philosophy of Symbiosis*, p. 29.
37  J. Boyer, 'La Ferronnerie d'Art et sa technique actuelle', *Nature*, 2701 (9 January 1926), p. 28; R. Froissart-Pezone, *L'art dans tout: Les arts decoratifs en Europe et l'utopie d'un art nouveau* (Paris: CNRS Editions, 2004).
38  G. Janneau, *Le fer à l'Exposition internationale des arts décoratifs modernes* (Paris: Contet, 1925), p. 1.
39  *Ibid.*, p. 3.
40  Brandt's premises were located on the corner of rue Erlanger and 101 Boulevard Murat in Paris. J. Kahr, *Edgar Brandt Art Deco Ironwork* (Argler: Schiffer Publishing, [1999] 2010), pp. 46; 57.
41  P. Sulzer, *Jean Prouvé Complete Works*, vol. 1 (Basel and Boston, MA: Birkhäuser, 1999), pp. 18–19.
42  The Musée des Arts Décoratifs staged a Robert retrospective as a preamble to the 1925 Exposition. T. Harlor, *Les Fers Forgés d'Émile Robert* (Paris: Éditions Gazette des Beaux-Arts, 1925).
43  G. Querrien, 'L'enseignement de Prouvé, transmission d'une culture constructive' in H. Vacher and C. Bauer (eds), *Jean Prouvé, de l'atelier à l'enseignement transmission d'une culture technique. Cahiers du LHAC*, 1:1 (2014), pp. 21–35.
44  Coley, 'Comité Nancy-Paris', p. 20.
45  V. Guillaume, 'Le Ferronnier Jean Prouvé', *L'Est Républicain* (7 April 1923).
46  *Ibid.*
47  A. Daum, 'Les Industries d'Art de Nancy Avant et Depuis la Guerre', *Mémoire de l'Académie Stanislas* (1924), p. 62, https://gallica.bnf.fr (accessed 1 November 2020).
48  Sloterdijk, *Foam*, p. 48.

# 11

# The stimulating atmosphere of the English public house, c.1945–75

*Fiona Fisher*

In the aftermath of the Second World War, English pub owners and breweries were faced with the task of rebuilding war damaged pubs and the chance to develop new pubs within such unfamiliar architectural settings as modern office blocks and shopping precincts, among others. Acknowledging a growing distinction between a pub's architectural setting and its interior design *The Architectural Review* observed that while a pub's context might now be unconventional, 'the atmosphere to be created inside it must be one that people feel is orthodox – at least it must not seem too unfamiliar'.[1] Similarly, the architect Basil Oliver, in his book *The Renaissance of the English Public House*, considered the relationship between design and comfort. 'The Englishman', he claimed, 'loves a sense of cosiness, warmth and security, and although to meet modern requirements rooms must be loftier and windows larger than in the traditional pub, the architect should endeavour to create such an atmosphere, or design his rooms in such a way that the atmosphere may grow'.[2] As such, the major challenge for the post-war pub designer was understood to be that of negotiating the pub's long history to create a credible pub ambience within such new architectural settings.

Atmosphere has been understood as an elusive, borderless or boundary-blurring phenomenon that encompasses emotional, sensory, social and spatial experience and which mediates the relationship between the body and the interior.[3] The positioning of atmosphere within discussions about modern public house design brought certain aspects of the sensory experience of the interior to the fore. Oliver's referencing of lofty rooms and large windows speaks to the hygienic reform of the pub, which had gathered pace in the interwar years, and it was often within discussions about modernization that sensory references to the pub's interior atmosphere appeared. Having visited northern England to see the latest in pub design in 1944, one Labour member of the committee for War Damaged Licensed Premises and Reconstruction, for example, reported having seen 'some most pleasant modern premises' with 'none of the stuffy, smelly "pub" atmosphere'.[4] However, for some public house customers the smell of the interior was a satisfying, emotionally resonant attribute of the social setting. As one writer to *The Builder* put it, in 1950, reflecting wider contemporary concerns over a lack of comfort in modern public house design: 'What is wanted in a pub is atmosphere – the pleasant smell of beer and baccy, not hygiene and disinfectant'.[5] While such remarks can be placed within the context of a longer history of deodorization and sanitary reform, it was in relation to changing post-war design practices that other sensory aspects of the pub's atmosphere began to be considered more fully.[6]

Focusing on examples of English pub interiors of the 1960s and 1970s, this chapter explores some of the ways in which their designers sought to engage the senses to create profitable and meaningful connections with consumers. It begins by considering how sensory experience figured in writings on pub design and within a wider context of discussions of interior design practice and education. It then looks at the work of a single designer, Ivan Speight, who was known for creating pub interiors in Victorian style, and at a model of interior for the larger pub, the indoor street scene or streetscape. These two examples, drawn from the mainstream of English pub design, both aimed to evoke a familiar pub atmosphere and attract a wide range of customers. While they can offer only a partial view of the sensorial strategies employed – those favoured by the designers of youth-oriented disco-pubs, for example, offer a radically different perspective – they provide useful insights into the entry of interior designers into the sphere of pub design and point to an emphasis on customer experience and an acknowledgement of the pub as a complex multisensory environment that helped shape new approaches to its design.

## Evolving practices of public house design

Writing in the foreword to F. W. B. Yorke's book *The Planning and Equipment of Public Houses* (1949), as a corrective to Yorke's highly practical and somewhat austere manifesto, the architect Clough Williams-Ellis expressed his wish that Yorke had been 'more explicit on this most interesting, illusive and important matter of atmosphere'.[7] Williams-Ellis went on to suggest that designing modern pubs of efficiency and comfort perhaps required 'two parents – of which the technical specialist would clearly be the father, someone less of a plumber and more of a poet, the mother'.[8] He noted that several progressive brewers had begun to test 'such pub-producing methods', dividing responsibility for the functional elements of a design from those undertaken by the 'ensemble producer', whose chief role was to create a relaxing setting for the customer.[9]

Another significant context in which the pub's atmosphere was considered was that of the architectural press, notably *The Architectural Review* which from the late 1940s played a leading role in establishing parameters for modern public house design.[10] Drawing on historical examples, it argued that 'interior pub design is more a matter of the right kind of furnishings, equipment, colour and material than of the architectural framework within which they are contained' and suggested 'intimacy and enclosure; interrupted vistas; mirrors and reflections; strong varnished colours; bold lettering; barrels and bottles; brightly coloured labels and advertisements' as its key constituents.[11] Interior pub design was in this way understood chiefly as a visual tradition directed at 'creating the right visual atmosphere'.[12] While Williams-Ellis, writing in the late 1940s, had understood the 'ensemble producer' as an architect, the post-war years were ones in which the professional landscape of design and associated 'pub-producing' methods were changing. As interior designers began to bring their specialist knowledge to the business of pub design, often working as consultants or alongside brewery architects, both the multisensory nature of the ensemble and the affective qualities of individual elements of a pub's interior design were explored for their potential to ease or stimulate the consumer.

*Inscape: The Design of Interiors*, edited by Hugh Casson and published by The Architectural Press in 1968, defined interior design as 'a field of design where all the physical senses are simultaneously alerted and at work' and understood space perception as multisensory, writing that 'space is *heard*, it is *smelt*, and it is *felt*'.[13] Sensory experience of such everyday spaces as pubs also came into focus within the intersecting and developing interdisciplinary field of environmental psychology.[14] A report on a summer school on alcoholism at Birmingham University in 1969, for example, noted one participant psychologist's view that 'the noise and smell of a pub, the feel of a glass and the chinking of bottles' had the same potential to relieve anxiety among drinkers as the alcohol itself, acknowledging the complexity of the social setting and its affective qualities.[15]

Within the sphere of retailing, efforts were also being made to develop a more systematic understanding of the effects of retail settings on the purchasing decisions of consumers. As Philip Kotler observed, in an influential article on 'Atmospherics as a Marketing Tool',

> One of the most significant features of the total product is the *place* where it is bought or consumed. In some cases, the place, more specifically the *atmosphere* of the place, is more influential than the product itself in the purchase decision. In some cases, the atmosphere is the primary product.[16]

In the case of eating and drinking environments sensory enjoyment was central to their success. As one hotel and catering trade representative explained, it was 'the one industry where all five senses have to be excited and appeased at the same time in well-planned form'.[17]

The structure of the licensed retail trade was also changing. Within the evolving organizational forms of the major breweries, in which English pub ownership began to be concentrated from the 1960s, a convergence of design and marketing functions positioned the pub interior ever more closely in relation to sales.[18] Associated with these productive expectations, the lifespan of commercial interiors began to shorten as the influence of Pop lifestyles, with their desire for novelty and stimulation, began to inform the creation of pub interiors for instant effect.[19] Noting the rapid pace of change, the architect and designer Misha Black suggested that the interior of a shop or restaurant was unlikely to last twenty-five years and often considerably less.[20]

## Acceptable authenticity: Ivan Speight's London pub 'Victoriana'

Ivan Speight qualified with a National Diploma in Design (Decorating and Interior Decorating) in 1958 and went on to specialize in pub design. Described as 'London's foremost designer of Victoriana', his projects from the 1960s and 1970s included the refurbishment of original Victorian pub interiors and the creation of new pubs within buildings of modern architectural design.[21] He completed several interiors for the Finch's chain, which owned thirty-five pubs in and around London by the early 1970s.[22] At The Hoop in Notting Hill, a modern pub that replaced an earlier pub of the same name, Speight created 'a spacious yet cosy' bar that was recognisable as the old pub 'but with some new and more comfortable seating and a gorgeous dark maroon-patterned paper on the ceiling and spotlights accentuating the darker corners'.[23] Speight considered the use of colour and theatrical lighting as central to the success of a pub interior and often drew on a colour palette of bright or dark reds and browns. As one article on Finch's described, 'Shining brass, glittering mirrors [...] highly polished wood, pillar-box red and brown paintwork' characterized his work for the firm.[24] While Speight's colour choices referenced those used within many late nineteenth-century pub interiors, they were made not only for reasons of style but with an understanding of the role of colour in creating the intimacy and cosiness that traditional pub customers desired.

Elaine Denby, in the Country Life book *Interior Design* of 1963, suggested that colour was perhaps 'the most powerful factor in defining the character and setting the mood' of sites of leisure and recreation.[25] While recognizing the affective quality of colour, contemporary guides such as Denby's often understood colour selection to be intuitive. In *Interior Design*, a Penguin handbook of 1964, Diana Rowntree noted that whereas much was 'said and implied about the psychological effects of colours [...] virtually nothing is known about the subject scientifically'.[26] A more scientific basis for colour selection was suggested in an *Interior Design* article of 1973, which, in considering the creation of the 'right' atmosphere for a pub, contended that '[w]arm "thirsty" colours are generally more appropriate than stark clinical whites or "cool" colours. Strong contrasts in yellows, browns, and reds are excellent to stimulate thirst'.[27] While no supporting evidence was offered, this suggestion of a close relationship between the visual experience of colour and contrast and the stimulation of thirst suggests a belief in the commercial potential of colour to activate the senses in support of commercial aims. Speight's designs were highly successful, one refurbished pub reportedly increasing its profits by 201 per cent in the first few months after reopening, the report itself indicating a direct expectation for a redesigned interior to enhance sales.[28]

Speight's mid-1970s interiors for The Witness Box, situated on the ground floor of a modern office block in London's Holborn, aimed to create a sense of familiarity and an impression of long existence in a modern architectural setting [Figure 11.1]. Designed for Watney's brewery, the pub's interiors were described as a 'fake-up' by their designer.[29] Speight lined the concrete shell of the building with natural materials, using second-hand London stock bricks to clad the concrete columns,

**Figure 11.1**  The interior of The Witness Box, designed by Ivan Speight, *Interior Design* (February 1978), p. 80.

fibrous plaster for the ceilings, cornices and beams, and reclaimed pine for counter fronts, back cabinets and glass racks. Using reclaimed materials that bore traces of their manufacture or past use alongside imitative finishes with irregular surface patterns and textures, Speight mobilized the complex relationship between visual and tactile experience, history and memory. This use of old and reclaimed materials was carried through the wider scheme of furnishing and decoration. A mid-nineteenth-century painted coat of arms, along with 'much of the furniture, light fittings, pictures, mirrors and clock' were bought and restored for the pub.[30] Speight was an early customer of Walcot Reclamation, a major architectural salvage specialist, and argued that using 'genuine stuff, particularly where the customers can touch it' helped to 'create some degree of authenticity'.[31] In this way, Speight's designs proposed a sense of historical continuity and a pubness rooted in the materiality of the interior, experienced visually and through touch. Similarly, his choice of antique door furniture and preference for natural textiles over modern synthetic fibres drew on a tradition of pub design while valuing tactile experience, communicating luxury and comfort, and representing and anticipating use and wear. As an article in *Interior Design* explained, 'the door furniture is old, the leather is hide not P.V.C., the velvet is mohair not Dralon, the Hungarian point upholstery is worsted and cotton not polyester, and though they are costly, they do attain as they wear, a regal shabbiness rather than a plastic shine'.[32]

Contemporary writings suggest ways in which surface textures were understood in relation to psychological experience, visual and spatial perception. Denby, for example, wrote that 'The imagined feel of a surface adds to its effect in a way comparable with the emotional impact of colour'.[33] Rowntree, in contrast, noted the close relationship between texture and spatial perception, observing that 'texture – as perceived by eye and not by touch – is surprisingly closely linked with our idea of space. It is therefore of basic importance to the designer, to be thought of as the skin of the interior, not as its overcoat'.[34] More recently, Juhani Pallasmaa has observed the way in which touch is mediated, writing: 'Our eyes stroke distant surfaces, contours and edges, and the unconscious tactile sensation determines the agreeableness or unpleasantness of the experience. The distant and the near are experienced with the same intensity, and they merge into one coherent experience'.[35] Designed to conceal their age, and to trick the eye and reassure the hand, Speight's interiors engaged the haptic dimension of visual perception, material choices working in consort: the feel of heavy upholstery lending veracity to a seemingly nicotine-stained ceiling, created with varnished grainers' scumble on flat oil rather than through long years of smoke. Supported by a 'theatrical' approach to lighting, the overall scheme was designed to draw the eye of the customer to 'what you want them to see, and away from what you want to hide'.[36] In this way, the lighting aimed to support the idea that the pub had evolved through social use 'rather than produced as an instant package deal'.[37]

Speight brought to his designs a knowledge of the history of pub design, an understanding of the relationship between visual and tactile experience, and an awareness of the association between age, patina and comfort. While such 'faked-up' surfaces as those at The Witness Box may well have gone unnoticed by customers – and it was Speight's belief that customers should not consciously notice the design, only the benefits that arose from it – their widespread use provoked contemporary criticism.[38] As architect Duncan Sharp commented, in an article in *Interior Design* of February 1974, '[y]ou cannot design into a new building that quality which is characteristic of a long established environment. That quality *is* its long establishment.'[39]

Speight's practical approach to the past balanced the immediate commercial expectations of his clients with the desires of customers for credible spaces of familiarity and comfort. Marrying 'faked-up' elements with reclaimed materials and good quality textiles helped create resonant yet unobtrusive settings of acceptable authenticity that depended on knowledge of the affective qualities of materials and the interplay between the senses for their success. While some aspects of Speight's design practice suggest a continuation of ideals of longevity and durability that had informed earlier approaches to pub interior design, others are more closely aligned with the sensory strategies employed in the creation of what were often short-lived themed pub environments of the 1960s and 1970s.

## Place-making and the senses: themed pubs and the interior street scene

Themed interiors and what Alastair Best referred to in *Design Journal* as 'escapist' interiors were much in evidence from the 1960s.[40] The architectural and design historian Alan Crawford has described that decade as 'The Age of the Gimmick' in public house design.[41] An *Interior Design* review of January 1971 showcased examples of recent pub projects for the major breweries, among them a pub on a funfair theme to appeal to young visitors to London's King's Road, a rural pub on a farmyard theme, a pub designed in tribute to the history of the London Fire Brigade and one on a costermonger theme. Market segmentation has been associated with the expansion of themed commercial and leisure environments in an American context.[42] In England, themed pubs evolved in response to similar marketing-led approaches as breweries with large pub portfolios began to introduce 'categorization' as a means of targeting specific types and groups of customer.[43] While themed interiors have been explored in relation to their visual and symbolic qualities, less has been said about other sensory aspects of their design and their effects on social experience.[44]

Part of a new area development in the City of London, the Sir Christopher Wren pub was designed for Watney's brewery by Alex Waugh and Patrick McNeil of Stewart, Henry and Smith.[45] Although frequented chiefly by city workers, its proximity to St Paul's Cathedral made it a popular summer destination for tourists.[46] Deplored by *The Architect's Journal* for its use of simulated materials, the pub's interiors were labelled a 'vulgarian flight into archaic fantasy'.[47] Alex Waugh, one of the pub's designers, was some-what curtly dismissed by virtue of his former employment in Hollywood as a designer of film sets for Metro-Goldwyn-Mayer.[48] Described in 1965, the pub's Wren Bar imitated an old London coffee house. Its restaurant was designed as a London street complete with 'a bookshop window (stocked by Longmans Green & Co with interesting manuscripts and books), original eighteenth-century doors and a collection of old veterinary instruments and carpenters' tools'.[49] The bookshop window reflected the long history of the area as a centre for publishing and bookselling. Background sound was provided 'by a specially programmed tape of tunes associated with London, interspersed with the street cries of old London'.[50]

Until the 1950s, the principal sounds of the pub had been those of service and sociability, with acoustic experience of the interior varying according to the spatial organization and furnishing of the different bars in line with their social use. Notable in this respect is a long history of using durable, easy-to-clean materials and hard surfaces in public bars, where customers might enter in working clothes, and of soft furnishings, such as curtains, upholstered seating, carpets and wallpapers in spaces aimed at middle-class customers and women. Such material choices contributed the creation of distinct atmospheres, the experience of sound, for example, varying significantly within hard-surfaced public bars and carpeted drink-ing and dining areas. Similarly, the visual openness of many public bars, and sense of seeing and being seen experienced by those drinking within them, can be contrasted with the relative visual seclusion of settings aimed at middle-class customers and women. Rooted in gendered and classed social behaviours, historical attitudes to privacy and supervision, and the planning of pubs with public and private sides, these distinctions began to break down as breweries and their designers developed interiors on more democratic and thematic lines.[51] Nevertheless, their legacy can be seen in settings in which a public bar or its equivalent was retained, and in new approaches to lighting and the use of music in the design of the modern pub lounge. The *Hop Leaf Gazette*, distributed to the staff and publicans of H & G Simonds, for example, advised choosing a 'well-lit effect for the public bar, and a rather more subdued scheme in the lounge bar' in line with expectations about custom.[52]

While music and radio had featured in some interwar pubs, the post-war introduction of jukeboxes and fruit machines altered the atmosphere. Their presence in more traditional pub settings was often unwelcome; the architectural historian James Stevens Curl, for example, grumbled: 'The insufferable noise is not conducive to enjoyment, and the machines themselves are so vulgar and ugly they wreck any interior'.[53] Pubs were also beginning to use background music in line with a growing interest in the commercial application of sound that included the use of 'piped' or 'canned' music to stimulate sales in such public settings as shopping centres and supermarkets. In 1960, Rediffusion's Reditune, the largest music service in Britain, claimed to create 'the perfect atmosphere for profitable business'.[54] Pubs reportedly favoured 'bright and breezy piano selections' or 'pleasant melodies' as these were said to 'keep customers in the lounge for an extra drink'.[55] Women's use of the pub had fallen significantly in the 1950s and was of major concern to breweries and pub owners.[56] Lounge bars were frequently introduced during pub refurbishments with the aim of attracting women. When the Prince of Wales at Byker in Newcastle was updated in 1972, for example, Camerons Brewery created a new lounge and replaced the pub's jukebox with 'soft background music' from Soundplay Limited of South Shields to create 'a nice friendly atmosphere' into which a husband would be happy to bring his wife.[57] In this way, the use and choice of recorded music supported social differentiation, subtly reinforcing other gendered and classed cues in the spatial organization, furnishing and decoration that distinguished the ambience of a lounge from that of a public bar, while, as the music providers argued, supporting the publican's sales.

In contrast to the use of background music, or the self-selected music of the jukebox, the incorporation of 'street cries' within the themed musical soundtrack at the Sir Christopher Wren lent coherence to the overarching interior theme of the London street. While these snatches of recorded sound were perhaps a relatively minor element of a complex interior setting, their evocation of the historical urban landscape suggests a more immersive, multisensory approach to design and place-making. This can be contrasted with a greater use of visual strategies in pub designs of the 1950s, such as the incorporation of motifs and murals depicting local historical figures, sites or trades.

Other examples of interior streetscapes of the 1970s addressed the challenge of creating an agreeable level of seclusion for customers of larger pubs. An interior street scene on a 'Western' theme was employed by Authentic Interiors in their 1978 redesign of the Downham Tavern in Bromley, which had been one of the largest pubs in England when it first opened in 1930 [Figure 11.2].[58] One of the major criticisms of such super-sized pubs was their lack of comfort, understood principally in relation to the visual openness of their bars and the sense of exposure and social

**Figure 11.2**    The interior of the Downham Tavern, designed by Authentic Interiors, *Interior Design* (January 1978), p. 15.

discomfort experienced within them. The interior streetscape offered a thematic pretext for the subdivision of interior space and the creation of a playful atmosphere that supported intimacy while using 'interrupted vistas' to mediate spatial experience in line with a tradition of English pub interior design.[59]

Like the Sir Christopher Wren, the design of the Geordie Pride in Newcastle aimed to create a sense of local identity and, as its name suggests, to engender feelings of pride and belonging among customers. The new pub, a large basement pub of 10,000 square feet with five bars and a restaurant, occupied a prominent island site opposite the city's central railway station. Conceived by Archon Design of Hexham, for the brewery Scottish and Newcastle, the interiors were devised to appeal to a wide age range and to promote a sense of nostalgia without turning the pub into a museum.[60] Described on its opening in August 1974, it was said to be the first pub to incorporate a 'walkabout' or 'vista and vision' design, pointing to a desire to encourage customers to roam while suggesting the importance of interior views in the realization and experience of the over-all theme.[61] The designers were tasked with creating 'a theme which would tie together a collection of trades, industries, characters and specific items which the people of Newcastle would identify themselves with', based on the view that 'the essence of good public house design is to make people feel at home and belong in the newly created surroundings'.[62] The interior incorporated 'a complete Victorian Street, 35 yards long, with paving, street lamps, shops, a Gunsmith's, a Bakery, Saddler's shop, Potter's shop, and a Chemist's'.[63] Each of these 'shops' served as drinking space with 'its own décor and atmosphere, enhanced with bric-a-brac'.[64] As customers moved through the interior different sounds evoked 'the hustle and bustle of an old Newcastle street'.[65]

Writing in the late 1960s, Hugh Creighton had observed that, while interior designers used colour and light to accentuate spatial transitions and bring contrast to an interior, 'the possibility of deliberately using the acoustical conditions to a similar end' did not appear to have been explored.[66] Similarly, Rowntree noted the role of sound in spatial per-ception, writing: 'The ear too plays its part in perceiving space. Where space flows unhindered, so does sound'.[67] An interest in the social experi-ence of sound is also evident in the contemporary emergence of the term 'soundscape' to describe 'the perceived acoustic environment of a place', understood in relation to human and natural factors.[68] At the Geordie Pride, sound was used to support the interior theme and to promote a relationship with the wider historical urban setting. Varying according to a customer's location, the background sounds enhanced customers' spatial perception of the unfolding interior scene, reflecting the 'walkabout' or 'vista and vision' design concept. As the architect and pub designer Ben Davis has observed, '[f]ew drinking areas are happier than a complex of loosely interconnected spaces, and where this does not exist in truth the appearance of it is a good substitute'.[69]

In recent years, an extensive literature has explored the influence of environmental factors on the social experience of eating and drinking environments and their commercial success.[70] Sensory marketing has also evolved rapidly as a recognized field of consumer marketing practice.[71] Writings on English pub interiors of the 1960s and 1970s point to explicitly productive expectations of the interior and a desire to forge rapid, profita-ble connections with consumers. In line with the rise of environmental psy-chology, a more scientific slant can be seen in some contemporary writings on public house design and interior design more broadly. These suggest a desire to understand more fully the potential of interior design to activate pleasurable forms of sensory experience and stimulate consumption. As the above examples indicate, pub designers proposed and embraced a

range of sensory strategies: the use of colour to stimulate thirst; the blending of 'fake' and 'authentic' materials to trick the eye and reassure the hand
and lend an acceptable authenticity and familiarity to an interior; the use
of recorded music to entice customers to linger for an extra drink; the thematic use of sound in place-making and to encourage customer identifica-
tion with the setting; and the employment of variations in recorded sound to
enhance the perception of a gradual unfolding of interior space which was
understood as an important element of a pub's atmosphere. While some
of these approaches drew on established methods of public house interior
design and supported what might be understood as conventional forms of
pub comfort, others, notably the use of recorded sound, contributed to the
production of immersive, thematic settings and positioned customers in a
playful multisensory relationship with the past.

## Notes

1 'The Pub Tradition Recaptured', *The Architectural Review*, 107:642 (June 1950),
  p. 396.
2 B. Oliver, *The Renaissance of the English Public House* (London: Faber and Faber,
  1947), p. 54.
3 M. Bressani and A. Sprecher, 'Atmospheres', *Journal of Architectural Education*, 73:1
  (2019), pp. 2–4; B. Anderson, 'Affective Atmospheres', *Emotion, Space and Society*,
  2:2 (2009), pp. 77–81.
4 Mrs L'Estrange Malone, Labour member of the London County Council and the
  Home Office Committee on War Damaged Licensed Premises and Reconstruction,
  quoted in 'Brighter "Pubs" Quiz to Women', *Daily Herald* (13 April 1944), p. 3.
5 'The Pub in the London Scene', *The Builder* (14 April 1950), p. 482.
6 On deodorization see M. S. R. Jenner, 'Follow Your Nose? Smell, Smelling, and
  Their Histories', *The American Historical Review*, 116:2 (April 2011), pp. 335–51.
7 C. Williams-Ellis in the Foreword to F. W. B. Yorke's *The Planning and Equipment of
  Public Houses* (London: The Architectural Press, 1949), p. 3.
8 Williams-Ellis in Yorke, *The Planning and Equipment of Public Houses*, p. 5.
9 *Ibid.*
10 M. Gorham and H. McG. Dunnett's 'Inside the Pub', a special issue of *The
  Architectural Review* of October 1949, was published as a book the following year
  and had a lasting influence on English post-war pub design.
11 'The Pub Tradition Recaptured', p. 396.
12 'Inside the Pub', a special issue of *The Architectural Review*, 6:634 (October 1949),
  p. 220.
13 H. Casson (ed.), *Inscape: The Design of Interiors* (London: The Architectural Press,
  1968), p. 17 and p. 41.
14 H. M. Proshansky and T. O'Hanlon, 'Environmental Psychology: Origins and
  Development' in D. Stokols (ed.), *Perspectives on Environment and Behavior* (New
  York and London: Plenum Press, 1977), pp. 101–27.
15 Birmingham Post Medical Reporter, 'Inn Is "Like Home" to an Alcoholic',
  *Birmingham Post* (9 September 1969), p. 1.
16 P. Kotler, 'Atmospherics as a Marketing Tool', *Journal of Retailing*, 49:4 (Winter
  1973–4), pp. 48–64.
17 The Scribe, 'Bognor Man's Diary', *Bognor Regis Observer* (24 January 1953), p. 4.
18 Breweries owned 25 per cent of pubs in 1960 and by 1972 owned 56 per cent. See
  C. Hutt, *The Death of the English Pub* (London: Hutchinson & Co, 1983), p. 70.

19  N. Whiteley, 'Toward a Throw-Away Culture: Consumerism, "Style Obsolescence" and Cultural Theory in the 1950s and 1960s', *Oxford Art Journal*, 10:2 (1987), p. 23.

20  M. Black, 'The Education of the Interior Designer' in Casson (ed.), *Inscape*, p. 83.

21  Advertisement for the Master Robert Motel in Hounslow, *Acton Gazette and Post* (31 August 1972), p. 5.

22  L. Dalton, 'Finch's: Following in the Family Tradition', *Kensington Post* (8 August 1969), p. 9; Advertising feature, 'Finch's: The Pub People', *Kensington Post* (21 April 1972), p. 43.

23  Advertising feature, 'The More It Changes the More It Remains the Same', *Kensington Post* (21 April 1972), p. 42.

24  Special feature, 'A Look at Finch's in 1969', *Marylebone Mercury* (8 August 1969), p. 10–11.

25  E. Denby, *Interior Design* (London: Country Life, 1963), p. 121.

26  D. Rowntree, *Interior Design* (Harmondsworth: Penguin Books, 1964), p. 182.

27  'Public Houses: Creating the Right Atmosphere', *Interior Design* (February 1973), p. 101.

28  'Finch's Win International Award', *Kensington Post* (26 June 1970), p. 58.

29  'The Witness Box, London', *Interior Design* (February 1976), p. 80; 'Talking to Ivan Speight', *Interior Design* (January 1978), p. 10.

30  'The Witness Box, London', p. 80.

31  T. Kay, 'Was Selfridges the Earliest Retailer to Reuse Salvage?', *Salvo*, 12 May 2015, www.salvoweb.com/salvonews/17963-was-selfridges-the-earliest-retailer-to-re use-salvage (accessed 11 January 2021); 'The Witness Box, London', p. 80.

32  'The Witness Box, London', p. 80.

33  Denby, *Interior Design*, p. 127.

34  Rowntree, *Interior Design*, p. 12.

35  J. Pallasmaa, *The Eyes of the Skin: Architecture and the Senses* (New York: John Wiley & Sons, 2012), p. 46.

36  'Talking to Ivan Speight', p. 10.

37  'The Witness Box, London', p. 80.

38  'Talking to Ivan Speight', p. 10.

39  D. Sharp, 'Public Houses: A Modern, Flexible Pub Vernacular is Needed', *Interior Design* (February 1974), p. 99.

40  A. Best, 'Flight of Fancy', *Design Journal*, 293 (May 1973), pp. 60–5.

41  A. Crawford, 'Birmingham's Victorian Pubs' in M. Binney and E. Milne (eds), *Time Gentlemen Please!* (London: SAVE Britain's Heritage, in association with CAMRA, The Campaign for Real Ale Ltd, 1983), p. 15.

42  M. Gottdiener, *Theming America: Dreams, Visions, and Commercial Spaces* (Boulder, CO: Westview Press, 1997), p. 74.

43  Tony Thornton has identified the main categories as: community pubs, destination outlets, young person's meeting houses, multifunctional, businessmen, parasites (i.e. pubs with a transient trade whose custom depends on their position). T. Thornton, *Brewers, Brands and the Pub in Their Hands* (Kibworth Beauchamp, UK: Matador, 2014), p. 17.

44  A. Bryman, *The Disneyization of Society* (London: Sage Publications, 2004); Gottdiener, *Theming America*.

45  'Grave Turning', *The Architects' Journal* (28 July 1965), p. 175.

46  'Night Out and Best Bars', *The Tatler* (10 December 1966), p. 48.

47  'Grave Turning', p. 175.

48  *Ibid.*

49  'The Christopher Wren by St. Paul's Cathedral', *The Red Barrel*, 5:5 (October 1965), pp. 8–9.

50  *Ibid.*

51  On privacy and supervision, see F. Fisher, 'Privacy and Supervision in the Modernised Public House, 1872–1902' in P. Sparke et al. (eds), *Designing the Modern Interior: From the Victorians to Today* (Oxford and New York: Berg, 2009), pp. 41–52.

52  R. Howie, 'Furnishing Trends', *The Hop Leaf Gazette*, 33:2 (Autumn 1959), p. 9.

53  J. S. Curl, 'Whatever Happened to the London Pub', *The Architect and Building News* (19 November 1970), p. 59.

54  Advertisement, 'Ring Up More Sales with Reditune', *The Cornish Guardian* (5 May 1960), p. 6.

55  'Swing-a-long Music Helps Shoppers in Supermarket Stores', *Coventry Evening Telegraph* (20 May 1965), p. 16.

56  J. McLeod, 'Drinks', *The Tatler* (9 April 1966), p. 56; David Gutzke, *Women Drinking Out in Britain since the Early Twentieth Century* (Manchester: Manchester University Press, 2014), p. 73.

57  Advertisement feature, 'A Modern Pub for "New" Byker', *Newcastle Journal* (26 January 1972), p. 7.

58  'The Downham Tavern', *Interior Design* (January 1978), p. 15. See also E. Cole, 'The Urban and Suburban Public House in Inter-War England, 1918–39', Historic England, Research Report Series 004–2016, Volume 1, pp. 32–3.

59  'The Pub Tradition Recaptured', p. 396.

60  'Where Geordie Tradition Meets the 20th Century', *Newcastle Journal* (9 September 1974), p. 5.

61  Advertisement feature, 'Geordie Pride', *Newcastle Evening Chronicle* (5 August 1974), p. 10; 'Where Geordie Tradition Meets the 20th Century', p. 5.

62  'Geordie Pride, Newcastle', *Interior Design* (February 1975), pp. 98–100.

63  Advertisement feature, 'Geordie Pride', p. 10.

64  'Geordie Pride, Newcastle', pp. 98–100; advertisement feature, 'Geordie Pride', p. 10.

65  'Geordie Pride, Newcastle', pp. 98–100; advertisement feature, 'Geordie Pride', p. 10.

66  H. Creighton, 'Skill 2: Interior Acoustics' in Casson (ed.), *Inscape*, p. 180.

67  Rowntree, *Interior Design*, p. 12.

68  J. Kang et al., cited in A. Fiebig et al., 'Assessments of Acoustic Environments by Emotions – The Application of Emotion Theory in Soundscape', *Frontiers in Psychology*, 11 (20 November 2020), p. 4, doi:10.3389/fpsyg.2020.573041.

69  Davis worked for Ind Coope in the 1950s and 1960s and was also involved in training for Allied Breweries. B. Davis, *The Traditional English Pub: A Way of Drinking* (London: The Architectural Press, 1981), p. 28.

70  C. Spence, 'Atmospheric Effects on Eating and Drinking: A Review' in H. L. Meiselman (ed.), *Handbook of Eating and Drinking* (Cham, Switzerland: Springer Nature Switzerland, 2020), pp. 257–75.

71  B. Hultén et al., *Sensory Marketing* (London: Palgrave Macmillan, 2009).

# 12

## Interiorizing the senses

### David Howes

This chapter presents a genealogy of the new 'Age of Aesthetics' proclaimed by American writer Virginia Postrel in *The Substance of Style*.[1] It does so from the standpoint of the sociology of consumption to begin with, and then follows up with an anthropologically inspired critique of certain current trends in design thinking that purport to be grounded in the science of sensory evaluation, evolutionary psychology, and cognitive neuroscience. Next, this chapter entertains the style counsel of the LA-based interior decorator Catherine Bailly Dunne, with a particular focus on their practice as grounded in a 'science of the concrete'. It concludes by offering an alternative model for design practice centring on the figure of the interior designer as sensory ethnographer.

## The new 'age of aesthetics'

HomeSense is a Canadian chain of discount home décor stores, with branches in the United States and UK. As the store's slogan suggests: 'It makes perfect HomeSense.'[2] The name of this store nicely expresses the theme of this chapter: interiorizing the senses. However, it is the cover of the Fall 2000 Pier 1 Imports catalogue that more sensuously captures the spirit – and the message – of what follows. Pier 1 is a home furnishings store that specializes in wood and wicker furniture, textured draperies (velvet, corduroy), faux tribal art, cast-iron candelabra, and scented candles – especially scented candles. The catalogue cover shows a miniature slate stone fountain, with earthy hues, suitable for a living room end table, or the garden.[3] Down the right side of the cover is a list of senses, each bordered by a different colour: feel (golden yellow), smell (grassy green), hear (hazy purple), taste (rose red), and see (burnt orange). Splashed across the image of the fountain is an advertising slogan: 'Get in touch with your senses™'. The implication is that we have lost touch with our senses; shopping at Pier 1 Imports can help us recover them.

The checklist approach to the senses exemplified by the Pier 1 home décor catalogue is emblematic of the current vogue for sensory design and sensory marketing.[4] This trend has been theorized by Virginia Postrel in *The Substance of Style*. According to Postrel,[5] we live in a new 'Age of Aesthetics' – an age in which 'design is everywhere, and everywhere is now designed'. Indeed, it is impossible to miss the burgeoning emphasis on the 'sense appeal' both of commodities and of the venues in which they are sold, such as Pier 1, or Anthropologie (HomeSense with its warehouse aesthetic not so much). Attractive design is no longer a luxury: 'We, … customers, demand it' (i.e. aesthetic pleasure), Postrel holds.[6] But do we demand it, or has it been inculcated in us by the 'consumer engineers' (in Sheldon and Arens'[7] apt phrase), who pay lip service to 'We, customers' all being kings or queens, while slyly manipulating our senses in the interests of moving merchandise?

In the sociological literature, Postrel's 'new aesthetic age' is referred to as 'the aestheticization of everyday life'. Mike Featherstone reflects on the derivation of this phrase in *Consumer Culture and Postmodernism*. In one of its senses, he writes: 'the aestheticization of everyday life can refer to the project of turning life into a work of art'.[8] Featherstone points to the example of the artistic countercultures that sprang up in mid-to-late nineteenth-century European urban centres, such as Berlin and Paris – the haunts of Baudelaire and company, most notably Comte Robert de Montesquiou (the subject of Benoit Beaulieu's contribution to this volume).[9] In its most salient sense for us now, however, 'the aestheticization of everyday life refers to the rapid flow of signs and images which saturates the fabric of everyday life in contemporary society'. Elaborating further, Featherstone states, in the current conjuncture 'we find an emphasis upon the effacement of the boundary between art and everyday life, the collapse of the distinction between high art and mass/popular culture, a general stylistic promiscuity and mixing of codes'.[10]

In *The Substance of Style*, Postrel argues that 'Aesthetics has become too important to be left in the hands of the aesthetes.'[11] So much for the dandies of the historical avant-garde and their contemporary counterparts! Rather more critically and perspicaciously, Featherstone points to how this appropriation or new valorization of the aesthetic paved the way for the growth of the so-called culture industries, 'with painting moving into advertising, architecture into technical engineering, [and] handicrafts and sculpture into the industrial arts, to produce a mass culture'.[12] The so-called democratization of luxury is intimately bound up with the proliferation of mass production and mass consumption. This development was fuelled by the transformation of the nineteenth-century regime of industrial capitalism into the consumer capitalism of today.[13] In place of the disciplining (and alienation) of the senses of the worker under the former regime, which attached a premium to productivity, thrift and moderation, in the twentieth century the worker was reborn as a consumer, and the onus shifted from moderation to instant gratification, conspicuous consumption, and the titillation of the senses (in place of having to curb them).

Digging deeper into the genealogy of the new 'Age of Aesthetics', following the lead of sociologist Stuart Ewen in *All Consuming Images*,[14] we find that in the early decades of the twentieth century (which is somewhat earlier than Featherstone or Postrel would allow) giant industrial corporations, such as AEG, began to develop multipurpose styling divisions. An industrial aesthetic was born, with a view to bringing coherence to the perceived 'disorder' of the marketplace. This development tipped the scales of capitalism, as consumption came to drive production and attractiveness came to override considerations of functionality or efficiency in the manufacture and marketing of products. Advertising companies sprang up and brought a new level of artistry to everyday life. A premium was attached to 'eye-appeal', but the so-called creatives of the day also turned their attention on the 'lower' senses, most notably touch, which were seen as having been repressed by civilization, and sought to capitalize on their appeal as well.[15] If 'art for art's sake' was the banner cry of the artists and 'life for art's sake' that of the aesthetes, 'art for control's sake' was the goal of the thoroughly modern designers and advertisers, or consumer engineers.

Alongside AEG, Dupont Chemical emerged as one of the leading drivers of the aestheticization of everyday life in the twentieth century. One of the products it visited upon 'We, customers' was shag carpeting. As architectural historian Chad Randl observes in 'Sensuality and Shag Carpeting',[16] shag fibre was a product of the 'synthetic revolution', but for all that – unlike plastic, for example – it is markedly *sensual*. According to Randl, shag fitted the post-war cultural preference for casual living, as exemplified by the practice of lounging on the floor watching TV or listening to LPs, instead of sitting upright on chairs or a sofa, and the new atmosphere of sexual permissiveness and experimentation that caught on in the 1960s and 1970s: shag carpeting, as an 'extension' of body hair, with all the same connotations, was especially popular in bachelor pads and honeymoon suites, but also used to line bathrooms. Soft, plush, 'natural' (fur-like, grass-like) shag fibres ushered in a new style of human sensuousness. Randl brings out well how this transformation in sensuality was directed by the style divisions of Dupont Chemical and other manufacturers, with their corps of consumer engineers all dedicated to actively (re)fashioning our sensory surroundings.

## Colour your world

Another driver of the 'new aesthetic age' has been the big paint company: Pantone, Sherwin-Williams, Benjamin Moore – there to help you 'colour your world'. In 1999, a watershed year, the main forecasting workshop of the non-profit Color Marketing Group was held in Montreal. Top of mind was the question: What will be the colour to usher in the new millennium? James Warren, a journalist with the *Chicago Tribune*, tuned in to the chatter of the other reporters and experts at the convention. Among other things, he reported that a certain Eliot Burrows of Engelhard Pigments and Additives Group had been lobbying for iridescent colours for many years prior but was consistently snubbed. Things changed in 1999, however, and Burrows' colour-vision triumphed:

> Whether it's the economy, or the millennium, or sheer boredom with the matters of the past, color-changing iridescents and metallics have broken free of the preteen lip-gloss niche and begun to appear in luxury footwear – to say nothing of office furniture and automotive, where the color parable of the moment is the back-order on silver Volkswagen Beetles.[17]

How fitting that the colour for the year 2000 should have been so liminal! It is tempting to surmise that Burrows was the proverbial 'man in the gaberdine suit' at the convention, but the record is silent regarding his personal sartorial preferences.

Colour experts are eager to start new trends and at the same time dissociate themselves from the trends of the past, which are instead referred to as crazes: for example, the 'craze' for avocado and harvest-gold appliances in the 1960s, which bordered on 'mass hysteria' in the opinion of most latter-day experts:

> Why avocado? Avocado's not pretty. Still, the tremendous pistons of industry pumped out a long line of avocado plastics, avocado dryers and avocado stoves, until a significant proportion of North America's homes were avocado-colored. Industrial color consultants still talk about the 'avocado syndrome' in tones of mild distaste, as if it were a germ.[18]

While the work of the non-profit Color Marketing Group continues, since the turn of the twentieth century the big colour companies have opted to proclaim (and profit from) their own prognostications. For example, the Pantone Color Institute predicted a blue trend – Classic Blue, to be precise – for 2020 which, given the onslaught of the novel coronavirus, seems prescient in retrospect (the mood of the pandemic being 'blue', not 'rosy', for example). For 2021, the Institute proposed not one but two 'Colour(s) of the Year': Ultimate Gray and Illuminating (a vibrant yellow). This selection was meant to communicate a message of 'strength and hopefulness', dependability and warmth, for uncertain times.[19] It is soothing to know that the big paint companies, like big pharmaceutical companies, have our psychological being so well in hand, isn't it? While big paint and big pharma are not in league, the question arises: What colour goes best with Prozac, or with Oxytocin? On second thought, maybe we shouldn't be asking that question. And maybe we should be anxious that the Pantone Color Institute fixed on two such contradictory 'Colours of the Year' for 2021. Might not this prove schizogenic for some?

## Psychophysics

A third driver is the Sensory Evaluation Laboratory, the haunt of the so-called sensory professional. While many such professionals are mainly concerned with designing food products for the mass market,[20] at Procter & Gamble and other like companies they also hone their senses on perfecting the sense appeal of household products, such as air-fresheners. Indeed, they have toiled mightily at capturing the essence of 'freshness' – synthetically, of course. They do so within the (top-secret) confines of the sensory research lab, with its white walls, fluorescent lighting, air-conditioned atmosphere, and rows of individual cubicles. There, ensconced in their respective cubicles, the expert panellists 'evaluate' the qualities of the products in development one-sensation-at-a-time, and one-sense-at-a-time (assisted by the use of blindfolds, ear defenders, gloves, and nose-clips). The tests they use include discriminative tests (to determine whether a difference exists among samples), descriptive tests (to identify the characteristics of a sample and gauge their intensity), and hedonic tests (to determine liking). The results are then tabulated and analysed statistically to arrive at the ideal (or at least, normative) 'sensory profile' for a product, before it is launched.[21]

Notably absent from this battery of tests is any sort of semantic test. A semantic test would yield information about the *meaning* or associations that products have for the panellists and hence potentially for consumers. This lacuna is due to the fact that the experimental protocol is grounded in psychophysics (a field of psychological research founded by Gustav Fechner in the mid-nineteenth century).[22] Psychophysics has no room (or 'headspace') for semantics, because its aim is to excavate beneath any associations the expert panellist might bring to the task – that is, beneath perception and beneath cognition – to focus on the *sensation* in and of itself. Immediacy is key; spontaneity is *de rigueur*.[23]

Given all the safeguards in place (sterile atmosphere, blindfolds, ear defenders, injunction to be spontaneous, etc.) one might suppose that the sensory professional is able to curb any associative leanings and assess the sensory properties of a product purely and simply. However, the fallacy of the whole superstructure of psychophysics is easily called into question. To cite one of the many examples discussed in *Aroma*:

> In one consumer test, a pine fragrance evaluated as 'fresh' and 'clean' was added to facial tissues. When the tissues were then tested, however, they were considered harsh and rough. This was because the pine fragrance also carried associations of 'rough' and 'hard' [not to mention prickly, like pine needles] – undesirable qualities for facial tissues.[24]

As this example suggests, cross-modal associations (here, scent/feel) can intrude into even the most carefully controlled laboratory conditions. The senses are not discrete channels; they intersect. Hence, the sensory checklist approach creates a mirage – the mirage of the dissociated sensibility. The experimental protocols of the sensory research lab are also dissociative in a further sense – namely, a social sense. They are modelled on the idea of the totally asocial individual in that each panellist, ensconced in their cubicle, is obliged to carry out their task in isolation and not utter a word, or even so much as a sigh (since this might influence the judgement of other panellists). Is it any wonder that 'bowling alone' (thinking of Michael Moore's film of the same name), like eating alone and sleeping alone, has increasingly become the new normal in US culture? Does sensory individuation in the laboratory breed isolationism in society?

Looking back on the craze for shag carpeting, the fad for avocado green, and the cult of (synthesized) freshness, 'We [latter day] customers' are wont to smile knowingly or roll our eyes like the colour experts do. If 'We, consumers' have any taste, our kitchen appliances all come in black or stainless steel, our countertops in marble or granite, and our floors are laid with synthetic wood, ceramic tile, or polished concrete. Before feeling too smug about our superior taste, however, we need to think about the 'avocado syndrome', and the rapid demise of shag carpeting:

> Shag functioned as a reassuring and expected accoutrement of sex [in the 1960s and 1970s]; its symbolic associations with physical pleasure were both suitably exotic and comfortably familiar. [However, as] popular tastes for what was increasingly seen as the decadence of 1970s design waned, shag, as perhaps the most prominent symbol of that decadence, went with it. Consumers linked shag with a tasteless lack of restraint and the cultural malaise and decline of the entire decade.[25]

The precipitous demise of the shag aesthetic illustrates an important point about the built-in dynamism of contemporary definitions of style:

> The power of style, and its emergence as an increasingly important feature in people's lives, cannot be separated from the evolution and sensibility of modernity. Style is a visible reference point by which we have come to understand life *in progress*. People's devotion to the acceleration of varying styles allows them to be connected to the 'reality' of a given moment. At the same time they understand that this given moment will give way to yet another, and another ...[26]

## (R)Evolutionary design

Sensory design and sensory marketing are booming, and we shall have more to say about these two trends presently. But the attention of many designers and marketers has shifted. The trendiest consumer engineers now have gone over to neuroscience (hence neurodesign and neuromarketing) and evolutionary psychology. In this way, they are able to take their discourse out of the realm of mere conjecture and dress it up as scientific fact, thereby augmenting its credibility and the fee their clients are willing to pay for their advice. For example, the evolutionary psychologist has an explanation for why most of us set our home thermostats to a uniform 17–23°C (63–73°F): that was the ambient temperature of life on the African savannah, the birthplace of humanity.[27] Air-conditioning manufacturers and home-heating companies will be pleased at this news.[28] Leaning on evolutionary psychology, they can also tell you why: 'The latest fitness trend – "the cavewoman workout" – an all-new "ancestral health" movement involving "exercise routines based on what humans naturally did 10,000 years ago, or moving like an animal"' is bound to be the *next* big thing.[29] And, like my marketing colleague Gad Saad,[30] author of *The Consuming Instinct: What Juicy Burgers, Ferraris, Pornography and Gift Giving Reveal About Human Nature*, they are happy to lecture you on the four key Darwinian drives that drive consumer behaviour in the Anthropocene just as they did in the Pleistocene.

Another much touted finding of neuroscience and evolutionary psychology is that we humans are drawn more towards open than closed rooms, and more towards round forms than angular ones (as revealed by having test subjects view pictures of different interiors while entombed in an fMRI machine so as to tell how their brain reacts). The latter finding was picked up on by Ingrid Fetell Lee, former director of IDEO design agency, New York. She counsels:

> Angular objects, even if they're not directly in your path as you move through your house have an unconscious effect on your emotions. They may look chic and sophisticated, but they inhibit our playful impulses. Round shapes do just the opposite. A circular or elliptical coffee table changes a living room from a space for sedate, restrained interaction to a lively center for conversation and impromptu games.[31]

It is not difficult to see through evolutionary psychology. Basically, evolutionary thinking eclipses history and posits a direct line of descent from the (presumed) conditions that prevailed in the 'cradle of humanity'. In other words, this style of reasoning abstracts and essentializes certain traits (of masculinity or femininity, for example), projects them back in time to the origin of our species, and then reads these traits forward into the present, all seamlessly. The circularity of such reasoning is vicious. It is ideology,

the ideology of 'genetic capitalism',[32] masquerading as natural philosophy. The most curious thing about evolutionary thinking, however, is how
timeless it is.

## The sensual home

According to the prevailing stereotypes, interior decorators tend to be
women, just as architects tend to be men. This perception is erroneous:
it masks more than it reveals.[33] Yet it is fruitful to consider it in relation
to the broader issue of how the division of labour by gender is bound up
with the division of the senses. Traditionally, in accordance with the longstanding Western hierarchy of the senses, men were associated with the
'higher', 'distance', 'public' senses of sight and hearing and women with
the 'lower', 'proximity', 'private' or 'intimate' senses of smell and taste
and touch.[34] It is only natural (or, we should say, cultural), therefore, that
women should be mistresses of the interior and men should be masters of
the exterior. Home decoration calls for a woman's touch just as architecture is beholden to the male gaze.

This opposition between sight and touch does not tell the whole story
of design (interior or exterior), however. Interestingly, as we shall see in
this section, *Interior Designing for All Five Senses* by Catherine Bailly Dunne
clearly demonstrates that women are not only 'into' touch[35] but also strive
to imagine and implement a *democracy of the senses* – that is, a regime
in which each sense is given 'equal consideration'[36] – and in so doing
subvert the standard Western hierarchy of sensing. In place of the 'visual
dominance' that rules in architecture, the onus is on 'balancing the senses'
within the home. In what follows, then, I offer a sensory content analysis
of the personal style counsel offered by Dunne, while at the same time
highlighting how the personal is social, which is to say socially constructed.

Dunne insists that 'the best person to decorate your home is you',
since you are the one best qualified 'to translate your past and express
your personality and desires'; a decorator such as herself can only advise
on how to choose things to 'make your surroundings look more beautiful'.[37] But the beautiful is nothing if it is not personal. A philosopher such
as Kant in his *Critique of Aesthetic Judgment* would insist that you must
legislate for all humanity when you declare something, such as a painting,
to be beautiful.[38] Dunne, by contrast, suggests that we should each make
exceptions of ourselves.

Dunne's second principle is that making your surroundings 'look more
beautiful' or 'pleasing to the eye' is *not* the end of interior design. For

> a room that looks right doesn't necessarily feel right, and doesn't always seem
> complete. In an age dominated by the visual, we've come to overlook the rest
> of our senses – and our world is blander and more irritating for it. Recognizing
> the power of the senses opens up new pathways of enjoyment.[39]

Hence her approach, which she calls 'Designing for All Five Senses'.

Before proceeding to treat each of the senses in turn, Dunne presents a series of rules of thumb. These practical tips include: have a plan, interview yourself about yourself (i.e. your fondest memories and favourite sensations), 'find your golden thread' (i.e. choose a theme or themes, by clipping magazines and scouting shops for ideas, so you can give your home and each room its own 'personality'), always go for quality over disposability (if you don't want your home to seem cheap), and be confident. This is all very sensible.

In the ensuing chapters, Dunne takes a checklist approach to the senses – sight, smell, touch, hearing, taste (in that order). However, unlike the approach of the sensory professional, she takes the framework for her analysis from the six-panel medieval tapestry known as *The Lady and the Unicorn* and proceeds to weave a tapestry of the senses. In other words, she arranges the senses, she does not just individuate and check them off. What is more, she demonstrates a modicum of understanding of the rich symbolism to be found in the six panels of the master tapestry (for example, she notes that the sixth panel is about the moral dilemma of choosing between reason and desire), unlike the sensory professional who never gives the symbolism of the senses the least thought.

## Contrasts and correspondences

Another way in which Dunne's approach departs from the industrial checklist is that she is a strong advocate for using sensory contrasts and for mixing or crossing the senses. She is not a purist. Thus, in a section called 'Contrast Is Key' she writes: 'Nature's genius is in its contrasts. The glory of a rose is the contrast of its soft, frail petals to its thick and thorny stems.'[40] Diverse textures will 'add punch to your decorating scheme', she states, and notes how 'I like pairing unexpected fabrics: silks and wovens, wool and gingham, mohair and chenille. I call these "touch contrasts," and they delight the fingers as well as the eyes.'[41] The evolutionary psychologist would be aghast at this, on account of the dissonances it creates – cognitive dissonance is bad.[42] Dunne, by contrast, delights in juxtapositioning sensations, and also creating correspondences: if there is a fruit or floral motif to your wallpaper then 'echo' it with a corresponding scent. Senses should resonate: it would not be wise to isolate them, for that would drain all the harmony from life. The Comte de Montesquiou, who *lived* Symbolism (the artistic movement), would approve of this advice (as Beaulieu's contribution to this volume also suggests).

The effects Dunne advocates often border on the synaesthetic: take a terracotta ring, place it on a lightbulb, add some drops of essential oil – voilà, 'fragrant light'; or, arrange some little conga drums or musical figurines on a side table – voilà, 'music for the eyes'.[43] Her favourite object would appear to be the conch shell (for the amusement of guests and family alike): 'Its texture and soft pink gradations of color make the conch shell a triple delight for the senses: it not only sounds good [when held up to the ear], it looks and feels good, too.'[44] No living room can be considered 'complete' without one.

I must confess to being quite smitten by Dunne's multi- and cross-modal aesthetics.[45] Her work provides a delightful antidote to what Caroline A. Jones calls the 'bureaucratization of the senses' under high modernism.[46] Modernism reached its zenith in the 1950s, when hi-fi audio systems were all the rage, when influential New York art critic Clement Greenberg declared painting to be 'for eyesight alone', and when research at the Monell Chemical Senses Center laid the groundwork for the hygienization of olfaction. At that point in time, 'genre purity' (e.g. colour-field painting, hi-fi, deodorization) was idealized, and 'miscegenation' demonized. By century's end, however, the sensory and social exclusivity of high modernism had come undone, due to the advent of postmodernism: mixing senses and blurring genres took over from demarcation.[47]

What most commends the work of Dunne to my way of thinking and sensing is not, however, its ostensible postmodernism[48] but the way it brings the original meaning of the term 'aesthetic' back in. This term was coined (or rather taken over from the Greek) by the philosopher Alexander von Baumgarten in the mid-eighteenth century. He defined it as 'the science of sense perception' and positioned it as a 'science of the lower cognitive power' (*gnoseologia inferioris*) in contradistinction to 'the higher cognitive power', or reason. In a novel move, Baumgarten held that reason (i.e. the intellect) was 'the poorer' for the fact that it traffics exclusively in 'distinct ideas', which are quite 'arid', as opposed to the 'confused and indistinct ideas' generated by the senses, which are quite 'vivid'. Sense perception could not yield the same self-evident, purely rational truths as the intellect (e.g. the truths of mathematics), Baumgarten allowed, but when exercised judiciously it could provide a sense of the 'unity-in-multiplicity of sensible qualities'.[49]

Dunne's sensuous design thinking circles back to Baumgarten and could equally be likened to Claude Lévi-Strauss' idea of 'the science of the concrete' (i.e. a science of 'sensible qualities', unlike the abstractions of modern physics), as set out in *The Savage Mind*, or the idea of 'sensuous cognition' suggested by recent advances in cognitive linguistics.[50] What is so nice about it is that it abjures calculation and instrumentalization (leave that for the evolutionary psychologist) in favour of sensualization.

There are moments when brain science rears its head and interrupts the sensuousness of Dunne's design thinking. But these (fortunately rare) moments are offset by references to other traditions, such as the aesthetics of the Japanese tea ceremony or the aesthetics of the Victorian period, as exemplified by Dunne's predilection for making seedballs (styrofoam spheres with colourful seeds glued to their surface) and using glass pens filled with coloured, scented ink to write her dinner invitations (also very Victorian).[51] These references to the ritualization of sensation (the Japanese tea ceremony) and the handmade (rather than mass-produced) artefact give her aesthetic its unique feel. As noted previously, touch is one of the cardinal home senses (not to be confused with HomeSense) and a prime 'feminine tactic'.[52]

While reserving a place for brain science (unwisely, in my opinion), Dunne and her sister-in-arms, the equally legendary designer Ilse Crawford, nevertheless put technological rationality in its place. Both Dunne and Crawford's ideal for the home borders on the pastoral ('every room needs a plant').[53] A home should provide respite from the technological dynamo of modernity, as 'the last bastion of the senses', and quiet is paramount (with allowance being made for nature sounds, such as birds chirping).[54] And if you must bring technology into the home, then be sure not to let its noises disturb the (all-important) 'balance': 'When purchasing an aire-conditioner [sic] system for your home (or a room), be aware of its level of noise. Keep in mind the delicate balance between the "touch" and "hearing" senses in your home.'[55]

## Other ways of sensing

This is all very sensual, but the question remains of just how well founded the style counsel of these design mavens is in 'the life of the senses' in the other cultural traditions (Asian, Arabic) and historical epochs (Victorian, ancient Egyptian) they draw on for inspiration. This is a serious question for the sensory historian and/or sensory anthropologist since it goes to the 'truth of materials' (always an important consideration for any designer worth their salt) and, at a deeper level, the 'truth' or integrity of other 'ways of sensing'.[56] The sensory anthropologist in me rankles at the promiscuous blending of materials and design motifs (culled from around the world at random) on the display shelves at Pier 1 Imports (or worse, Anthropologie) for this risks adulterating 'the sense of the senses *in situ*' (to coin a phrase) and generating so much non-sense, however pleasing or 'hedonic' the items may be. Hedonics in the absence of semantics creates 'floating signifiers' that are ultimately vacuous, and potentially perverse.

'Truth to other cultures' isn't likely to catch on as a selling proposition, and Anthropologie (for all the exotic imports it offers) was never meant as an ethnographic museum, admittedly. So let me (begrudgingly, temporarily) set aside my campaign for the reform of the marketplace,[57] and offer a few suggestions for the reform of design pedagogy instead. In my estimation, design school does not instil the optimal sensibility in the design student, for while the curricula of design school may be aesthetic, they are not sufficiently historic or ethnographic in orientation. Design students need schooling in history and anthropology. Were they better trained in anthropology, for example, they would be able to counsel a future client who is enamoured of, say, Persian motifs of the corresponding sociology and cosmology of the Persian home, with its separate door knockers for male and female visitors, its intergenerational home entertainment (storytelling), its inner courtyard (obviating the need for air conditioning or artificial lighting), and (re)creation of 'Paradise' on earth.[58] Supplementing the hedonics of the Persian home with some knowledge of its semantics would instil in the client an 'enlargement of mind' through their coming to be 'of two sensoria' about things (own and other culture's), in place of pandering to some (unalloyed) pleasure. Furthermore, the design student schooled in anthropology would be adept at sensory ethnography (which employs the methodology of participant-sensation), so they could arrive at 'embodied sensory knowledge' of their client's habitual ways of sensing and aspirations, and therefore be able to advise them more knowingly and empathically.[59] This seems preferable to leaving clients to 'interview themselves', the way Dunne would do.

There is actually an already abundant and growing ethnographic literature on 'the sensory home',[60] 'the sensory office' (which requires a different balance),[61] and 'the sensory hospital',[62] for that matter, so no need to start from scratch. The design student will want to get reading this literature right away,[63] secure in the knowledge that the best way to engage both the intellect and the affects in the design of 'your interior' (own or future client's) is through engaging the senses.

## Notes

1 V. Postrel, *The Substance of Style* (New York: HarperCollins, 2003).
2 Especially for the more impecunious amongst us, HomeSense being a discount store.
3 To view the cover image of the Pier 1 catalogue see Figure 1 at www.percepnet.com/cien01_07_ang.htm.
4 E. Lupton and A. Lipps, *The Senses* (New York: Cooper Hewitt, 2018); A. Krishna, *Sensory Marketing* (New York: Routledge, 2010).
5 Postrel, *Substance*, p. 24.
6 *Ibid.*, p. 5.
7 R. Sheldon and E. Arens, *Consumer Engineering* (New York: Arno Press, 1932).
8 M. Featherstone, *Consumer Culture and Postmodernism* (London: Sage, 1991), p. 66.
9 De Montesquiou was the real-life figure after whom the character of Des Esseintes was modelled in J.-K. Huysman's *Against the Grain* (New York: Dover, 1969). For an account of his sense-life see C. Classen, *The Color of Angels* (London: Routledge, 1998), pp. 113–16 and B. Beaulieu, 'Sensitive design' (Chapter 2 in this volume). See further, regarding the aesthetes who came after, J. Potvin, *Deco Dandy* (Manchester: Manchester University Press, 2021).
10 Featherstone, *Consumer Culture*, pp. 67, 65.
11 Postrel, *Substance*, p. 4. 'To succeed, hard-nosed engineers, ... and MBAs must take [over] aesthetic communication, and aesthetic pleasure' from such dilettantes, Postrel writes.

12  Featherstone, *Consumer Culture*, p. 73.

13  D. Howes, 'HYPERAESTHESIA' in D. Howes (ed.), *Empire of the Senses* (Abingdon: Routledge, 2005).

14  S. Ewen, *All Consuming Images* (New York: Basic, 1988).

15  '*Make it snuggle in the palm*', suggest Sheldon and Arens, *Consumer Engineering*, p. 101.

16  C. Randl, 'Sensuality and Shag Carpeting', *The Senses and Society*, 5:2 (2010), pp. 244–9.

17  J. Warren, 'Color Trendsetters Emerge from the Shade', *Chicago Tribune* (8 January 1999).

18  *Ibid.*

19  L. Boone, 'The Pantone Color of the Year for 2021', *L.A. Times* (9 December 2020).

20  J. Lahne and C. Spackman (eds), 'Accounting for Taste', *The Senses and Society*, 13:1 (2018), pp. 1–5.

21  D. Howes, 'The Science of Sensory Evaluation' in A. Drazin and S. Küchler (eds), *The Social Life of Materials* (London: Routledge, 2015), pp. 81–97.

22  C. Salter, *Sensing Machines* (Cambridge, MA: MIT Press, 2022).

23  G. Teil, 'Learning to Smell', *The Senses and Society*, 14:3 (2019), pp. 330–45.

24  C. Classen, D. Howes and A. Synnott, *Aroma* (London: Routledge, 1994) p. 194.

25  Randl, 'Sensuality', p. 248.

26  Ewen, *All Consuming*, p. 23.

27  C. Spence, *Sensehacking* (London: Viking, 2021) p. 29–30.

28  There is a much simpler and more sustainable 'design solution', of course: 'Just the sound of running water makes us feel cooler', observes Ilse Crawford, in *The Sensual Home* (New York: Rizzoli, 1997), p. 58.

29  Spence, *Sensehacking*, pp. 203–4. Of course, it is not mere physical fitness the latter day cavewoman aspires to, it is 'reproductive fitness' as *demanded* by her genes that motivates her to forgo her home gym equipment and 'move like an animal'.

30  G. Saad, *The Consuming Instinct* (New York: Prometheus, 2011).

31  Lee quoted in C. Spence, 'Senses of Place', *Cognitive Research*, 5:46 (2020), p. 6.

32  M. Sahlins, *The Use and Abuse of Biology* (Ann Arbor, MI: University of Michigan Press, 1976).

33  On the gendered and sexual history of design, which complements the sensory history presented here, see J. Potvin, 'Fags, Queens and Fairies: (Re)locating the Professional Gay Decorator in the History and Historiography of Interior Decorating' in P. Sparkes and P. Lupkin (eds), *Shaping the American Interior* (London: Routledge, 2018).

34  Classen, *Color of Angels*, p. 61–106.

35  *Pace* the philosopher Luce Irigaray. See Classen, *Color of Angels*, pp. 63, 175–6.

36  C. Bailly Dunne, *Interior Designing for All Five Senses* (New York: Golden Books, 1998), p. 16. Per Dunne's sister-in-arms Ilse Crawford in *The Sensual Home*, p. 16: 'the sensuous home needs to feel and smell and even taste as good as it appears'.

37  Dunne, *Interior*, p. 3.

38  Kant imposed much the same strictures on moral reasoning. Do not lie. Do not contract in bad faith. Do not make an exception of yourself. The 'good will' (which is to say the moral self) wills for everybody when they act.

39  Dunne, *Interior*, p. 3.

40  *Ibid.*, p. 112.

41  *Ibid.*, p. 91.

42  Spence, 'Senses of Place', p. 16–18.

43  Dunne, *Interior*, pp. 73, 121.

44  *Ibid.*, p. 135.

45  Perhaps I reveal my class colours by admitting this. In any event, it must be said that Dunne's style counsel is quite classy, even though she (disingenuously) professes

it to be classless: 'This is a book for everyone, whether you live in a mansion or a one-room apartment'. This is why I recommend reading Dunne together with P. Bourdieu, *Distinction: A Social Critique of the Judgment of Taste* (Cambridge, MA: Harvard University Press, 1984).

46 See C. A. Jones, 'The Mediated Sensorium' in C. A. Jones (ed.), *Sensorium* (Cambridge, MA: MIT Press, 2006), pp. 5–49.

47 See Featherstone, *Consumer Culture*; Jones, 'Mediated Sensorium'.

48 And it (Dunne's style) isn't postmodern, not really, anyway.

49 D. Howes, 'Introduction' in D. Howes (ed.), *Senses and Sensation*, vol. IV (Abingdon: Routledge, 2018), pp. 4–5.

50 C. Lévi-Strauss, *The Savage Mind* (Chicago: University of Chicago Press, 1966); R. Caballero and J. E. Diaz Vera (eds), *Sensuous Cognition* (Berlin: De Gruyter, 2013).

51 Dunne, *Interior*, pp. 112, 64–9.

52 C. Classen, 'Feminine Tactics' in C. Classen (ed.), *The Book of Touch* (Abingdon: Routledge, 2005), pp. 228–39.

53 Dunne, *Interior*, pp. 50, 142; Crawford, *Sensual Home*, p. 12–13, 16–17, 25–6, 53, 126, 130.

54 Crawford, *Sensual Home*, pp. 12–17, 25, 38.

55 Dunne, *Interior*, p. 104; Crawford, *Sensual Home*, pp. 15, 41.

56 C. Bardt, *Material and Mind* (Cambridge, MA: MIT Press, 2019); D. Howes and C. Classen, *Ways of Sensing* (London: Routledge, 2014).

57 D. Howes, 'Decommodifying Indianness' in D. Howes (ed.), *Cross-Cultural Consumption* (London: Routledge, 1996).

58 M. M. Tehrani and M. Duffy, 'The Sensuous Host', *Journal of South Asian Studies*, 3:3 (2015), pp. 351–61. On the Persian home see also M. Bille, 'Ecstatic Things', *Home Cultures*, 14:1 (2017), pp. 25–49, on the Bedouin home.

59 S. Pink, *Home Truths* (London: Bloomsbury, 2004).

60 *Ibid.*; S. Pink, *Doing Sensory Ethnography* (London: Sage, 2009).

61 See S. Warren, 'Empirical Challenges in Organizational Aesthetics Research', *Organization Studies*, 29:4 (2008), pp. 559–80, and her many subsequent works. K. Messer, *How to Work with Space: Spatial Knowledge in Organizations and Research Practice* (London: Palgrave Macmillan, 2023).

62 Howes and Classen, *Ways of Sensing*, pp. 37–62; A. Harris, *A Sensory Education* (Abingdon: Routledge, 2021).

63 With the recent launch of the 'Explorations in Sensory Design' project, based at the Centre for Sensory Studies (http://centreforsensorystudies.org/), there will be even more literature integrating design studies with sensory studies coming soon (see https://www.sensorydesign.ca/).

# 13

# Sensorial worlds and atmospheric scenes in Terence Conran's *The House Book*

*Ben Highmore*

## Introduction

One suggestion given to homeowners looking to sell their property is to have some coffee brewing and bread baking when prospective buyers arrive: it will induce a sense of homeliness. Does the smell of coffee and fresh bread alter the house or apartment in any way? Does it make slightly ill-fitting windows shift from being perceived as dilapidated to charmingly quirky? Certainly, this sort of multisensory 'cueing' is now a major aspect of the food industry, with product designers making sure that food packaging produces just the right level of noise to solicit a perception of freshness and crispness in a potato chip, for instance.[1] The wine producers Campo Viejo involved almost 3,000 participants in an experiment in a custom-built 'colour lab' combining coloured lighting and music to show how the environmental conditions of colour and sound altered the perception of taste. Apparently red rooms with Erik Satie's *Trois Gymnopédies* playing improves the taste of the wine by almost 10 per cent (from a 'neutral' state of the room without music and standard white lighting).[2] This overlapping and interlacing of the senses suggests that the best way of investigating the sensorial dimensions of interior design and the history of interior architecture is going to be through a synaesthetic approach.

The aim of this chapter is twofold. Initially the task is to suggest that a historical sense of what an interior 'feels' like, whether it feels 'homely', 'fabulous', 'convivial', 'sacred', and so on is dependent on a synaesthetic mix of sensorial materials, and that these are perceived (though this term will need some nuancing) through orchestrations of the visual, the haptic, the auditory, and the olfactory. In other words, while emphasis has been placed on the look of interiors, we need also attend to the whole somatosensory experience of interiors: the way that our feet 'touch' and move through a space; the way warmth, coolness, and humidity are felt by the skin and in the body; the way that scale (vastness, intimacy) is heard and felt; and so on. The second task is to suggest an approach that tries to grasp the synaesthetic effect and affect of space through a vocabulary that is capacious enough to register multisensory affects. Through the terms 'atmosphere' I want to suggest a way of grasping the gestalt of the sensory scene of the interior. But sensing is an interactive affair, and while atmospheres are active agents in interiors so too are the subjects that congregate there: 'attunement' names the symbiotic assemblage of attuning environment and attuned and attune-able subject. To give material form to these approaches I use the case study of Terence Conran's *The House Book* (from 1974) and the domestic aesthetics that Conran and the shop Habitat developed from 1964.

## Orchestrating the senses

In his 1936 essay 'The Work of Art in the Age of Its Technological Reproducibility', Walter Benjamin famously declared that we experience buildings and their interiors both visually and tactilely:

> Buildings are received in a twofold manner: by use and by perception. Or, better: tactilely and optically. Such reception cannot be understood in terms of concentrated attention of a traveller before a famous building. On the tactile side, there is no counterpart to what contemplation is on the optical side. Tactile reception comes about not so much by way of attention as by way of habit.[3]

He goes on to say that 'even the optical reception of architecture', when treated as part of habitual, everyday life, 'takes the form of casual noticing, rather than attentive observation'.[4] Perception, then, has different levels – from concentrated attention, through casual noticing, on to something less apparent – something that we might name both vaguely and accurately as 'feeling'. The word 'feeling' and 'feels' (like the word 'atmosphere') simultaneously names a metaphorical condition and a material aspect of the world (the sense of touch, the gaseous environment surrounding the earth). When we say we 'feel' our way in the dark, we are both literally using the sense of touch to feel for a wall or a step while also using other 'sensing' abilities (night-vision, echolocation) to 'see' where we are going. And when we say we feel an atmosphere we are often using the senses but also going beyond them to use our associative, imaginative, allusive capacities to narrate and speculate.

    Benjamin's emphasis on tactility (touch, and haptic experience more generally) in relation to both use and habit is an important reminder that in everyday life the optical has a less exalted status and takes its place alongside other modes of senses. It also alerts us to the difficulty of consciously registering the other senses. When I step away from this desk and walk downstairs to make a cup of coffee, which I then bring back to my desk, I only have a vague sense of what I have done partly because it is such a routine, habitual activity. Much of what I'm 'sensing-out' in my micro-journey are routine acts of 'feeling my way' that are almost entirely nonconscious. It is my body (my feet, my hands, my deportment) that does most of the work, that 'knows' when floorboards turn to carpeting, or the depth and width of each stair, or where the coffee mugs are and how to use a kettle. But even in totally unfamiliar environments, when I'm in utility-mode, say, rather than contemplating-space mode, I'm using senses other than vision in navigating my way through a building. One of the first things I'm likely to register, but relatively unlikely to comment on, is the floor surface. The slight bounce of floorboards compared to concrete, the smoothness of linoleum compared to the embrace of carpeting are felt, and this feeling is mediated through shoes (or the lack of them) and feeling depends on whether I'm wearing stiff shoes or softer soled trainers (sneakers). And yet this flooring isn't simply registered by my feet. When walking through the corridors of a luxury hotel, I see and feel the carpet, but I also hear the plush hush of luxury. In a large church I can see the flagstones and feel the ungiving and unforgiving surface, but I also hear the reverberating vastness that encourages me to whisper.[5]

Phenomena that seem to be aimed at one of the senses on closer investigation reveal multisensory experience. Lighting is a good example of a sensorial realm that at first glance seem to be entirely visual but has a panoply of other sensorial effects (and affects) that are essential to it. Candlelight offers the most emphatic example of this. Clearly candles smell (both unscented and scented), sometimes they can make a slight noise as they hiss and splutter, and they also produce heat (however limited in capacity). The kind of light produced by candles alters the physical experience of a space. The light dances on surfaces, picking out tactile characteristics that would be imperceptible with another form of lighting. We think of candlelight as producing intimacy because it shrinks space, altering the geography of a room. A table or a chest experienced in candlelight has a different mass, a different density, than the same object seen in daylight or under fluorescent lighting. Shadows make solid forms merge with each other and with the background. When you enter a room in candlelight you feel it on your skin, in your bodily response to space, with your eyes, but often on the surface of your eyes: materials feel different; the orchestration of the senses is being recalibrated.

How do we deal with this multisensory orchestration that involves at least four of the five senses (though many domestic spaces are directly concerned with eating and drinking)? And how do we include those other senses that seem so internal to our bodies? For instance, how might we explore something that has been so historically important for cold climates as the shift from located forms of heating (the fire*place*) to the ambient and diffuse heating of 'central heating'? Or in hot climates the extensive but often ambient chilling through air conditioning? How do we understand so many of our furnishings that disappear from view when they are put to use? A chair, for instance, might be highly patterned or plain, but when we are sitting on it, we are experiencing it via proprioception rather than visually. The work of phenomenologists and those working in their wake might be particularly useful here.

## Atmospheres and attunements

One area of research that is proving to be particularly useful for thinking holistically about sensual space has focused on 'atmospheres and attunements'.[6] Thinkers in this field are often working from a phenomenological perspective. This is an area that is having its biggest impact within marketing and within contemporary architecture and design.[7] Here is not the place to offer a detailed rehearsal of the philosophy of phenomenology (nor would it be possible) but it is worth noting three general aspects of existential phenomenology (which might see Martin Heidegger as the source of its inspiration) that make it particularly conducive to an approach to multisensory space. First, phenomenology works to overcome the dualism of subjects and objects, minds and bodies. It works with a much more distributed sense of consciousness, and a much more diffuse sense of self and things. Thus, in thinking about a room's atmosphere it neither imagines that this atmosphere is somehow embedded in the room, nor as a quality that a person simply brings into a room or subjectively 'finds' there. An atmosphere might be a form of subjectivity that we receive externally (objectively) but experience as if it emanates from inside us. Second, despite having a dauntingly technological sounding title, existential phenomenology often uses vernacular terms to suggest that in our everyday speech we are often already operating with a phenomenological sensitivity. Words, like 'mood', 'feeling', 'atmosphere', 'care', and 'being', are the sorts of words that phenomenology puts in play. Phenomenology often deals with words that have a necessary vagueness to them because what they are describing are ordinary experiences that are amorphous and ambient. In ordinary speech we often say things such as 'how's it going?' or 'what's happening?' where neither the subject nor the verb seems to have a specific referent. The happenings and goings of 'it' (our being-in-the-world) is phenomenology's topic. Phenomenology treats experience and being as a process and a relationship that is ongoing. Third, phenomenology's terms are value-neutral. For a phenomenologist words like 'mood', 'atmosphere', 'care' aren't qualities that only pertain to certain phenomena. While we might say 'wow, that bar has atmosphere' what we really mean is something like 'wow, that bar has a really convivial atmosphere and manages to enable an ethos of easy-going sociality' or 'that bar has an old-world charm that feels really authentic'. Similarly, when we say that the motorway service station has 'no atmosphere' we mean something like 'these services have an atmosphere of cold utility to them that seemed to discourage any form of social enjoyment'. From a phenomenological perspective all scenes, all spaces have an atmosphere – to remark about the absence of atmosphere is just a short-hand way of describing a particular atmosphere. The general applicability of the term atmosphere is one of its strengths and means we can investigate the atmospherics of a hospital, a restaurant, a living room, a kitchen, a mosque, and so on.

In the field of architectural and design history, the focus on atmosphere and attunement offers considerable possibilities and challenges. One of the leading exponents of an atmospheric approach to architecture and interiors is the German philosopher Gernot Böhme. For Böhme, 'atmosphere' doesn't name an aspect of phenomenology's aesthetic approach; it is its overriding subject. Atmospheres are central to an engagement with aesthetic life primarily because they allow for a holistic approach to space:

> *Atmosphere* itself is something rather vague, indeterminate or even indeterminable. The reason for this is related to the fact that atmospheres are totalities: they flood out over everything, they tinge the entire world or sight, they let everything appear in a certain light, and they aggregate a multiplicity of impressions into an overall mood.[8]

A concern with aggregation, and the concomitant realization that atmospherics can't be determined by isolated elements (such as the smell of newly baked bread), alerts us to the way atmospheres are established by orchestrations of a relationship between phenomena, as well as between the perceiver and perceived. Thus, for Dora Zhang: 'The failure of attempts to itemize and to break down an atmosphere into its components demonstrates that this concept names, in effect, the spatialization of relationality. The problem is that we are dealing with a kind of relationality that is total, the kind that has been called ecological, global, or cosmological.'[9] The 'spatialization of relationality' might be a useful way of connecting with interior design history where an audit of elements (even if they are sensitive to their sensory properties) would miss the overarching orchestral arrangement of the sensorial situation that is both designed and lived.

Importantly, attention to atmospheres is a challenge to a form of attention that has been dominated by a representational logic that privileges the symbolic, the ideational, and the referential. A representation logic asks us to interpret a space; an atmospheric logic asks us to feel space. Thus an atmospheric approach is particularly valuable for a multisensory enquiry that wants to move away from a semiotics where a particular piece of furniture, for instance, signifies 'cultural capital' or 'social status', and on to a sensorial sensitivity that is attentive to the materiality of the furniture.

As Kathleen Stewart writes in her essay 'Atmospheric Attunements', when you are attentive to atmospheres 'things matter not because of how they are represented but because they have qualities, rhythms, forces, relations, and movements'.[10] One way of attuning ourselves to an atmospheric sensitivity is to treat spaces as stagings. As Böhme often argues, the world of theatre and particularly the art of scenography offers an emphatic example of how atmospheres are deliberately created as well as how they are never simply the result of individual responses (if we all responded to a staging of *Macbeth* differently there would be little point in scenography). For Böhme atmosphere is

> not just something one feels but something that can be generated deliberately by specific, indeed material constellations. The paradigm here is the art of scenography, where stage designers habitually produce a *climate* by arranging things, spatial constellations, light and sound in specific ways. As a result, a space of a particular basic mood arises on stage, within which the drama can then unfold.[11]

As a way of demonstrating the productivity of an atmospheric approach to the sensorial dimensions of interiors, I now turn to the example of Terence Conran.

## Terence Conran and the Habitat aesthetic

Terence Conran (1931–2020) was a furniture designer, a restaurateur, a shop designer, a retailer, a museum creator, and an assembler of teams of designers, display specialists, and publicists. I mention this list of activities not as a way of showing the extent of his accomplishments but to notice the multisensory dimensions of his career. I think that an argument could be made to claim that Conran worked primarily in the business of staging and atmospherics. There is no doubt that the single most important contribution he made to the cultural landscape was through the shop Habitat. The first Habitat shop was opened in London in 1964 and in the words of Barry Curtis 'combined the informality of the boutique with the abundance of a warehouse'.[12] Twenty years later there were forty-four Habitat stores across the British Isles; twenty-three stores in France and Belgium; and a further eight shops in Japan and eight in the USA (trading under the name 'Conran'). While Habitat was indebted to the department store ethos of everything-under-one-roof, it adapted and transformed this ethos in two significant ways. Firstly, as Curtis points out, Habitat nurtured a sense of informality: shop assistants were specifically told not to 'hustle' customers; everything was available to handle whereas department stores kept most items in drawers and cabinets that were mediated by sellers. Secondly, and perhaps most crucially, whereas department stores catered for a range of tastes and styles, Habitat promoted a loose unilateral taste: everything went with everything else. Habitat taught the consumer modern 'good taste': as Penny Sparke argues, rather than asking them to choose styles they were 'being asked to trust his [Conran's] taste decisions and to purchase whole interior settings from his shop'.[13] While shopping in general might seem to encourage the sort of concentrated contemplation that Benjamin associated with the tourist's approach to famous buildings, Habitat drew out the tactility of modern consumption by encouraging touch, while also staging a shopping experience more attuned to Benjamin's ideas of casual noticing through attention to the ambient environment – floors and ceilings had a Habitat feel to them, piped music created a sense of up-to-date-ness, lighting modulated and 'dramatized' spaces.[14] Habitat sought to bring the same energy of instant gratification to shopping for furnishings as was available for clothing and music.

What was so significant about this chain of shops was the way they staged their goods and also staged a multisensory atmosphere of the domestic interior. In a previous article I adopted a scenographic approach to analysing what I called the Habitat taste formation across three aspects of Habitat: the store itself; the annual catalogue; and Conran's *The House Book* as a piece of advice literature that was directly and indirectly associated with Habitat (you could order it through the catalogue or buy in the stores, but it also showed you how to get the Conran/Habitat 'look' without necessarily shopping at Habitat).[15] But I think that story would benefit from being articulated within the atmospheric-attunement paradigm because the emphasis on the 'good life' that Habitat promoted was always gustatory as well as visual, haptic as well as auditory: herbs, kitchenware, textiles, and hi-fi systems were all sold at Habitat. When Conran died commentators tended to credit him with popularizing the duvet in Britain, as well as a lifestyle that favoured sensual pleasure and spontaneous sociability, Mediterranean food, and a more informal style of domestic life. In a tonally ambivalent obituary of his one-time boss, Stephen Bayley correctly paints a portrait of a man who was more an *animateur* than an originator, and notes how much of the Conran look is down to other agents (Caroline Conran, Oliver Gregory, Vico Magistretti, to mention just three). Bayley's assessment is that Conran's 'achievement was to put middle Britain in touch with the pleasure principle. Habitat was meant to make houses cheerful. Thus, there was a sort of missionary ethos.'[16] Conran, then, was as much a brand as an author, as much a collective enterprise as a designer. His name designates a plurality of agents.

It is worth noting one aspect of his design education that is important for considering the multisensory aesthetic of the Habitat taste. Conran attended the Central School of Art and Design at the end of the 1940s working primarily in the textile department with Eduardo Paolozzi.[17] The School followed the principles of the Bauhaus, with a strong emphasis on the distinctive characteristics and affordances of materials. Such an ethos is summed up by the architects Alison and Peter Smithson who also taught there and who were part of the same cultural circle as Paolozzi: 'we were concerned with the seeing of materials for what they were: the woodness of wood; the sandiness of sand'.[18] The New Brutalism aesthetic that the Smithsons and others developed signalled this emphasis partly with the phrase 'as found': the phrase signalled a commitment to using materials in their 'as found' state, whether that was bricks or plastic. But it also signalled an attention to the environment 'as found', which included a strong empathy for vernacular forms (terraced housing, crofters' cottages, etc., but also the *objet trouvé*). Conran drew insistently from this heritage in Habitat's emphasis on items that stress their 'rough and ready' qualities, things such as sisal floor matting, quarry tiles, wooden spoons, butcher's blocks, and so on. And he also drew from this heritage by attempting to make a trip to Habitat somehow equivalent to the 'lucky find' from a small hardware shop or a French market. Much of the material that was sold was simply sourced by buyers rather than designed by Habitat. The design correspondent for the *Guardian* newspaper, Fiona MacCarthy, described the shop like this:

> Here, pre-assembled and impeccably displayed, were all the things the design pundits had hunted for and gloated over all these many years: workmen's mugs and rustic cooking pots and sturdy peasant furniture, baskets, cheap pub glasses, butchers' aprons, wooden toys, an overall good humour and indomitable Britishness.[19]

The 'Britishness' that MacCarthy points to describes a graphic style that was something of a cross between Aubrey Beardsley and Heath Robinson, yet the objects themselves were often distinctly un-British: plain, unfussy vernacular items from France, Italy, and Scandinavia.

The sensorial world of Habitat had two distinct atmospheres: the upstairs floors favoured tableaux, where selected items would be arranged in a way that suggested they were already part of a domestic *mise-en-scène*, already part of a scene of improvised sociability (a large plant, a sofa, a coffee table, an armchair, a scattering of magazines; the ensemble arranged as if it were the staging of some kind of conversation). Downstairs the atmosphere was designed to replicate the informal abundance of a market: 'I wanted to re-create the feeling of abundance and plenty that I had experienced in French markets and make Habitat brim over with merchandise. All the packaging was removed so that the products could be not only seen but also touched – I always recognized the emotive value in customers handling our products.'[20] These overflowing stacks of earthenware pots or wicker baskets were known within Habitat as 'dump displays'. The sensual landscape of the shop deployed different styles of lighting: ambient for the market areas; spotlights for the tableaux. Reviewers at the time were sensitive to the particular sensuality of the shop:

Any food addict will be interesting in the cooking side, kitchen equipment from all over the world (though some of the most covetable is resurrected from forgotten British sources); packeted Provençal herbs, pungent and aromatic; pastoral flowery mugs in soft browns and blues, enamelware in innumerable colours; sensibly thick, cheap and simple china is resurrected from forgotten reminiscent of Edwardian café crockery; traditional wine glasses.[21]

The sensuality of Habitat was, I would argue, meant to elicit an atmosphere of the 'good life', where the good life looked forward to modern 'classless' forms of sociability and relaxed informality (no strict adherence to British aristocratic or bourgeois propriety), while also looking backwards to an idealized peasant culture of pastoral plenty.[22] Yet the full sensorial world could not simply be purchased new from a Habitat; to be a true Habitater (so to say) required finding items that could never be bought from a chain store, however dedicated it was to authenticity. *The House Book* was an attempt to provide an extensive pedagogy in atmospheric attunement. It was designed to offer practical and imaginative attunement in the larger sensorial world of Conran and Habitat.

## The House Book

*The House Book* was an immediate success, selling more than two-and-a-half million copies in multiple editions and various translations. It existed in dynamic tension with Habitat, primarily because it seemed to encourage what we now call recycling and upcycling, and refused the off-the-peg interiors championed by Habitat and its annual catalogues.[23] While there were examples of interiors fitted out with brand-new furnishings the emphasis was on the weathered. One of the lessons that *The House Book* taught was the sensual pleasure of the battered, the old, the impoverished. Perhaps as significant as popularizing duvets, the taste transformation associated with Conran and Habitat performed the *retuning* of the basic well-used pine kitchen table. I purposefully use the word 'retuning' here rather than a term like 'recoding' because it is not just the meaning of the table that is changing; it is the sensorial registration that is being altered, retuned. During the 1960s and 1970s the battered pine kitchen table moved from being an item associated with the poor and utility, a bygone age of 'below stairs' servitude, to becoming something that could stage a new alignment with a sensual world of gustatory pleasure and easy sociability. A key here was the furniture itself shifting from something to be looked at (which might be associated with social status) to something that had a tactile presence. Of course, as Benjamin pointed out, any building, any interior, any piece of furniture can be a thing to contemplate and a thing to use: part of the retuning *The House Book* was performing was to shift contemplation from the symbolic to perceiving the sensorial tactility of a useable thing.

The weathered kitchen table takes pride of place in *The House Book*. It is the first colour image in the book, and it is given a full page [Figure 13.1]. The page is captioned 'Style/1'. The photograph is captioned with the following words: 'The hub of the farmhouse is its kitchen, and the hub of that kitchen is the table: old, huge and scrubbed, a reminder of endless gargantuan meals that have been prepared and eaten there. Here, all abiding warmth and comfort comes from an Aga recessed in the beautiful old chimney breast – such a welcome for a farmer returning from his fields – or a fugitive from the city rat-race'.[24] If the writing wants to evoke memories

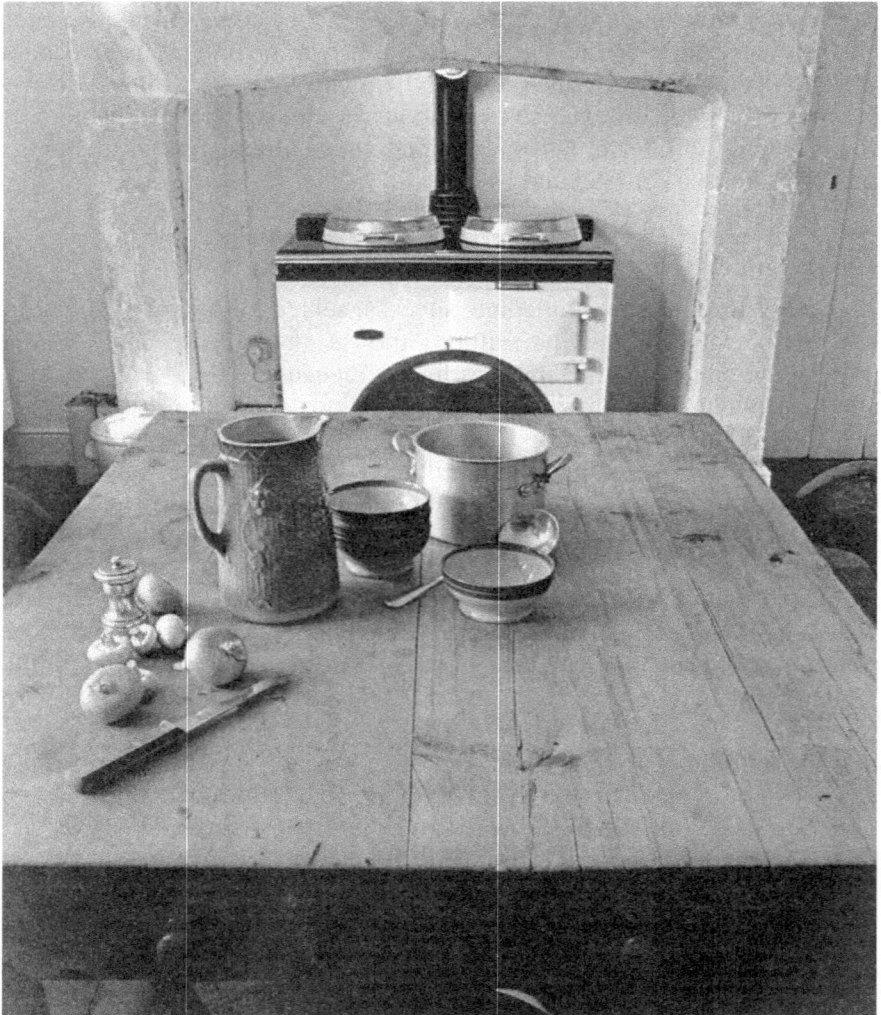

**Figure 13.1**   From *The House Book*, p. 9.

(real or imagined, it doesn't seem to matter), then the image is designed to emphasize the table as both historical (the foregrounding of the table's edge with its notches and splits) and gustatory (the scattered arrangement of onions, mushrooms, and peppermill, and the cooking and consuming utensils). Habitat and *The House Book* set out to ensure that a consumer didn't have to live on a farm to enjoy the idealized ruralism being performed in the 'farmhouse style'. As MacCarthy noted, Habitat sold a rurality aimed squarely at city folk: 'Piled high on the chests and dressers and plain scrubbed trestle tables there are stoneware kitchen crocks, apothecary jars, preserving pans, giant pestles and mortars, rural English china with pictures of cows paddling lugubriously in brooks. People lug them off to countrify their cottages in Fulham.'[25] This was a rurality being performed in the newly gentrifying areas of London (Islington, Fulham, and Chelsea in the 1960s and later Notting Hill in the 1970s) by relatively young members of the 'new middle classes'.

Here is not the place to pursue these arguments about the social affects and effects of this retuning of kitchen tables. Instead what I want to puzzle is how the cultural historian, faced with an archive that is often sensorially limited to images and writing, can go about attuning themselves to the multisensory atmospherics of past interiors. I think that one of the ways of doing this is by being particularly attentive to light and lighting in images. Light, as we have seen, is crucial to the atmospherics of Habitat, but it is also, for the atmospherically attuned phenomenologist, the basic element for perceiving matter:

> It is only through the play of light on things that appearance as such acquires a character: things appear to us in a certain way. This type of light phenomenon is extraordinarily significant. One may well say that, in design, cosmetics or architecture, the deployment of materials is essentially determined by how their surfaces interact with light.[26]

Böhme's privileging of light is not unproblematic as it seems to de-emphasize olfactory and haptic forms of perception which might also have ways of perceiving character, yet it is particularly useful when looking at images. We could say that it is partly the diffuse warm lighting of the table's foreground in Figure 13.1, coupled with the direct spot of sunlight at the corner of the table and the glow of the fireplace, that reveals the sensual character of the table, as a place where utility has morphed into gustatory and sociable pleasure, and where the wood itself is 'thick' with past repasts.

Figure 13.2 is from the section on flooring. It is showing us a floor made up of quarry tiles and we can assume that the floor is old or rather that it is not a pristine example of a newly quarry-tiled floor. The grouting is irregular, the tiles look slightly chipped in places, and the floor looks uneven. But what gives the flooring character, what reveals (for us) its

**Figure 13.2**   'Non-porous floors (slate, ceramic and quarry tiles)', *The House Book*, p. 60.

sensorial atmosphere is the lighting falling on both the floor and the flowers and container, chair, curtains, and French windows. It would, I think, have been relatively easy to show the tiles in such a way that they look like examples of bad flooring, but instead the image discloses the homely open atmosphere of the floor. The light both falls across the floor, warming it up, and refracts some of the reflective quality of tiles that have been smoothed into a shine over years of use. As with the table we are not simply looking at a hard, unforgiving surface but a surface saturated with memories, of pleasurable sociability. For Böhme: 'If atmosphere is a tuned space, or an environment that appears to people in a certain way, then the lighting of a space or scene is of decisive importance. Colours, light, distribution of light, intensity, concentration or, conversely, diffusion of light are what endow a space, or a scene, with a certain atmosphere.'[27]

The textures of material are never simply revealed as an *essence*. Even in a hardware shop a plank of wood is never outside an atmospheric situation that orients us in certain ways. We are attuned to particular material and sensorial sensitivities in a myriad of ways. The smell of coffee and newly baked bread might be part of an orchestration of atmospherics in some scenes, but clearly such elements are missing from *The House Book*. What we have instead, though, is a staging where some mushrooms or quarry tiles are enmeshed in an atmospheric situation that is always something more than the itemizing of the sensual qualities of the things included.

## Conclusion

Hopefully I have shown that an attunement towards atmospheres is a productive way of approaching the history of the interiors of the built environment. But is it just *another* tool, an *expansion* of how we might go about doing historical work? I would argue that an approach that is attentive to atmospheres and attunements has the capacity to get a better understanding of how the material realm attunes our historical sensorium (our capacities for enjoyment, disdain, our socialities, our sense of comfort and care, our sensorial inclusions and exclusions) and that this understanding is essential for critically engaging with the everydayness of our life worlds. As Dora Zhang has it what 'we need is to cultivate *more* attunement to the atmospheres around us and to the possibilities they encourage or deter':[28] in other words, atmospheres stage the actualization of our social potentiality. To alter a bullying, fearful atmosphere it is not enough to outlaw abusive language or to reprimand aggressive bosses; the atmosphere itself needs to change. If an atmosphere of 'reciprocal care' is desired, then an accumulation of sensorial adjustments can count for a great deal. In the building where I work, a large shared office went from having a bleakly unconvivial atmosphere to feeling extraordinarily hospitable and this was achieved by rearranging the space, bringing in some new people, but mostly by the fact that everyone started bringing in large plants to tend. The office became a garden of horticultural attention: people's orientations were redirected, bodies moved in a different manner, the light and the smell of the room shifted dramatically.

For Böhme,

> the critical potential of an aesthetics of atmospheres is […] initially positioned against the condemnation of the *lower spheres* of the aesthetic and shows the legitimacy of an aestheticization of everyday life […] it is also a critique of the aestheticization of everyday life and the world, namely in all instances in which it becomes a law unto itself, and where its power has to be resisted.[29]

Böhme's dialectic asks us to be attentive to those aesthetic elements that have been ignored through a sense of aesthetic hierarchy, but also to have a critical-historical sense of how 'atmospherics' are fashioning the world for us. Here, I would argue, it is not a question of condemning or condoning atmospheric attunements such as those found in *The House Book*. It is not enough to champion these stagings as the liberation of the domestic interior from formal propriety, aristocratic taste, and austere parenting, and nor is it enough to bemoan them as the materialization of a neoliberal emphasis on individualism, as offering a scenography of gentrification and white entitlement. Both evaluations are probably true to some degree, but the atmospherics and attunements of the book offer us something more; a historical sensitivity to how taste changes are not about the alteration of a symbolic universe but about the lived sensorial tuning of our everyday worlds.

## Notes

1  M. Zampini and C. Spence, 'The Role of Auditory Cues in Modulating the Perceived Crispness and Staleness of Potato Chips', *Journal of Sensory Studies*, 19 (2004), pp. 347–63.

2  R. Ross, 'Colour and Sound Proven to Affect Wine Taste', *The Drinks Business* (20 June 2014), www.thedrinksbusiness.com/2014/06/colour-and-sound-proven-to-affect-wine-taste/ (accessed 13 February 2021).

3  W. Benjamin, *The Work of Art in the Age of Its Technological Reproducibility, and Other Writings on Media* (Cambridge, MA: Belknap Press of Harvard University Press, 2008), p. 40.

4  *Ibid.*

5  See, for instance, T. Ingold, 'Culture on the Ground: The World Perceived Through the Feet', *Journal of Material Culture*, 9:3 (2004), pp. 315–40.

6  See, for instance: S. Ahmed, *Queer Phenomenology: Orientations, Objects, Others* (Durham, NC: Duke University Press, 2006); G. Böhme, *Atmospheric Architectures: The Aesthetics of Felt Space* (London: Bloomsbury, 2017); K. Stewart, 'Atmospheric Attunements', *Environment and Planning D: Society and Space*, 29:3 (2011), pp. 445–53; A. Pérez-Gómez, *Attunement: Architectural Meaning After the Crisis of Modern Science* (Cambridge, MA: MIT Press, 2016); and D. Zhang, 'Notes on Atmosphere', *Qui Parle*, 27:1 (2018), pp. 121–55.

7  For a review of the literature in business research see L. W. Turley and R. E. Milliman, 'Atmospheric Effects on Shopping Behavior: A Review of the Experimental Evidence', *Journal of Business Research* (2000), 49, pp. 193–211. For architecture and design see C. Borch (ed.), *Architectural Atmospheres: On the Experience and Politics of Architecture* (Basel: Birkhäuser, 2014) and M. Sloane, 'Tuning the Space: Investigating the Making of Atmospheres through Interior Design Practices', *Interiors*, 5:3 (2014), pp. 297–314.

8  Böhme, *Atmospheric Architectures*, p. 159.

9  Zhang, 'Notes on Atmosphere', p. 130.

10  Stewart, 'Atmospheric Attunements', p. 445.

11  Böhme, *Atmospheric Architectures*, p. 119.

12  B. Curtis, 'A New Domestic Landscape: British Interior Design, 1960–73' in D. A. Mellor and L. Gervereau (eds), *The Sixties: Britain and France, 1960–1973, The Utopian Years* (London: Philip Wilson, 1997), p. 190. Before Habitat had opened Conran and his design team had been actively involved in developing a 'boutique aesthetic' by designing the interior of Mary Quant's *Bazaar* store in London's Knightsbridge in 1957.

13  P. Sparke, 'At Home with Modernity: The New Domestic Scene' in C. Breward and G. Wood (eds), *British Design from 1948: Innovation in the Modern Age* (London: V&A Publishing, 2012), p. 131.

14  One of my informants, who managed a Habitat shop in the 1970s, remembers Mike Oldfield's *Tubular Bells* (Virgin, 1973) endlessly being played when it was released.

15  B. Highmore, 'Habitat's Scenographic Imagination', *Journal of Design History*, 30:1 (2017), pp. 33–49; see also B. Highmore, 'Feeling It: Habitat, Taste and the New Middle Class in 1970s Britain', *New Formations*, 88 (2016), pp. 105–22 for a more cultural historical account of Habitat.

16  S. Bayley, 'Sir Terence Conran obituary', *Guardian* (12 September 2020), www.the guardian.com/culture/2020/sep/12/sir-terence-conran-obituary (accessed 15 February 2021).

17 See B. Phillips, *Conran and the Habitat Story* (London: George Weidenfeld and Nicolson, 1984).

18 A. Smithson and P. Smithson, 'The "As Found" and the "Found"' in D. Robbins (ed.), *The Independent Group: Postwar Britain and the Aesthetics of Plenty* (Cambridge, MA and London: MIT Press, 1990) p. 201.

19 F. MacCarthy, *A History of British Design 1830–1970* (London: George Allen & Unwin, 1979), pp. 103–4.

20 T. Conran, *My Life in Design* (London: Conran Octopus, 2016), p. 50.

21 Press cutting from Habitat Archive, V&A (AAD/1995/12/15/1), the *Observer*, unpaginated and dated just October 1966.

22 As I argue in 'Feeling It', 'classlessness' was a particular class identity for the 'new middle classes' that were emerging in post-war Britain in the wake of the Welfare State, new forms of industry and much larger education sector.

23 The book included items that could be purchased from Habitat and elsewhere alongside older 'found' furnishings. In many ways it could be read as Conran's response to criticism that Habitat offered 'instant good taste' in an ersatz form.

24 T. Conran, *The House Book* (London: Mitchell Beazley, 1974), p. 9.

25 F. MacCarthy, 'Geared Up', *Guardian* (16 January 1965), p. 6.

26 Böhme, *Atmospheric Architectures*, p. 155.

27 *Ibid.*, p. 156.

28 Zhang, 'Notes on Atmosphere', p. 129.

29 Böhme, *Atmospheric Architectures*, p. 31.

# 14

# Aesop's sensory experience

## D. J. Huppatz

The past two decades have seen significant changes in the design and perception of retail stores. While media claims about the 'death' of bricks and mortar and the 'retail apocalypse' proved to be exaggerations, the rise of online shopping resulted in both store closures and anxiety about retail's future viability.[1] Defying this trend, luxury skincare brand Aesop grew from a single store in Melbourne, Australia, in 2008, to over 230 stores around the world by the end of 2021. Aesop's success was due – at least partially – to its design of distinctive, immersive interiors. Smells of citrus, cedar and lavender, soothing music, visual order and tactile materials combine with the ritual of applying skin products and washing hands to create an engaging sensory experience for the customer.

Focusing particularly on Aesop's Melbourne stores, this chapter analyses the company's retail interiors within the context of two recent directions in design practice: experience and sensory design. The first, prompted by Joseph Pine and James Gilmore's influential work on the 'experience economy', describes how brands employ designers to integrate product, graphic, interior and digital design into compelling experiences.[2] The second describes architecture's 'phenomenological turn', advocated by practitioner-theorists such as Peter Zumthor and Juhani Pallasmaa, whose works have prompted a renewed emphasis on design that engages with our senses. The Aesop store – a carefully curated, immersive interior – occupies the intersection of these two directions, making it a compelling case study of sensory experience design.

## Designing an ethos

Aesop began as a series of haircare products sold from Dennis Paphitis' Melbourne hairdressing salon in the 1980s. Paphitis was interested in the possibilities of natural ingredients and essential oils and, with the help of a chemist, began to experiment on a broader range of products. In 1987, he launched Aesop as a brand of skincare products. He distributed these through existing Australian stores, slowly gained a local clientele, then secured distribution in up-market department stores in the United States and Europe.

Fundamental to Paphitis' brand ethos was a design-consciousness, exemplified by Aesop's distinctive bottles and minimal packaging. Aesop's amber bottles looked like old-fashioned apothecary bottles; their black and white labels with sans serif typography contained only essential information (ingredients and use). No promises of eternal youth, perfection or sex appeal. In fact, Paphitis was determined to avoid the traditional marketing strategies of the beauty industry: Aesop's advertising does not feature models or celebrities. Instead, they focus on ethical and environmental statements. 'Vegan', 'cruelty-free' and 'plant-based' highlight the company's ethical stance and, like the minimal design and packaging, gesture towards environmental sustainability.

But even in the late 1980s, this was not an entirely novel concept. In establishing an ethical, environmental ethos, Aesop followed in the footsteps of The Body Shop, founded by Anita Roddick in Brighton in 1976. As it grew into a national, then global brand, The Body Shop became 'a model of Green conscience: all products are biodegradable and natural; animal testing is avoided; containers are basic and can be refilled; and packaging is minimal'.[3] The Body Shop eschewed traditional advertising, instead promoting their brand through interviews, launches, events and public advocacy of environmental, fair trade and social justice issues.[4] But a 1994 exposé by Jon Entine in *Business Ethics* magazine and ensuing articles questioned the company's 'natural' ingredients and ethical sourcing of exotic ingredients, and described their branding as 'greenwashing'.[5]

Among other brands, Lush Cosmetics adopted the ethical skincare mantle. Mark and Mo Constantine (who had previously supplied The Body Shop with products) founded Lush in 1995 and centred their brand ethos on natural ingredients, cruelty-free products and 'a marketing strategy strongly integrated around transparency, fair trade, human rights, and justice'.[6] Lush also adopted a promotional strategy with no celebrity endorsements and regularly partnered with nonprofits and charities to support social and environmental causes. By the 1990s, the marketing of these and other cosmetics companies around no animal testing was certainly an attempt to promote an ethical high ground in what was (and remains) a complex subject, particularly when the ingredients of any cosmetic or skincare product are considered.[7]

Both companies created distinctive if uninspiring interiors. The original Body Shop store design, by Brian Lowe Design consultancy, 'featured a dark green modular system constructed in timber, and extensive use of dark green tones on both the facia and in the interior'.[8] The Body Shop deployed the same 'green box' into thousands of stores globally in the 1980s and the 1990s. Similarly, Lush stores (over 900 worldwide as at the end of 2021) had a consistent aesthetic: raw, recycled timber joinery and boxes filled with unwrapped, candy-coloured 'bath bombs' and soaps, with white, handwritten script on the labels of their black plastic tubs and transparent bottles. Perhaps most distinctive is the Lush store's reputation for an intense, overpowering clash of fragrances that extends beyond the interior.

While Aesop's brand ethos is clearly indebted to the ethical, natural and sustainable ideals of these precedents, Paphitis forged an alternative reputation by engaging with high culture, architecture and design. An intellectual emphasis would prove a distinctive foil within a broader skin-care industry peopled with superficial images of models and celebrities. From Aesop's inception, Paphitis turned to literature. The brand is named after Aesop, the legendary ancient Greek figure whose fables functioned to instruct correct behaviour or convey a moral lesson. With Aesop as a key motif, the brand immediately carried connotations of ancient Greek wisdom and literature yet in an accessible mode.[9]

This attachment to literary and ancient Greek intellectual culture continues to the present. A section of the 2021 Aesop website titled 'The Athenaeum', for example, features short articles such as 'Anti-Oxidants in Skincare' alongside the more intellectual 'View from Above: A Stoic Practice for Daily Perspective', an article that ends with a quote from Roman Stoic and emperor, Marcus Aurelius.[10] The Aesop web-site is sprinkled with inspirational quotes from famous writers, and some of these also appear on the walls of the stores. Writers Walt Whitman and Virginia Woolf, intellectuals Baruch Spinoza and Walter Benjamin, composers Frédéric Chopin and Felix Mendelssohn are all represented by one-line aphorisms – bite-sized intellectual snacks for a busy, information-saturated customer. The Aesop Foundation, the brand's charity arm, is dedicated to literacy and storytelling, and Aesop publishes its own online literary journal, *The Fabulist*, featuring short fiction and non-fiction.[11]

Aesop also employs an in-house design team, comprising architects, graphic designers, copywriters, videographers and photographers that maintain the brand's visual coherence. The Aesop aesthetic, based on simplicity, sharp contrasts and muted colours, remains consistent across social media. Aesop's Instagram feed, for example, appears more like an architecture or design magazine than a skincare company. Images and videos of Aesop stores, meticulously staged bottles and close-ups of raw ingredients feature prominently, while people appear only incidentally in Aesop's image-world. These are interspersed with book covers, art, and music videos (broadly 'ambient' or 'chill') commissioned by Aesop.

## Designing a weighty gold charm bracelet

Despite their initial success in building a brand, Aesop remained a whole-sale company that sold products in department stores and other retail outlets. According to CEO Michael O'Keeffe, around 2003, the company implemented a conscious shift from 'product-centric to retail-centric'.[12] Modest brown bottles with black and white labels, he recalled, could not compete on a glittering department store cosmetic counter. So, O'Keeffe's strategy was to create Aesop stores that could complement the products.[13] The first trial store in 2003, a collaboration with local architectural practice Six Degrees, was a small, narrow space in an underground carpark below the Prince Hotel in Melbourne's gentrifying suburb of St Kilda. Though modest (and temporary), it allowed Aesop to curate their own environment. The unusual space, lack of overt signage and minimal fittings resonated with their customers.

Then Aesop opened their first permanent store in the heart of Melbourne's shopping district. The Flinders Lane store began as a temporary installation in 2008 designed by March Studio's Rodney Eggleston. Given a fortnight and a brief that stipulated the use of recycled cardboard, Eggleston's studio staff folded, cut and arranged recycled cardboard into an installation of boxes that functioned both aesthetically and as product shelves [Figure 14.1]. The repetition of the bottles and jars in rhythmic patterns within the beige cubes suggested a 1960s Minimalist art installation and this repetition became a consistent feature of Aesop's interiors. Along the opposite wall, Eggleston left stacked cardboard sheets exposed so customers could see the interior structure of the industrial-grade material. The prominent use of unadorned cardboard helped reinforce the brand's ethos around sustainability while the absence of artificial colours and materials complemented Aesop's emphasis on natural ingredients.

This installation remained until 2015 when Aesop's in-house design team redesigned the Flinders Lane store, maintaining continuity through the use of recycled cardboard. But this time, the designers created an undulating, sculptural form that curves around one wall, with rows of bottles lining shelves on another. They first modelled the forms digitally, then constructed them from cut and stacked layers of cardboard, hand-finished into seamless contours. Spotlights create dramatic hollows that contribute to the store's cave-like ambience; the calm atmosphere contrasts the busy laneway outside. As with the original iteration, this store also contains no barriers or partitions separating customers and staff, no clearly delineated counter which might form a spatial separation between buyer and seller. This later iteration includes an essential feature of later stores missing from the 2008 original: a central sink to highlight the sensual experience of applying lotions and washing them off.

**Figure 14.1**    Aesop store, Flinders Lane, Melbourne, design by March Studio, 2008.

Another Melbourne store continued this refined vision of the Aesop interior. Also designed by March Studio, the North Melbourne store is located on a corner, with large windows open onto the street. Here, the designers left the existing structure intact and created the store by adding a few signature pieces and painting the walls pale pink. The central focus is an old archive drawer from the Art Gallery of New South Wales, used to display rows of Aesop bottles [Figure 14.2]. The other feature is the row of three fountains from the streets of Vienna. Rusty around the edges and with German type, these ornate fountains display the overt patina of age. This juxtaposition of recycled objects is a design strategy consistent with Naomi Leff's classic Rheinlander Mansion for Ralph Lauren (1986), a series of stage sets containing historical props.[14] Unlike a museum installation, here, customers can touch the old archive drawers and wash their hands in the fountains. There is in this tactile engagement something of a bricolage – materials that resonate with the customer, specifically curated in order to resonate with a cultured customer's knowledge, memories and sensory experiences.

Adaptive reuse is a key part of Aesop's signature stores and aligns with the brand ethos of sustainability. Minimal intervention is also a means of integrating a new store modestly into existing neighbourhoods. Aesop's Upper West Side store in New York, for example, retained the façade of an old French laundry store, including the original signage and stainless-steel store front. Working with rather than against the existing streetscape is

**Figure 14.2**   Aesop store, North Melbourne, design by March Studio, 2013.

also evident in March Studio's Gough Street store in Hong Kong. Here, the designers embraced the unusual corner site, leaving much of the original interior exposed and unadorned, adding a floor and counter made from glass bricks [Figure 14.3]. To the right of the entrance, a row of three of Aesop's moisturizer dispensers invite passing pedestrians to try before they enter [Figure 14.4]. These sidewalk samples are also a means of engaging with the local neighbourhood and extending Aesop's sensory experience into the street.

Utilizing these strategies, Aesop's signature stores around the world have been designed in collaboration with some well-known designers and architects, such as Ilse Crawford (who designed the first London store in 2008), Fernando and Humberto Campana (who designed the Vila Madalena store in Sao Paulo in 2016) and Snøhetta (who designed stores in London, Singapore, Oslo and Berlin). But the majority of Aesop's collaborators are not famous but smaller, local studios such as Paris-based Ciguë and Melbourne-based March Studio (who have designed seventeen stores to date). To highlight their importance, the website 'Taxonomy of Design: An Archive of Aesop Spaces' showcases short videos with designers describing their interiors and photos highlighting each store's distinctive materials, fixtures and furniture.

**Figure 14.3**    Aesop store, Gough Street, Hong Kong, design by March Studio, 2018.

**Figure 14.4**    Aesop store, Gough Street, Hong Kong, design by March Studio, 2018.

Part of the appeal of the Aesop interiors is that, despite their consistency, each one is also unique and carefully designed to interact with its local context. Paphitis described his horror at the idea of Aesop developing into a 'soul-less chain', instead describing the series of stores 'as the equivalent of a weighty, gold charm bracelet on the tanned wrist of a glamorous, well-read European woman who has travelled and collected interesting experiences'.[15] His characterization is telling – the cosmopolitan, intelligent and affluent woman is also an ideal Aesop customer. But, to take up his metaphor, it is easy to imagine a design-conscious clientele desiring to travel to all of the Aesop stores – most of which are located in fashionable neighbourhoods of global cities.[16]

In retrospect, launching a chain of retail stores in the decade following 2008 seemed an unlikely road to success. Aesop's Flinders Lane opened in the midst of the Global Financial Crisis of 2007–8 (though, to be fair, Australia escaped this relatively unscathed) and at the same time as the first iterations of Apple's iPhone. The latter is important, again in retrospect, as this marks the beginning of an era in which the affordability and accessibility of mobile internet technologies and online shopping also began to take off. Yet, despite constant poor forecasts for 'bricks and mortar' retail, Aesop expanded its stores around the world between 2008 and 2021. But their stores did not simply sell skincare products in unusual interiors; they encapsulated an experience.

## Design and experience

In their influential 1998 essay, 'Welcome to the Experience Economy', Joseph Pine and James Gilmore argued that 'staging experiences' was the key to a corporation's future prosperity.[17] Designing a compelling experience, they argued, required creating a coherent set of 'cues' comprising product design and packaging, interiors, staff uniforms and scripts. This approach centred on designing a holistic experience for the customer similar to a theatrical or cinematic one – immersive, seamless and, most of all, emotionally appealing. Part of this includes what Pine and Gilmore refer to as to 'sensorialize', or design each product and detail to accentuate 'the sensations created from its use'.[18]

In contrast to goods that are tangible, and services that are intangible, Pine and Gilmore argued that experiences:

> are inherently personal. They actually occur within any individual who has been engaged on an emotional, physical, intellectual, or even spiritual level. The result? No two people can have the same experience – period. Each experience derives from the interaction between the staged event and the individual's prior state of mind and being.[19]

In their definition, an experience is a subjective phenomenon, an event evoked by the experience-designer that is extracted by the customer – on reflection – as memorable. The senses play a crucial role here as the holistic combination of sights, sounds, smells and touch experiences, such as in an Aesop store, condense into a memorable impression.

In the wake of Pine and Gilmore's original article, a 'second generation' of theorists of the experience economy both extended and critiqued their original account of 'staging experiences'.[20] First, they observed, Pine and Gilmore's analysis is directed solely at management and not at the customer, who 'is consistently viewed as a more or less passive target for the company'.[21] Aimed at a managerial and business audience as a guide to increasing revenue, it is hardly surprising that the customer was positioned by Pine and Gilmore solely as source of potential income. Second, in Pine and Gilmore's staged experiences the customer's status is defined as an instrumental one, 'with interaction between spectators as isolated entities, thereby conceiving experiences as means to reach pre-given ends'.[22] Experience is characterized as individual and immediate, and the customer is assured that their actions have no painful consequences. That is, they have no responsibilities nor duties other than self-satisfaction.

In a 2011 update, Pine and Gilmore continued to proclaim the experience economy as the next stage in an inevitable economic progression but added a further stage. 'Once the Experience Economy has run its course in the decades to come', they argued, 'the *Transformation Economy* will take over'.[23] Though this is only sketched briefly, Pine and Gilmore distinguish between experiences and transformations:

> With an experience, the employees of a staging company are actors performing parts, creating roles, and building characters to engage guests in entertaining, educational, escapist, and/or esthetic ways. With a transformation, all these experiential realms merely set the stage for helping *the customer* learn to act.[24]

Authenticity seems an essential theme in the new economy – or, as Pine and Gilmore put it, 'the management of the customer perception of authenticity becomes the primary new source of competitive advantage – the new business imperative'.[25] The *perception* of authenticity and how this is managed are important distinctions here.

Authentic, transformative experiences are defined by other critics as *meaningful* experiences.[26] Pine and Gilmore argue that transformations are created through increasingly customized experiences, or '"individualization" – creating more and more value for individuals by getting closer and closer to what each individual truly wants and needs, culminating in the individual-changing offerings of transformations'.[27] Here, Aesop's interiors offer a transformative individual experience, as General Manager Suzanne Santos explained in a 2013 interview:

To be able to give a person an opportunity to understand Aesop through demonstration, whether the person actually wants to put it on their face, or if they just want the pleasure of it on their hands, is vitally important to us. We invite the individual to become involved. It beckons you to be part of it. Companies generally try to force their own culture onto you, but we'd rather invite you to immerse yourself in it.[28]

An Aesop store is the stage for an individual to immerse themselves in a sensual experience, cocooned within a calm atmosphere with attentive staff – no images of models' unattainable beauty paired with mirrored surfaces as in the department store beauty counter – an authentic experience reinforced by 'natural' odours and the touch of 'raw' materials.

Of course, Aesop are not unique in designing this kind of retail immersive experience. Another retail success story of the first two decades of the twenty-first century that offers an unlikely parallel is Apple. Although selling completely different products – consumer electronics and skincare – both developed a similar visual language across digital media, minimal packaging and branding, and their carefully curated interiors. The common modernist design language, in which every detail is stripped of excess colour, decoration and ornament, is understood as inherently 'good' due to its lack of waste and rigorous, functionalist logic.

From their first retail store in 2001, Apple's staged experience was intimately connected with their minimalist aesthetic, developed through devices such as the iPod, iPhone and iPad. Beyond simply a surface aesthetic, one design writer celebrated Apple's approach to product design as synonymous with 'integrity, essence, deference, style, and honesty'.[29] This celebrated style extended not only across their physical devices, but across Apple's distinctive interface design, ensuring a coherent and consistent user experience. As the company expanded, Apple translated this minimal, refined design language into the clear, sober interiors that complement the props they staged. Like Aesop, Apple pursued the strategy of creating and curating their own retail experience that would differentiate their products and brand from the competition. Both stores' minimalism serves to centre customers' attention, eliminate distractions and concentrate their focus on interaction with the products.

Above all, Apple stores emphasize the luxury of space. Clear and simple signage and spotlessly clean surfaces offer a calm and orderly respite, particularly for busy city dwellers. The minimal interiors contained little furniture – typically only Alvar Aalto stools and rows of plain timber tables – and few visible fixtures. As with Aesop stores, the Apple stores do not feature a distinguishable cashier area, suggesting their main purpose is not selling products. Instead, the interiors borrow from the language of the modern art gallery, channelling the customer's attention onto the few significant objects on display. But, unlike in a gallery, customers are invited by eager staff to interact with the devices on display. This interactivity with the props is a crucial part of both the Aesop and the Apple store experience.

An alternative approach to the Aesop interior experience lies in parallel developments in fashion boutiques. Interiors for high fashion brands 'are often financially and sensually extravagant, short-lived and rely as much on publicity as on their own physical form for their effect'.[30] Certainly the Aesop stores fit the 'sensually extravagant' part of this definition and, like the fashion boutique, designerly qualities differentiate them from the mass market. Starting in the 1990s, collaborations between architects and fashion houses to create distinguished interiors began in earnest. Prada, in particular, forged a reputation for their distinctive interiors, beginning with Rem Koolhaas' New York flagship store (2001). Similarly, Renzo Piano's Hermès headquarters in Tokyo (1996–2001) and Louis Vuitton's architect-designed spaces became destinations for transformative experiences, each one unique yet consistent with the brand's ethos.[31]

But beyond this high architectural sense, fashion boutiques have always offered a transformative experience. As Mark Pimlott notes about the 1960s boutiques such as those of Mary Quant and Chanel: 'The products of these boutiques in some way *represented* the interests and desires of their consumers. Shoppers often left the shops wearing their purchases, as though their visit to the boutique was part of their own personal transformation'.[32] Such fashion boutiques and their transformative experiences set the scene for the later retail experience of flagship stores that could express an aura of uniqueness, distinction and authenticity.

Aesop's careful curation of the retail experience builds upon these precedents. Their interior experience includes the employees, who are not only expected to be knowledgeable and passionate about the brand, trained on the products and consultation techniques, but also adhere to a set of rules regarding a ban on takeaway coffee cups or personal objects, and refraining from talking about the weather or a customer's clothes.[33] Eliminating distractions and focusing on the customer's experience are crucial. More than this, Aesop staff are trained to wash a customer's hands – a particularly intimate sensory experience – and advise on appropriate skin treatments. The Aesop store as an immersive environment serves to focus on an individual customer's sensory experience while engaging with the products.

## Designing a sensory experience

Yet the modest Aesop store offers customers a different experience to an architect-designed fashion boutique or an Apple store. Instead, the company's design programme drew upon another architectural tradition that emerged (or reemerged) in the 1990s. This 'phenomenological approach' to design has its roots in the work of architects and theorists such as Christian Norberg-Schulz, Peter Zumthor, Steven Holl and Juhani Pallasmaa. It comprised designers who were working in opposition to a modernist tradition that emphasized form, scale and detail but not the 'experiential' aspects of architecture.[34]

Norwegian architect and educator Norberg-Schulz popularized the idea of *genius loci*, the 'character' or atmosphere of a place.[35] In contrast to modernists of the 1970s who assumed space to be universal and anonymous, Norberg-Schulz argued that designers should engage with the particularities of a site, its local history and culture. Understanding the *genius loci* is a starting point for designers of Aesop stores. As we saw above, the stores are typically inserted into the shell of an existing building, retaining as much as possible of the past. Store designers also use recycled local materials that evoke memories – recycled timber or tiles from a local school or warehouse – worn and marked by traces of past use.

Building upon Norberg-Schulz's sense of locality, architects such as Peter Zumthor and Juhani Pallasmaa highlighted a renewed interest in design for the senses. In response to what he termed the 'hegemony of vision' in architectural culture, Pallasmaa argued that 'the inhumanity of contemporary architecture and cities can be understood as the consequence of the neglect of the body and the senses, and an imbalance in our sensory system'.[36] Spaces of our technological world, he argued, engender feelings of detachment and alienation. To counter this, designers should situate the sensory body as central to architectural experience, such as in Zumthor's iconic spa complex in Vals, Switzerland.

Following this tradition, the first impression one gets entering an Aesop store is the distinctive smell – citrus, cedar, lavender or some kind of botanical scent. Different Aesop stores have different scents and change them according to the local seasons.[37] As well as being notoriously difficult to describe in words, the sense of smell typically goes unnoticed in design and architectural projects. Yet what Walter Benjamin described as 'the inaccessible refuge of the *mémoire involontaire*', the involuntary memory evocatively expressed by Gaston Bachelard's raisins drying on a wicker basket is often associated with intensely personal and intimate memories.[38]

Along with smell, touch is the other essential part of the Aesop sensory experience. Beside the sink or basin, staff espouse the botanical ingredients and cleansing effects as they apply creams, hydrators, oils and serums to a customer's hands and wash them off again. Engaging our sense of touch is not only important for a skin care brand, but such intimate rituals engender a sense of care. While this sense of touch is obvious, in a more subtle way, the materials of the interiors are also designed to evoke our tactile sense. The walls of the Nolita Aesop store in New York, for example, are composed of tightly stacked copies of the *New York Times*. Customers are drawn to feel the walls and flip their fingers through the pages. This desire to run your fingers over a worn stone basin or trace the grain of aged timber is a compelling part of the Aesop experience.

More recently, theorists have begun to discuss this sensory approach to design in terms of 'atmospheric' qualities.[39] Atmosphere is a term that attempts to encapsulate that elusive resonance or vibrations of an interior, 'perceived by the felt-body in a given space, but never fully attributable to the objectual set of that space'.[40] For Zumthor, atmosphere is something we perceive 'through our emotional sensibility'.[41] He writes of the immediate, spontaneous response to a building or a space, and how this holistic perception affects our body akin to listening to music. This initial experience of architecture, argues Pallasmaa, is not only multisensory 'but it also involves judgements beyond the five Aristotelian senses, such as the sense of orientation, gravity, balance, stability, motion, duration, continuity, scale and illumination'.[42] This embodied experience, perceived in a diffuse and peripheral manner 'fuses perception, memory, and imagination'.[43]

An Aesop interior encapsulates this holistic, embodied experience. In contrast to Marc Augé's 'non-places', alienating and anonymous airport terminals and shopping malls filled with artificial surfaces and 'non-human mediation',[44] the Aesop store offers customers an individual, sensual experience and the opportunity to be part of a perceived community. As General Manager Santos puts it:

> I'm always reluctant to categorise our customers – they really are such a diverse range of people – yet I do believe there's a shared consciousness amongst them, there's a belief in the ability to make change through their cosmetic purchases.[45]

While the combined sensory impressions are subjective and personal, this shared consciousness suggests some general principles. The tranquil, sparse environments with a carefully curated collection of materials products evoke a museum or art gallery. Their situation within dense, urban neighbourhoods offers a respite from the noise, distractions and speed of the city: a moment of self-care and sensual indulgence.

Academics, critics, architects and designers are accustomed to analysing architectural spaces objectively, from a safe distance. Yet if we take the idea of sensory experience seriously, interiors are 'ambient environments delimited by the aura of affect and subjectivity'.[46] This seems particularly acute when considering the Aesop store. We inhale its scents, touch its surfaces, consume its visual order and interact with its materials and products physically, emotionally and in our imaginations *before* we can rationally reflect on the experience. Could an interior such as this transform us? Philosopher and psychoanalyst Teresa Brennan suggests that 'the transmission of affect, if only for an instant, alters the biochemistry and neurology of the subject. The "atmosphere" or the environment literally gets into the individual'.[47] In this way, the sensory experience of an Aesop store gets *under* our skin to (ever so subtly) transform our bodies.

## A fable

It seems appropriate to end a chapter about Aesop stores with a fable-like conclusion. Return for a moment to Paphitis' well-travelled, wealthy European woman, or at least someone who aspires to be part of this set. She is above the glossy, shallow lifestyles of models and celebrities reflected in overpackaged, glitzy brands such as L'Oréal or Estée Lauder. Instead, the Aesop customer revels in the sophisticated yet modest stores and their particular character and interactions with their fashionable neighbourhood. Yet, in their hometown of Melbourne, Aesop stores also appear in several suburban shopping malls.[48] In these stores, Aesop's signature sensory experience is not only diluted by restrictions on retail fit-outs but limited by its context in a row of uniform chain stores. As the legendary Aesop himself might have put it, this is how a weighty gold charm bracelet becomes just another plastic wristband.

## Notes

1  Also referred to as the 'retail apocalypse' or 'retail meltdown' of 2015–17; see, for example, D. Thompson, 'What in the World Is Causing the Retail Meltdown of 2017?', *The Atlantic* (10 April 2017): www.theatlantic.com/business/archive/2017/04/retail-meltdown-of-2017/522384/ (accessed 30 March 2022).
2  B. J. Pine and J. H. Gilmore, 'Welcome to the Experience Economy', *Harvard Business Review* (July–August 1998), pp. 97–105.
3  N. Whiteley, *Design for Society* (London: Reaktion Books, 1993), p. 50.
4  *Ibid.*, p. 54.
5  J. Entine, 'Caring Capitalism', *Sunday Times* (31 December 1995), http://archives.jonentine.com/reviews/caring_capitalism.htm (accessed 30 March 2022). See also Jon Entine's 'Social and Environmental Audit': https://jonentine.com/a-social-and-environmental-audit-of-the-body-shop-anita-roddick-and-the-question-of-character/ (accessed 30 March 2022).
6  Melissa Aronczyk, 'Market(ing) Activism: Lush Cosmetics, Ethical Oil and the Self-Mediation of Protest', *JOMEC: Journalism, Media and Cultural Studies Journal*, 0:4 (2013), https://jomec.cardiffuniversitypress.org/articles/abstract/10.18573/j.2013.10256/ (accessed 30 March 2022).
7  For example, the European Union regulations on cosmetic testing began in 1993 and by 2004 animal testing for finished products was completely banned. See European Commission, 'Ban on Animal Testing', online: https://ec.europa.eu/growth/sectors/cosmetics/ban-animal-testing_en (accessed 30 March 2022).
8  T. Kent and D. Stone, 'The Body Shop and the Role of Design in Retail Branding', *International Journal of Retail and Distribution Management*, 35:7 (2007), p. 536. The Body Shop currently has over 3,000 stores globally, though most are operated by franchisees.
9  In contrast, imagine a skincare brand called 'Aristotle'.

10 See www.aesop.com/au/r/the-athenaeum/view-from-above/ (accessed 30 March 2022).

11 See www.aesop.com/fr/en/r/the-fabulist (accessed 30 March 2022).

12 D. Powell, 'How Aesop Chief Executive Michael O'Keeffe Helped Craft a $250 Million Business Model', *Smart Company* (9 September 2016), www.smartcompany.com.au/entrepreneurs/influencers-profiles/how-aesop-chief-executive-michael-okeeffe-helped-craft-a-250-million-business-model/ (accessed 30 March 2022).

13 The company's global success after the launch of their retail strategy led to Brazilian giant Natura buying a majority share in the company in 2012. Natura attained full ownership in 2016.

14 See D. J. Huppatz, 'Fashion Branding: Staging Identities' in G. Riello and P. McNeil (eds), *The Fashion History Reader: Global Perspectives* (London: Routledge, 2010); D. J. Huppatz, 'The Spaces of Interiors: Staging Fantasies' in T. Vaikla-Poldma (ed.), *Meanings of Designed Spaces* (New York and London: Fairchild Books, 2013). However, Aesop does not engage in Lauren and Leff's aristocratic fantasies.

15 M. Fair, 'Interview with Dennis Paphitis', *Dezeen* (10 December 2012), www.dezeen.com/2012/12/10/dennis-paphitis-aesop-interview/ (accessed 30 March 2022).

16 In the UK, for example, Aesop has seventeen stores in London, two in Edinburgh and one in Bath.

17 Pine and Gilmore, 'Welcome to the Experience Economy'.

18 B. J. Pine and J. H. Gilmore, *The Experience Economy* (Boston, MA: Harvard Business Review Press, 2011), p. 18.

19 *Ibid.*, p. 17.

20 A. Boswijk, J. P. T. Thijssen and E. Peelen, *The Experience Economy: A New Perspective* (Amsterdam: Pearson, Prentice Hall, 2005); J. Sundbo and F. Sørensen (eds), *Handbook on the Experience Economy* (Cheltenham: Edward Elgar, 2013).

21 Boswijk, Thijssen and Peelen, *The Experience Economy*, p. 6.

22 B. A. Christensen, 'Connecting Experience and Economy – Aspects of Disguised Positioning', *Integrative Psychology and Behavioral Science*, 47 (2013), pp. 77–94 (p. 83).

23 Pine and Gilmore, *The Experience Economy*, p. 255.

24 *Ibid.*, p. 284.

25 B. J. Pine and J. H. Gilmore, 'The Experience Economy: Past, Present and Future' in Sundbo and Sørensen, *Handbook on the Experience Economy*, p. 29.

26 See Boswijk, Thijssen and Peelen, *The Experience Economy*.

27 Pine and Gilmore, 'The Experience Economy: Past, Present and Future', p. 33.

28 K. Bezar, 'Suzanne Santos Is the Brains behind Aesop', *Dumbo Feather* (31 March 2013), www.dumbofeather.com/conversations/suzanne-santos-brain-behind-aesop-brand/ (accessed 30 March 2022).

29 C. Shelley, 'The Nature of Simplicity in Apple Design', *The Design Journal*, 18:3 (2015), p. 441.

30 D. Vernet and L. de Wit (eds), *Boutiques and Other Retail Spaces* (New York and London: Routledge, 2007), p. xi.

31 On Louis Vuitton's architectural programme see https://eu.louisvuitton.com/eng-e1/la-maison/architecture (accessed 30 March 2022).

32 M. Pimlott, 'The Boutique and the Mass Market' in Vernet and de Wit, *Boutiques and Other Retail Spaces*, p. 4.

33 K. Hall, 'A Post-It Ban and No Weather Talk: The Weird and Wonderful Secrets of Working at Aesop', *Mamamia* (1 March 2017), www.mamamia.com.au/working-for-aesop (accessed 30 March 2022).

34 J. Pallasmaa, 'Space, Place, and Atmosphere: Peripheral Perception in Existential Experience' in C. Borsch (ed.), *Architectural Atmospheres: On the Experience and Politics of Architecture* (Basel: Birkhäuser, 2014), p. 19.

35  C. Norberg-Schultz, *Genius Loci: Towards a Phenomenology of Architecture* (New York: Rizzoli, 1979), pp. 10–11.

36  J. Pallasmaa, *Eyes of Skin* (Chichester: Wiley, 2005), p. 21.

37  See Tam Gim Ean's interview with Aesop retail architectural manager Denise Neri, 'Aesop Store Speaks Sensitively to Local Surroundings, Honouring Neighborhoods and Heritage', *Options* (9 February 2020), www.optionstheedge.com/topic/haven/ aesop-store-design-speaks-sensitively-local-surroundings-honouring-neighbour hoods-and (accessed 30 March 2022).

38  W. Benjamin, 'Some Motifs in Baudelaire' in W. Benjamin, *Selected Writings, Volume 4, 1938–1940* (Cambridge, MA: Harvard University Press, 2006), p. 335; G. Bachelard, *The Poetics of Space*, trans. M. Jolas (Boston, MA: Beacon Press, 1994), p. 13.

39  See C. Borsch (ed.), *Architectural Atmospheres: On the Experience and Politics of Architecture* (Basel: Birkhäuser, 2014).

40  T. Griffero, *Atmospheres: Aesthetics of Emotional Spaces*, trans. S. de Sanctis (Farnham: Ashgate, 2010), p. 6.

41  P. Zumthor, *Thinking Architecture* (Basel: Birkhäuser, 1998), p. 13.

42  Pallasmaa, 'Space, Place, and Atmosphere', p. 19.

43  *Ibid.*, p. 19.

44  M. Augé, *Non-Places: Introduction to an Anthropology of Supermodernity*, trans. J. Howe (London: Verso, 1995), p. 118.

45  Bezar, 'Suzanne Santos Is the Brains behind Aesop'.

46  J. Preston, 'In the Midst of' in 'Interior Atmospheres', *Architectural Design*, 78:3 (May/June 2008), p. 8.

47  T. Brennan, *The Transmission of Affect* (Ithaca, NY and London: Cornell University Press, 2004), p. 1.

48  Not surprisingly, these stores do not appear on the 'Taxonomy of Design' website.

# Index

EU authorised representative for GPSR:
Easy Access System Europe, Mustamäe tee 50,
10621 Tallinn, Estonia
gpsr.requests@easproject.com